About the Author

"If a statue is ever erected to honor the person who has done the most for American investors, the hands down choice should be Jack Bogle."
—**Warren Buffett**, Chairman, Berkshire Hathaway

"Jack Bogle's remarkable career spans the spectrum from lonely iconoclast to celebrated rock star. His conception and development of index funds transformed the investment world for individuals and institutions alike. Countless millions of investors have purchased index funds because of Jack."
—**David F. Swensen**, Chief Investment Officer, Yale University

"What Gutenberg was to the printing press, Henry Ford to the automobile, and Shakespeare to the English language, Jack Bogle is to finance."
—**William J. Bernstein**, bestselling author of *The Investor's Manifesto: Preparing for Prosperity, Armageddon, and Everything in Between*

"One hundred years from today, historians will remember only two investors from this era—Warren Buffett and Jack Bogle. The two books they will note? Buffett's bible, Ben Graham's *The Intelligent Investor*, and . . . anything written by Jack Bogle. In a world of investment foxes, Jack remains a stalwart hedgehog."
—**Steve Galbraith**, Managing Member, Kindred Capital

"Jack Bogle has given investors throughout the world more wisdom and plain financial horse sense than any person in the history of markets."
—**Arthur Levitt**, Former Chairman, U.S. Securities and Exchange Commission

"Jack Bogle is one of the most lucid men in finance."
—**Nassim N. Taleb**, PhD, author of *The Black Swan*

Praise for *Stay the Course*

"Only one man could've created Vanguard and only one man could've written this book. I'm thankful Jack has done both. Investing for the many has been forever changed for the (much) better by him. Read the story of how it happened."

—**Clifford Asness**, Managing and Founding Principal,
AQR Capital Management, LLC

"Jack Bogle has done more for the individual investor than perhaps anyone on the planet. His seminal insights and relentless tenacity revolutionized the mutual fund industry, permanently and for the better. Yet for me, the signature of his greatness lies first and foremost in his passion to serve as an inspired teacher to us all. With nearly seventy years of disciplined thought on the topic of investing, Bogle's incisive mind and considered wisdom shines through always in his well-chosen words."

—**Jim Collins**, bestselling author of *Good to Great*,
co-author of *Built to Last*

"It's a rare privilege to be handed a backstage pass into the mind and motivation of the man who democratized finance, which is what this remarkable book has done. More than any other single individual, Jack Bogle has improved the lives of millions of investors, allowing us to save and invest for our future at lowest cost, so we really can stay the course. I can't think of a more important story to tell, and Jack tells it beautifully."

—**Andrew W. Lo**, Charles E. and Susan T. Harris Professor,
MIT, author of *Adaptive Markets*

"Jack Bogle—a man with a mission.

For a long while, it seemed to me, an almost 'mission impossible' to push the Wall Street establishment into providing individuals and investment institutions alike with practical and economical means for keeping up with the stock markets.

Book after book—twelve in all—drive home the point. It's rare, extremely rare, for even the most astute investors to beat the stock market averages year after year. And it was expensive to try; fees were high and active trading has costs.

Jack Bogle has won the point. 'Indexing' has swept much of the investing field. Now Jack has provided his valedictory: the saga of a determined boy whose family struggled financially but who thrived at boarding school and Princeton, and then in the investing world, fighting off both the investment establishment and a congenitally weak heart along the way.

Stay the Course puts it all in the broader perspective. Professional and personal battles, won or lost, give way to the larger responsibilities: to family, to communities large and small, to the nation itself."

—**Paul A. Volcker**, Chairman, Federal Reserve Board
1979-1987, author of *Keeping at It*

"I served on the Vanguard board for 28 years. I can attest that every policy that came before the board was resolved by applying a simple criterion: Was the policy good or bad for the individual shareholder? It is small wonder that Jack Bogle has been called 'the best friend the individual investor has ever had.'"

—**Burton G. Malkiel**, Chemical Bank Chairman's Professor of
Economics, Emeritus, Princeton University, and bestselling
author of *A Random Walk Down Wall Street*

STAY THE COURSE

STAY THE COURSE

The Story of Vanguard
and the Index Revolution

JOHN C. BOGLE

WILEY

Dedication

Dedicated to the wonderful human beings who have helped to shape my life— the family of my heritage and the family of my procreation; my teachers and my mentors; the colleagues who have supported me during my long career; the Vanguard shareholders who have inspired me (and paid my salary!); and my friends from all walks of life.

Becoming 90

Even as I approach my 90th year on this Earth, I strive to follow the impassioned advice expressed by the Scotsman Sir Harry Lauder (1870–1950):

Keep Right on to the End of the Road

Every road through life is a long, long road,
Filled with joys and sorrows too,
As you journey on how your heart will yearn
For things most dear to you.
With wealth and love 'tis so,
But onward we must go.

With a big stout heart to a long steep hill,
We may get there with a smile,
With a good kind thought and an end in view,
We may cut short many a mile.
So let courage every day
Be your guiding star always.

Keep right on to the end of the road,
Keep right on to the end,
Though the way be long, let your heart be strong,
Keep right on round the bend.
Though you're tired and weary still journey on,
Till you come to your happy abode,
Where all the love you've been dreaming of
Will be there at the end of the road.

Contents

About *Stay the Course*

T his book tells the story of how my career began, how it was abruptly cut short, and what followed once I resumed that career. It is a story of creativity and innovation; of victory and defeat; of laughter and tears; of pure coincidence and sheer luck; of commitment to high values; of determination, stubbornness, and cussedness. All in the name of serving investors, small as well as large, simply by giving thrifty human beings–directly or through their employers' savings plans–their fair share of whatever returns the financial markets bestow on our investments.

It is also the story of a revolution. No, there are no Molotov-cocktail-throwing radicals involved. Just one man with a truly financial-world-changing idea called the index mutual fund. That idea has spread like a meme, maybe even a religious sect. It is *The Index Revolution*, and Vanguard has been its clear leader.

For as long as I can remember, I've used the phrase "stay the course" to urge investors to invest for the long term and not be diverted by the daily sound and fury of the stock market. In this book, as you'll see, "Stay the Course" also has been my motto in building Vanguard, holding fast to a long-term business strategy and overcoming both adversities and adversaries, none of which were able to halt our rise.

What This Book Contains

Part I is the heart of the book. "The Story of Vanguard" proceeds more or less chronologically, from my time at Blair Academy and Princeton University through my early years at Wellington Management Company;

my rise to leadership and my descent into failure; my career saved by my creation of the upstart Vanguard in 1974, then, quickly, the index fund in 1975. Vanguard's mutual structure and index strategy defied convention; together they drove Vanguard to its place as the largest mutual fund complex in the world.

Along the way, you'll pass a series of "Landmarks." These Landmarks are highlights of the key events that were required to transform Vanguard's initially skeletal structure into today's complete fund complex—engaged in fund administration, marketing and distribution, and investment management—able to compete with our peers on a level playing field. Without this transformation, Vanguard would have been unable to join in the price competition that pervades today's powerful index fund industry.

Part II recounts the history of major Vanguard funds, including Wellington Fund, our index funds, Windsor funds, PRIMECAP funds, and bond funds. In Part III, "The Future of Investment Management," I discuss the future of investment management and reflect on some of the major changes that I see for the years ahead.

In Part IV, "Personal Reflections," I move from those financial subjects and offer a memoir of sorts (with a weird format!) of personal reflections on life, on the institutions that I've done my best to serve, and some unforgettable quotations that hold special memories for me.

Stay the Course: The Story of Vanguard and the Index Revolution should be of interest to investors, financial historians, entrepreneurs of all stripes, business people, academics, students, and, yes, any reader who simply enjoys a good story with a happy ending.

Striving for Accuracy

I've written the story of Vanguard and the index revolution in part because I've lived it and led it, in part because no one else who was involved in all of Vanguard's long saga still lives. I've done my best to be totally objective (you have a right to challenge that!) and to stick to the facts, revealed partly in my files and partly in my memory, reinforced by the notes I've taken along the long journey.

That said, I've had to write without access to primary sources of information. My request to review the corporate minutes of the Vanguard mutual funds during the long period in which I served as chairman was denied by Vanguard, a decision finally ratified by Vanguard's board of directors. Of course I could have let that inexplicable denial stop me from writing my book. But I decided to, well, stay the course, and persevere on my own.

I've had assistance from the many people who have worked with me to produce this book (Michael Nolan, Emily Snyder, Kathy Younker) or provided editorial comments (Cliff Asness, Andrew Cassel, Andrew Clarke, Rafe Sagalyn, Bill Falloon, and especially Monie Hardwick and Susan Cerra). I take this opportunity to thank each one.

Finally, *Stay the Course* represents my own candid and deeply held opinions. They are not necessarily those of Vanguard's present management.

Enjoy!

JCB
September 1, 2018

Postscript: All of the underlying information that supports the data in the book is available electronically at www.johncbogle.com.

Foreword

Burton G. Malkiel

I t is an honor for me to write the foreword to this important history of the unique and extraordinary financial institution that is Vanguard. Many institutions that call themselves "mutual" are mutual in name only. The Vanguard that Jack Bogle created is truly mutual in practice. Owned by those who have entrusted their money to it, Vanguard is run with only its shareowners in mind. Any "profits" are returned to its owners in the form of reduced fees. New investment instruments are created only if they promise to provide real benefits for investors.

I served on the Vanguard board for 28 years. I can attest that every policy that came before the board was resolved by applying a simple criterion: Was the policy good or bad for the individual shareholder? It is small wonder that Jack Bogle has been called "the best friend the individual investor has ever had." Perhaps my favorite testimonial to Jack was written by a group of acolytes, the Bogleheads, devoted to propagating Bogle's investment ideas: "While some mutual fund founders chose to make billions, [Jack created Vanguard] to make a difference."

And what a difference it was. In an industry known for imposing high fees, Vanguard's were invariably the lowest. Moreover, the complex was run with the objective of distributing any economies of scale back to the shareowners and inexorably lowering the fees over time. Jack's own research made clear that fees were the most important determinant of investment performance. If you want to own a mutual fund with top quartile performance, you are most likely to do so if you buy a fund with bottom quartile fees. As Jack so presciently remarked, "This is a business where you get what you don't pay for."

But lowering fees was only part of the reason for Vanguard's commercial success in now having over $5 trillion under management. Vanguard was also enormously innovative in bringing countless new financial instruments to market to better serve investors with different objectives and in different circumstances.

Vanguard was the first to offer tax-exempt bond funds with three distinct maturities: short, intermediate, and long. It then extended the idea to taxable bonds. It created the first total bond market index fund and then the first balanced index fund, holding both total bonds and total equities. In its drive to continuously lower costs, it created the "Admiral" series of funds. It even initiated the now-popular method of factor investing by bringing to market the first "value" fund in 1992.

But eclipsing any of these innovations, by far the most important was the creation by Vanguard of the first index fund available to the investing public. In my judgment, the index fund is the most important financial innovation that has been created for the individual investor.

Financial innovation is frequently disparaged. It is often associated with financial engineering and complex derivative instruments that were not well understood by their creators and certainly misconstrued by rating agencies and investors. The fallout from this misadventure was not confined to the hapless investors and global financial institutions that suffered punishing losses. The existence of complex mortgage-backed securities helped fuel an enormous housing bubble. When the bubble deflated, a sharp recession followed, and the repercussions practically brought down the entire world financial system. One can understand the animus toward this sort of financial technology, and it is not surprising that many observers have suggested that the only worthwhile financial innovation over the past century has been the ATM machine.

We can readily accept that not all financial innovations have benefited society and that some have actually been toxic. But it would be a serious mistake to brand all new financial instruments as having little or no benefit. For me, the index fund is unquestionably the most important financial innovation of our time, and it has unambiguously been of enormous benefit to the individual investor saving and investing to achieve a secure retirement.

Index funds that simply buy and hold all of the stocks in a broad-based stock market index guarantee that their investors will earn the rate of return generated by the market. Because they involve little turnover, they minimize trading costs and are extremely tax efficient. Index mutual funds and exchange-traded funds can be purchased at expense ratios close to zero, and thus for the first time enable the individual investor to earn the full return generated by the market.

According to Standard & Poor's research, over 90% of actively managed funds underperformed their benchmark indexes over the 15-year period ending in 2017. The average active fund underperformed its equivalent index by a full one percentage point per year. Index funds don't provide average performance: they give the investor top decile returns. The index fund has provided the ideal instrument to invest savings and receive the highest returns available.

When Jack Bogle created "The First Index Investment Trust" (the original name of today's Vanguard 500 Index Fund), it was greeted with derision by the professional investment community. It was variously called "Bogle's folly" or "doomed to failure" and even "un-American." Not even Jack would have predicted that it and its sister Total Stock Market Fund would become the two largest mutual funds in the world. But he did know that his innovation would give the ordinary investor a fair shake, and that managing the Vanguard organization exclusively for the benefit of those who entrusted their money to it would fundamentally change the ability of millions of people to achieve financial security.

Think of a person of modest means who made an initial $500 investment in the Vanguard 500 Index Fund at the start of the fund's life at the end of 1977 and then added $100 of savings each month thereafter. The following table presents the results through the end of 2017. With the most modest of investments, the individual would end up with a $0.75 million nest egg. With $150 per month of savings, the individual would be a millionaire. Small wonder that the index fund has been called the "best friend an investor could have," and that Jack has been called "the greatest investor advocate ever to grace the fund industry."

ILLUSTRATION OF DOLLAR-COST AVERAGING WITH VANGUARD 500 INDEX FUND

Year Ended December 31	Total Cost of Cumulative Investments	Total Value of Shares Acquired
1978	$1,600	$1,669
1979	2,800	3,274
1980	4,000	5,755
1981	5,200	6,630
1982	6,400	9,487
1983	7,600	12,783
1984	8,800	14,864
1985	10,000	20,905
1986	11,200	25,935
1987	12,400	28,221
1988	13,600	34,079
1989	14,800	46,126
1990	16,000	45,803
1991	17,200	61,010
1992	18,400	66,817
1993	19,600	74,687
1994	20,800	76,779
1995	22,000	106,944
1996	23,200	132,768
1997	24,400	178,217
1998	25,600	230,619
1999	26,800	280,565
2000	28,000	256,271
2001	29,200	226,622
2002	30,400	177,503
2003	31,600	229,524
2004	32,800	255,479
2005	34,000	268,933
2006	35,200	312,318
2007	36,400	330,350
2008	37,600	208,941

Year Ended December 31	Total Cost of Cumulative Investments	Total Value of Shares Acquired
2009	38,800	265,756
2010	40,000	306,756
2011	41,200	313,981
2012	42,400	364,932
2013	43,600	483,743
2014	44,800	550,388
2015	46,000	558,467
2016	47,200	625,764
2017	48,400	762,690

Source: Vanguard

In 2016 investors pulled $340 billion out of actively managed mutual funds while investing over $500 billion in index funds. The same trends continued in 2017 and 2018. Today over 45% of investment funds are indexed. A sea change was occurring in the fund industry. Active managers could no longer claim superior investment results, so they fought back by inventing new criticisms of indexing. Indexing is now alleged to pose a grave danger both to the stock market and to the general economy.

One of the most respected research houses on Wall Street, Sanford C. Bernstein, published a 47-page report in 2016 with the provocative title "The Silent Road to Serfdom: Why Passive Investment Is Worse Than Marxism." The report suggested that a capitalist market system in which investors invest passively in index funds is even worse than a centrally planned economy, where government directs all capital investment. Indexing is alleged to cause money to pour into a set of investments independent of considerations such as profitability and growth opportunities. It is active managers who ensure that new information is properly reflected in stock prices.

Could it be possible that if everyone invested only in index funds, indexing could grow so large that stocks could become massively mispriced? If everybody indexed, who would ensure that stock prices reflect all the information available about the prospects for different companies? Who would trade from stock to stock to ensure that the market is reasonably efficient? The paradox of index investing is that the stock market needs some active traders who analyze and act on new information so that stocks are efficiently priced and sufficiently liquid for investors to be able to buy and sell. Active traders play a critical role in determining security prices and how capital is allocated.

Active managers are incentivized to perform this function by charging substantial management fees. They will continue to market their services with the claim that they have above-average insights that enable them to beat the market even though, unlike in Garrison Keillor's mythical Lake Wobegon, they cannot all achieve above-average market returns. And even if the proportion of active managers shrinks to as little as 10 or 5% of the total, there would still be more than enough of them to make prices reflect information. We have far too much active management today, not too little.

But as a thought experiment, suppose everybody did index and individual stocks did not reflect new information? Suppose a drug company develops a new cancer drug that promises to double the company's sales and earnings, but the price of their shares does not increase to reflect the news. In our capitalist system it is inconceivable that some trader or hedge fund would not emerge to bid up the price of the stock and profit from the mispricing. In a free-market system we can expect that advantageous arbitrage opportunities are exploited by profit-seeking market participants no matter how many investors index.

The evidence indicates that the percentage of active managers outperformed by the index has actually increased over time. If anything, the stock market is becoming more efficient – not less so – despite the growth of indexing. The following figure presents the data. The solid line shows the growth of indexing over time and measures the percentage of equity investment funds that are indexed. The dots on the exhibit show the percentage of actively managed equity funds that are outperformed by the Standard & Poor's 1500 benchmark index. The data shown are three-year averages taken from the 2018 S&P report comparing active manager performance versus index returns through year-end 2017. What is clear is that the proportion of funds that have outperformed the broad S&P 1500 index has declined over time even as the proportion of funds that are passively managed has increased.

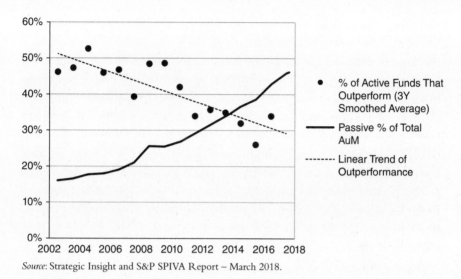

Source: Strategic Insight and S&P SPIVA Report – March 2018.

To be sure, index investors are free riders. They do receive the benefits that result from active trading without bearing the costs. But free riding on price signals provided by others is hardly a flaw of the capitalist system; it is an essential feature of that system. In a free-market economy we all benefit from relying on a set of market prices that are determined by others.

A second criticism of indexing is that it has produced an unhealthy concentration of ownership that has not been seen since the days of the Rockefeller Trust. Two academic papers, a law review article, and a widely circulated op-ed have hypothesized that common ownership of companies in the same industry may produce unwanted anti-competitive effects and invites remedies to prevent losses for the economy as a whole.[1]

---

[1] See T. F. Bresnahan and S. C. Salop, "Quantifying the Competitive Effects of Production Joint Ventures," *International Journal of Industrial Organizations* 4, no. 2 (1986): 155–175; J. Azar, M. C. Schmalz, and I. Tecu, "Anti-Competitive Effects of Common Ownership," *Competition Policy International* 1, no. 3 (2016); E. Elhauge, "Horizontal Shareholding," *Harvard Law Review* 129 (March 10, 2016): 1267–1317; and E. Posner, F. S. Morton, and G. Weyl, "A Monopoly Trump Can Pop," *New York Times*, December 7, 2016.

The argument by Azar, Schmalz, and Tecu is that common owner-ship can reduce the incentive to compete. If the same asset manager is the largest shareholder of all the airline companies, that manager will be loath to see vigorous fare competition that would reduce the profit margins of all the companies in the industry. The authors find that changes in ownership concentration over time in the airline industry have been associated with anti-competitive incentives and have led to ticket prices being 3 to 5% higher than they would be under separate ownership. Elhauge has proposed that the regulatory authorities as well as the private plaintiffs' bar bring antitrust claims against institutional investors who engage in horizontal shareholdings. Posner et al. propose that institutional investors limit their shareholdings to no more than 1% of the total equity stake in the industry when holding shares in multiple companies. Any of these remedies would deal a fatal blow to the ability of companies such as Vanguard to offer index funds to their shareholders.

The argument that common ownership could produce anti-com-petitive effects is certainly a plausible one. But it is important to note that there is absolutely no direct evidence of the mechanism that implements the behavior to cause higher prices. The empirical support for a finding of competitive harm is far from definitive so as to sup-port a blanket remedy. And there is no consideration to the harm that would be caused if low-cost index funds become unavailable.

In my own experience as a longtime director of Vanguard, there was never an instance where a vote was made that would encourage anti-competitive behavior. There is simply no evidence that anti-com-petitive practices have actually been encouraged by other indexing giants such as BlackRock and State Street because of their common ownership of all the major companies in an industry. Nor would it be in their interest to do so. The same investment companies control a sizeable portion of the common stock of every major company in the market. Perhaps banding together to encourage the airline companies to raise their prices would benefit their holdings of airline stocks. But this would mean higher costs for all the other companies in their portfolio that depend on the airlines to facilitate business travel. Index funds have no incentive to favor one industry over another. Indeed, since index funds have encouraged managements to adopt compensation systems based on relative rather than absolute performance, they have explicitly promoted vigorous competition among the firms in every industry.

Index funds have been of enormous benefit for individual investors. Competition and economies of scale have driven the cost of broad-based index funds very close to zero. Individuals can now save for retirement far more efficiently than ever before. Indexing, pioneered by Vanguard, has transformed the investing experience of millions of investors. It has helped them save for retirement and meet their other investment goals by providing efficient instruments that can be used to build diversified portfolios. They represent an unambiguous benefit for society.

Good public policy requires that the interests of all stakeholders be considered when contemplating blanket measures that have the potential to interfere with the ability of households to accomplish their long-run financial goals. When considering a hypothetical cost against the benefits from the most consumer-friendly innovation in history, it seems clear where the net benefit comes out. Even if it could be proved that institutions' cross-holdings are related to less competition, disruptive requirements on organizations such as Vanguard would be the last remedy that should be pursued.

Part I
The Story of Vanguard

Chapter 1
1974
The Prophecy

I n July 1974, I was in Los Angeles at the headquarters of the American Funds, meeting with friends that I had made as a governor and two-term chairman of the Investment Company Institute. Jon Lovelace, then the head of American Funds and son of the firm's founder, Jonathan Bell Lovelace, came into the meeting and said that there was an urgent matter that he needed to discuss with me. Jon had a reputation for integrity, independence, and wisdom, so I was eager to speak with him.

Following my visit to his firm, however, I had a scheduled dinner meeting before flying back to Philadelphia on the 7:30 flight the next morning. "That's fine," Jon said, "I'll meet you at the LAX breakfast room counter at 6 a.m."

Jon was already seated at the counter when I arrived. After a few pleasantries, he got right to his point: "I understand that you're planning to create a new mutual fund complex that will actually be *mutual*, owned by the fund shareholders." Yes, I responded, I hoped to build such a firm. To put it mildly, Jon was not amused. I still remember his exact words, "If you create a mutual structure," he said sternly, "you will destroy this industry."

More than four decades later, it is clear that Jon Lovelace was on to something. If he had amended his dire prediction to say, "you will destroy this industry *as we now know it*," today we could credit him with almost perfect foresight.

Structure and Strategy

Then again, nobody in 1974 really could have predicted that an upstart firm, founded at the bottom of a vicious bear market, would overcome all odds and not merely survive, but ultimately dominate the mutual fund industry. The firm's mutual structure – owned by its fund shareholders and operated on an "at-cost" basis – had never been tried before.

We were compelled by our own directors to retain an external investment adviser with a previous record of failure. Our role was initially limited to fund administration, for we were barred from portfolio management or share distribution. And we would soon stake our future on an unprecedented strategy: a stock portfolio that would not rely on an investment adviser.

If those liabilities were not burdensome enough, the firm had a brand-new name: **Vanguard**.

The new organization would be the first – and to this day, the only – *mutual* mutual fund organization, run on an "at-cost" basis, not by an external management company seeking to earn high profits for its own shareholders, but by the funds themselves, and ultimately by the funds' shareholders. We called it "The Vanguard Experiment" in mutual fund governance.

It may be useful to see how the Vanguard mutual structure differs from the conventional industry structure followed by (literally) all of our peers. (See Exhibit 1.1.)

Exhibit 1.1   Mutual Ownership Structure versus Traditional Corporate Structure

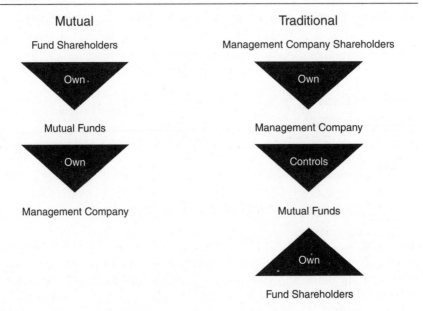

Mutual	Traditional
Fund Shareholders	Management Company Shareholders
Own	Own
Mutual Funds	Management Company
Own	Controls
Management Company	Mutual Funds
	Own
	Fund Shareholders

2018: The Prophecy Fulfilled

Yet during the decades that followed, the name Vanguard – along with its unique structure and an unprecedented strategy built around the creation of the world's first index mutual fund – would unquestionably change the nature of the mutual fund industry as we then knew it.

Call it creative destruction. Call it disruptive innovation. Call it luck. Call it, as some have, my attempt to salvage my career. (There's some truth in that.) But more than anything else, call it good karma, along with a healthy dollop of good timing. For surely the passage of time would have eventually awakened the investment world to this fundamental truth: before costs are deducted, the returns earned by investors as a group precisely equal the returns of the market itself.

After those costs, therefore, investors earn lower-than-market returns. The irrefutable fact: the only way for the 100 million families whom the mutual fund industry serves to maximize their share of the financial-market returns they earn as a group is by minimizing their costs. Paraphrasing the words of our nation's Declaration of Independence in 1776, "We hold this truth to be self-evident." Vanguard took the leadership role in bringing down the costs of investing, ultimately becoming the world's lowest-cost provider of mutual funds.

Vanguard: Lowering Costs for Investors

Since our founding in 1974, Vanguard has been focused on lowering the costs of investing. As a result, the Vanguard that we know today is a colossus. Worldwide, we manage more than $5 trillion on behalf of some 20 million clients – more than our two largest competitors *combined*. Our near-25% share of long-term mutual fund assets is almost double the previous high of 15%, reached earlier by three different firms, and our 65% share of the industry's entire net cash flow during the past five years is also without historical precedent.

In recent years, investors have entrusted an average of some $1 billion each business day to Vanguard's care, an amazing endorsement by the investing public, also without precedent in our industry.

Index Strategy Follows Mutual Structure

What accounts for Vanguard's acceptance in the marketplace? Surely our growth is rooted in that mutual structure that so concerned Jon Lovelace, and the strategy that it entailed. Thanks largely to the rock-bottom costs generated by our mutual structure, the long-term returns earned by the Vanguard funds for their investor/owners frequently rank among the highest in the industry. Such acceptance would not have been imaginable during the stormy and uncertain years following our founding. Indeed, at the outset we experienced 83 consecutive months of net cash *outflows* from our funds.

Nor would it have been imaginable that such a structure would almost compel the design of a strategy focused on index funds, which were not even a blip on the horizon when Vanguard began. But it took no genius to realize that "strategy follows structure," and within a year of Vanguard's founding, we created the world's first index mutual fund.

"The Emperor's Clothes"

Almost a century has passed since the first U.S. mutual fund was incorporated in 1924, yet only during the past two decades have investors come to fully embrace the truth that Vanguard holds self-evident. Rather than wearing the clothes of market-beating "professional management," the mutual fund emperor was wearing no clothes at all. In fact, it wasn't only the mutual fund emperor who was naked, it was the entire mutual fund empire, an industry unable to deliver on its prime, if tacit, promise: that professional money managers as a group would enhance the returns earned by fund investors.

The concept that fund managers could not add value to their clients' wealth, once considered nearly heretical, is now broadly accepted. It has led to a disruptive revolution in the mutual fund industry, largely driven by the rise of index funds. The index revolution, in turn, has been led by Vanguard.

The odds against Vanguard's ever coming into existence, let alone surviving that first decade, were staggering. To paraphrase a line from the hit musical *Miss Saigon*, Vanguard was "conceived in Hell and born in strife." Its creation was the result of an unsatisfactory compromise that ended an ugly fight for control of Wellington Management Company, a fight that cost me my job as CEO and made it appear for a time that my career in the industry I loved was over. But, by a series of unlikely but happy events, even coincidences, I made a comeback. Result: Vanguard oversees $5 trillion of assets in mid-2018, has become the world's largest mutual fund firm, broadly respected for its low-costs, its investment returns, and its ethical values.

How did that turnabout come to pass? Let's begin at the beginning.

Chapter 2
1945–1965

The Background – Blair, Princeton, Fortune, and Wellington

The story begins a long time ago, in September 1945, when I entered Blair Academy, a top New Jersey boarding school. I spent my junior and senior year there, thanks to a generous scholarship and demanding jobs, first as a waiter, then as captain of the waiters. I received a splendid college preparatory education. By graduation, I was ranked second in my class and named "Most Likely to Succeed."

My academic success at Blair was hard-won, and was instrumental in gaining admission to Princeton University as a member of the class of 1951. Once again, scholarships and jobs sustained me, but I found my early years at Princeton challenging. The low point came in the autumn of 1948, my sophomore year, when I took my first course in economics. Our textbook was the first edition of Dr. Paul Samuelson's *Economics: An Introductory Analysis*. Truth told, I found the book tough going, and fared poorly in my first stab at this new (to me) subject.

The low midterm grade in that course at the start of my sophomore year (D+), had it persisted through the semester, would have cost me my scholarship – and hence my Princeton career, for I had not a sou of outside financial support. But I pressed on as best I could, and closed out the semester with a grade of C–. It was a small triumph, but a triumph nonetheless.

1949: "Big Money in Boston"

Fate smiled on me a year later. I had determined to write my senior thesis on a subject that no student had previously tackled. Thus, Adam Smith, Karl Marx, and John Maynard Keynes were out. But what topic should I choose? Late in my junior year, in one of the many appearances of good luck in my long life, I found myself in the reading room of the then-brand-new Firestone Library, leafing through the December 1949 issue of *Fortune* magazine. I paused on page 116, and began to read an article describing a business I knew nothing about, one that I had never even imagined. The headline read, "Big Money in Boston." I immediately realized that I had found the subject of my thesis.

The bold-faced subhead below it confirmed my intuition, "But money isn't everything, according to the Massachusetts Investors Trust, which has prospered by selling the small investor peace of mind. It's invention: the open-end fund. The future: wide open." In the 10 fact-filled pages that followed, the article described the history, policies, and practices of Massachusetts Investors Trust. M.I.T., founded in 1924, was the first and then by far the largest "open-end" fund.[1]

In those ancient days, the term "mutual fund" had not yet come into general use, perhaps because "mutual" funds, with one notable exception, are *not* mutual. In fact, in direct contradiction of the principles spelled out in the preamble to The Investment Company Act of 1940, they are organized, operated, and managed in the interests of the management companies that control them, rather than placing the interests of their shareowners first.

"The 'Mutual' Fund"

Manuel F. Cohen, chairman of the U.S. Securities and Exchange Commission from 1964 to 1969, clearly addressed this lack of mutuality in mutual funds:

> *The fee structure [of mutual funds] has provided a real opportunity for the exercise of the ingenuity for which fund managers have established an enviable reputation. After all, that is where the money is,*

---

[1] An "open-end" fund redeems its shares on demand and (usually) continuously offers them for sale. A "closed-end" fund holds a fixed pool of capital and does neither.

and despite the common use of the word "mutual," the principal reason these funds are created and sold is to make money for the people who sell them and those who manage them. [2]

The *Fortune* article never used the term "mutual." It relied largely on terms such as "investment companies," "trusts," and "funds." Yet in its discussion of the embryonic industry's future, *Fortune* was optimistic that this tiny industry – which it described as "pretty small change" in the overall market – was nevertheless "rapidly expanding and somewhat contentious." More importantly, the industry "could become immensely influential . . . the ideal champion of the small stockholder in controversies with . . . corporate management."

1951: "The Economic Role of the Investment Company"

That serendipitous moment would shape my entire career and my life. The *Fortune* article was the springboard for my decision, made on the spot, to write my thesis on the history and future prospects of open-end investment companies. My title: "The Economic Role of the Investment Company." (As I mentioned earlier, the term "mutual fund" had not yet come into popular usage, so I used the term "investment company," the standard at the time.) I threw myself into the task with intensity, spending a year and a half researching and writing the thesis, meanwhile falling madly in love with my subject. I was convinced that the "tiny" $2 billion mutual fund industry would become huge, and would remain "contentious." I was right on both counts: today's $21 trillion mutual fund colossus is among the nation's largest and most dominant financial sectors.

My thesis conclusions, reached after an intense analysis of the industry, follow:

- "Investment companies should be operated in the most efficient, honest, and economical way possible."
- "Future growth can be maximized by reducing sales charges and management fees."

---

[2] From "The 'Mutual' Fund," a speech by then-SEC chairman Manuel Cohen before the Conference on Mutual Funds, Palm Springs, CA, March 1, 1968.

- "Funds can make no claim to superiority over the market averages [indexes]."
- "The principal [activity] of investment companies is the management of their investment portfolios. Everything else is incidental."
- "The principal role of the investment company should be to serve its shareholders."
- "There is no reason [an investment company] should refrain from exerting its influence on corporate policy. . . . Mutual funds seem destined to fulfill this crucial segment of their economic responsibility."

Yes, there was a lot of idealism in those conclusions. But, barely out of my teenage years, I was a typically idealistic scholar. Six-plus decades after I first read that *Fortune* article, my idealism has hardly diminished. Indeed, likely *because* of my lifelong experience in investing, that idealism is even more passionate and unyielding today. There's little question that many of the values I identified in my thesis would constitute the core of Vanguard's remarkable growth. Whatever was in my mind all those years ago, the thesis clearly put forth the proposition that mutual fund shareholders ought to be given a fair shake.

July 1951: Enter Wellington and Walter Morgan

The countless hours I spent researching and analyzing the industry in my carrel in Firestone Library were rewarded with a top grade on my thesis, and a magna cum laude diploma from Princeton. Even better, following my 1951 graduation, Walter L. Morgan, another Princeton alum (Class of 1920), read my 130-page opus and offered me a job with his Philadelphia firm, Wellington Management Company. "Largely as a result of this thesis," he would write to his staff, "we have added Mr. Bogle to our Wellington organization." Although I wasn't so sure at first, it was the opportunity of a lifetime.

Mr. Morgan – my mentor and the great hero of my long career – was an industry pioneer. Wellington Fund, which he had founded in 1928, had assets of $150 million when I joined the small firm in July

1951. It was one of 125 mutual funds operating in the United States, with aggregate assets of $3 billion. Ten firms, among them Wellington, then accounted for almost three-fourths of industry assets.

Boston was the center of the fund universe, home to 22 of the 50 largest funds, representing 46% of the industry's assets. The largest firm was Massachusetts Investors Trust, with assets of $438 million in 1951 – a market share equal to 15% of the industry. M.I.T. was not only the dominant firm, but it was also by far the lowest-cost provider, with an expense ratio of 0.29%. (In 1961 its expense ratio would reach a low of 0.17% of assets.) Funds based in New York then represented 27% of industry assets, followed by Minneapolis with 13%, and Philadelphia with a mere 7%.

Modus Operandi 1951: One Fund per Manager

In those days, most firms in the fund industry, including Wellington, managed but a single fund (and sometimes a second fund that was usually tiny). For example, the five M.I.T. trustees of that era also managed Massachusetts Investors Second Fund (hardly a name that would appeal to today's mutual fund marketers, and later changed to Massachusetts Investors Growth Stock Fund). With assets of just $34 million, the Second Fund represented but 8% of M.I.T.'s $472 million asset total.

I first walked into Wellington's Philadelphia offices on July 9, 1951. There I found the perfect environment for the start of my career – small, friendly, and laden with opportunities for a young college graduate. I was welcomed by the small (60-person) staff, and was soon involved in every phase of the firm's activities – administration, marketing and distribution, securities analysis, and shareholder relations. I began drafting letters to our investors for Mr. Morgan, and within a few years was writing his President's Letter in the Wellington Fund Annual Report. By the time a decade had passed, I was viewed as the heir apparent to Mr. Morgan. I assumed that I would be at Wellington forever.

Those years at Wellington were filled with joy and challenge. I eagerly jumped at the opportunity to lead the drafting of the prospectus for the 1958 initial public offering (IPO) of Wellington Equity Fund (now Windsor Fund), adding a stock fund to supplement our balanced fund.[3]

The Power of Conservative Investing

During my first 14 years at Wellington, our primary focus on a balanced fund was our great strength, and it helped make us the respected leader of the industry's balanced fund sector. The industry of that era could accurately be described as "conservative," with most fund portfolios diversified among high-quality common stocks. Because we balanced stocks with bonds, Wellington was considered one of the most conservative of all. As our motto of that day put it, Wellington Fund offered "a complete investment program in one security."

But the stability I hoped for at Wellington Management would not last. By the time of my rocket-like ascent to the company's presidency in April 1965, the traditional mutual fund industry that I described in my Princeton thesis had changed, and not for the better. The "Go-Go" era was in full swing, and investors were abandoning conservative balanced funds such as Wellington in droves, drawn by the siren song of quick profits being earned by high-flying aggressive stock funds. Still, one way or another, I would deal with these challenges – and many new challenges – for the rest of my long career.

Staying the Course

The mutual fund industry had been a major part of my life since 1949, when "Big Money in Boston" first inspired me. My career at Wellington Management Company was set, and in 1965 I was called to

---

[3] In 1960, I also took the lead in preparing the IPO prospectus for the public offering of Mr. Morgan's (non-controlling) shares of Wellington Management Company.

lead the firm. That proved to be the pinnacle of the early years of my career. Paradoxically, however, Wellington had overstayed its conservative course in a marketplace that, for almost a decade, would thrive on speculation. In the challenges that lay ahead, I would need a guiding star and a motto that encapsulates it. That that motto was, and still is, "Stay the Course."

Chapter 3

1965–1974

The "Go-Go" Era, the Aftermath, and the Formation of Vanguard

	12/1965	9/1974	Annual Rate of Growth
Wellington* Assets (Billions)	$2.2	$1.5	−2.6%
Industry Assets (Billions)	$35.2	$34.1	−0.2
Wellington* Market Share	6.3%	4.4%	—
			Annual Return†
S&P 500 Index	92	61	−1.1%
Intermediate-Term U.S. Government Bond Yield	4.9%	8.0%	5.7%
60% Stocks/40% Bonds	—	—	1.9

*Vanguard's predecessor company.
†Includes dividends and interest, respectively.
Source: Yahoo! Finance.

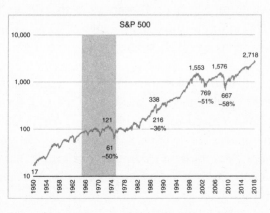

The beginning of the pre-Vanguard era saw stocks rise, driven first by speculative stocks with great stories but weak (or nonexistent) balance sheets, and then great growth companies that reached excessive valuations. Inevitably, a 50% market crash followed, which finally ended on October 1, 1974.

The "Go-Go" Era

During the mid-1960s, the fund industry began to move away from its conservative tradition. This was the "Go-Go" era, during which many new fund managers began to offer funds investing largely in speculative stocks, and many established fund managers followed suit. These stocks came with sweet stories, but were typically backed by neither substance nor nutrients. Gone was the industry's focus on a relative handful of middle-of-the-road equity funds and balanced funds holding "blue-chip" stocks, replaced by a far more speculative group of high-flying equity funds.

Bagels Out, Doughnuts In

To use a culinary metaphor, Wellington was the industry's bagel – hard, crusty, and nutritious. But by 1965, the industry had developed a tasted for doughnuts – sweet, soft, and bereft of nutritional content.[1] Doughnut shops, as it were, proliferated. Bagel buyers almost vanished. We could only watch helplessly as the balanced-fund share of industry sales fell from a high of 40% in 1955 to 17% in 1965 to 5% in 1970. By 1975, it would tumble to a mere 1%. What was the owner of the bagel shop to do? The strategy for survival was obvious: start selling doughnuts.

To survive, Wellington needed to compete with the "hot" sellers of doughnuts. Fidelity was one of the Go-Go era's leaders, and two of its funds proved to be gold mines – for Fidelity's management, but not, ultimately, for its clients. Financial buccaneers began to jump on the "junk" bandwagon. Marginal accounting standards produced performance records that would prove to be ephemeral, sometimes even fraudulent.

One particularly egregious example was the Enterprise Fund. In 1967, this Los Angeles–based newcomer would report a dubious return

---

[1] In hindsight, the nutritional content of both the traditional mutual fund industry and the bagel proved overrated.

of 117%, built largely on the acquisition of previously privately owned stocks acquired by the fund at discounts of as large as 50% from market price, later marked up to 100% of market price.

In the following year, Enterprise drew the largest annual cash flow in the previous history of the fund industry, an unheard of $600 million. The fund's assets grew to $950 million by the close of 1968. But reality finally returned to the marketplace. Enterprise Fund's assets fell 84% to less than $150 million in 1977, and the fund suffered negative net cash flow in 22 of the 25 years from 1970 to 1994. By 2011, Enterprise had ceased to exist.

"I Was Too Conservative"

Early in the spring of 1965, Mr. Morgan had become concerned about the growing trend toward speculative funds. He recognized the serious threat to his conservative philosophy and his business, with its near-total dependence on the balanced Wellington Fund. "I was too conservative," he told *Institutional Investor* magazine. At age 66, he decided that it was time for new leadership and took a radical step. In April, he called me into his office and told me that I would immediately take charge of Wellington Management as his successor. I still remember his exact words: "Jack, I want you to take charge and do whatever it takes to solve our problems."

I was but 35 years old (and looked a lot younger!). But after working with me for almost 15 years, Mr. Morgan had come to trust my judgment. Perhaps overly self-confident, I thought the solution was obvious. Imagine you run that bagel shop that I described earlier and your customers are deserting you in droves, buying doughnuts from the shop across the street. To survive – or so I reasoned – you must start selling doughnuts yourself.

I determined that the best way to secure Wellington's survival was by merging with a fund firm that had a strong equity presence. I quickly approached three firms that I believed offered such an opportunity. While none of the three managed the kind of aggressive fund that was that era's darling, each emphasized stock funds and each would have immediately reduced Wellington's dependence on a single balanced fund.[2] My plans were to merge with such a firm, and then grow the combined firm from a stronger foundation.

Three Strikes . . . but Not Quite Out

I first approached the American Funds group of Los Angeles, a respected manager of equity funds, then overseeing $1 billion of mutual fund assets. With 3% of the industry's total assets, American[3] was its fifth-largest firm. Failure. Next, I approached Incorporated Investors, a stand-alone stock fund in Boston, later to become part of the Putnam fund complex. Again, failure.

Then I turned to Franklin Custodian Funds, a then-tiny multi-fund complex with assets of just $17 million but lots of potential. Another failure. Owner Charles Johnson made a wise decision not to do the merger I proposed. The remarkable growth of the funds managed by what is now Franklin Templeton Investments – whose assets had grown to $415 billion by 2018 – has made his family billionaires at least 10 times over.

The Merger

By happenstance, a fourth candidate was brought to my attention: Thorndike, Doran, Paine & Lewis, Inc. This small Boston firm, owned by four young managing partners, ran an apparently successful Go-Go fund named Ivest with just $17 million in assets as well as a growing pension advisory business. It seemed to offer investment talent that, I then believed, could more effectively manage the portfolio of our then-faltering Wellington Fund. We agreed to merge.

On June 6, 1966, Mr. Morgan approved the deal. The merger terms were set. The price was paid, not in dollars, but in shares of Wellington

---

[2] We formed our first stock fund, Wellington Equity Fund (now Windsor Fund) in 1958, but it was tiny ($92 million in assets compared to Wellington Fund's $2 billion-plus), and its returns through 1965 were not impressive. Windsor Fund's history is recounted in Chapter 13.

[3] Led by Jon Lovelace, whom we met at the start of this book.

Management Company, which by then had substantial public ownership – a result of Walter Morgan's 1960 public offering of much of his stock. Mr. Morgan had retained his controlling "B" shares, and divided them among the new managers.

Collectively, the four Boston partners held 40% of the firm's shares, effective voting control. I controlled 28%. Public shareholders owned the remaining 32%.[4] As CEO of the combined firm, I was confident in my ability to work with my new partners, to set our course, and to captain the new ship successfully.

The "Peace Dollar"

Not that I wasn't nervous. At the celebration of the merger, I gave each of my new partners a small silver tray on which I had cemented a $1 coin with "peace" engraved on its face, known as the "peace dollar." I feared that peace with my partners would not endure, but I hoped that we could make it work.

Together, we five whiz kids whizzed high for a few years. (We were featured on the cover of *Institutional Investor* magazine.[5]) Then, the investment climate turned against us, and we whizzed low. The Go-Go era "went-went." It was superseded by something distinctively different, but, as it turned out, even worse: The "Nifty Fifty" craze, in which the stock prices of the nation's fastest-growing companies lost all touch with their intrinsic values. The simple principle: "Don't worry. High valuations don't matter. Earnings growth will ultimately bail you out."

The Bubble Bursts

Stocks such as Xerox, Polaroid, IBM, Avon Products, and Digital Equipment Corporation soared. These stocks, at their peaks, were valued

---

[4] I was not unaware that, were there ever to be a proxy fight, the legacy shareholders would likely vote with me.

[5] "The Whiz Kids Take Over at Wellington," *Institutional Investor,* January 1968. The cover showed me as a four-armed quarterback, handing off a football to each of my new partners.

at 50 times earnings or more. But reality finally took over. Their stock prices collapsed, leading the bear market downward. Like the "New Economy" bubble that developed in the late 1990s, the Nifty Fifty bubble burst in 1973.

Participants in that bubble included not only mutual fund managers, but the vast majority of institutional investors, including once-staid trust companies, insurance companies, and even college endowment funds. (The manager of the endowment fund of the University of Rochester, Bert Tripp, the guru of the craze, was so embarrassed that he had the cover of its annual report printed in red ink.) From its high in early 1973 to its low in early October 1974, the U.S. stock market fell by 50%.

1970–1974: Bear Market Follows Bull Market

At that same time, Wellington's new business model began to fail. Three of the four new funds that our aggressive new managers brought into our fold (or soon formed) collapsed. From high to low, Ivest Fund saw its asset value sink by 65%. It would later go out of existence, consigned to the dustbin of financial history.

Two of the Go-Go cousins formed by my partners performed equally badly and finally failed. Worst of all, under its aggressive new managers, the asset value of the once-conservative Wellington Fund tumbled big time. During the decade from 1966 to 1976, this premier balanced fund turned in the worst performance of any balanced fund in the land. (See Chapter 11, "Wellington Fund.")

In the 1960 IPO, Wellington Management Company's owner, Walter Morgan, had sold more than half of his shares. With the stock now public, we were able to issue new shares to our merger partners. Yet, even during the merger's remarkably successful early years, I questioned whether our public ownership structure was best for our mutual fund shareholders, and for our firm's competitive position in the industry.

Fiduciary Duty . . . but to *Two* Masters?

To state the obvious, we managers had a fiduciary duty *both* to our mutual fund shareholders *and* to our management company shareholders. But when a privately held management company becomes publicly held, this conflict of interest is exacerbated. In September 1971, I candidly expressed my concerns. Speaking at the annual gathering of our firm's investment professionals, I began my remarks with this excerpt from a speech delivered by Justice Harlan Fiske Stone at the University of Michigan Law School in 1934:

> Most of the mistakes and major faults of the financial era that has just drawn to a close will be ascribed to the failure to observe the fiduciary principle, the precept as old as holy writ, that "a man cannot serve two masters." . . . Those who serve nominally as trustees but consider only last the interests of those whose funds they command suggest how far we have ignored the necessary implications of that principle.[6]

It was high time, I added, that any conflicts between the profession of investing and the business of investing be reconciled in favor of the client.

I then suggested that one way of resolving this conflict could be "a mutualization, whereby the funds acquire the management company, . . . or internalization, whereby the active executives own the management company, with contracts negotiated on a 'cost-plus' basis, with incentives for both performance and efficiency, but without the ability to capitalize earnings through public sale." When I spoke those words, I could not possibly have imagined that, within three short years, I would not only *talk the talk* about mutualization, but would *walk the walk*.

The Wrong Scapegoat

As the 1973–1974 bear market took hold, the happy partnership formed by the 1966 merger fell apart. Bad markets and bad fund returns meant bad business and, buttressed by power politics, destroyed any semblance of trust between Wellington's merger-acquired money managers and me. Assets of our flagship, the conservative Wellington Fund, had tumbled from a high of $2 billion in 1965 to less than

---

[6] Reprinted as Harlan Fiske Stone, "The Public Influence of the Bar," *Harvard Law Review* 48, no. 1 (November 1934), 6.

$1 billion, on the way to a low of $480 million. The earnings of Wellington Management Company plummeted, and its stock price followed suit, dropping from a high of $50 per share in 1968 to a low of $4.25 in 1975.

My Boston partners quickly found a scapegoat. Not among themselves, despite their responsibility for the terrible performance of the mutual funds whose portfolios they managed. They chose me as their scapegoat, the chief executive responsible for the merger that wreaked such havoc on the returns earned by the investors who had trusted us. Yet I had ceded substantial voting power to the new managers to accomplish the merger. In the midst of the bear market, on January 23, 1974, they banded together and fired me. Then they replaced me as chief executive of Wellington Management Company with their leader, Robert W. Doran.

"Ex-Fund Chief to Come Back"

I leave it to wiser heads than mine to explain the perverse logic involved in that outcome. But it was the most heartbreaking moment – actually, until then, the *only* heartbreaking moment – of my entire career. I decided to fight back. Typical of the mutual fund industry, there was a considerable overlap in board membership between the funds and the manager. But the funds, as required by law, were overseen by a majority of independent directors.

On January 24, 1974, the day after my firing at Wellington Management Company, the board of directors of the 11 Wellington mutual funds met in New York. As chairman of each of the funds, I called the meeting to order and promptly proposed that we declare our independence from Wellington Management Company, mutualize our funds, elect our own officers, appoint our own staff, and empower them to operate the funds on an "at-cost" basis.

The resulting power struggle between the funds and their independent adviser was without precedent. It had never before occurred in our industry, and it hasn't since. I doubt that it will ever occur again. Even the *New York Times* couldn't figure out what was happening. In the *Times* early edition of March 14, 1974, the headline read "Ex-Fund

Chief to Come Back." In later editions, the story and the photo of me were unchanged. But the original headline now ended with a boldface question mark. A few excerpts:

Ex-Fund Chief to Come Back?

John C. Bogle, who was forced out of his $100,000-a-year job as president and chief executive officer of the Wellington Management Company in late January, is expected by his associates to try to fight his way back at the next board meeting, scheduled to be held within a week…. Mr. Bogle is understood to believe that this may be the appropriate time for the funds to "mutualize," or take over, their investment advisers.

That haunting question mark in the headline hinted at the uncertainty of the outcome of the struggle that was going on behind the scenes.

The Board Meeting That Changed Everything

At the January 1974 board meeting, the directors of the Wellington funds had requested that I provide a study of the options available to them for dealing with the crisis. The situation was, as far as I know, unique in the annuals of the mutual fund industry: an extraordinary confrontation between a group of mutual funds with its own CEO (me) and its long-time investment adviser, Wellington Management Company, then holding virtually complete control over the funds' affairs. WMC's new CEO was Robert Doran, my former partner.

I sought – and relished – the opportunity that the board presented to me. My young staff assistant, Jan Twardowski, and I would ultimately produce an analysis covering corporate goals and fund returns; costs; advisory and distribution contracts; industry practices; and future prospects for the funds. Our study would ultimately total more than 250 pages. We titled our paper "The Future Structure of the Wellington Group of Investment Companies."

LANDMARK 1. JANUARY 1974

"The Future Structure of the Wellington Group of Investment Companies"

The "Future Structure" study, as it came to be known, began by listing seven options available to the board:

- Option #1 – Status Quo: Continuation of all existing relationships.
- Option #2 – Internal administration by fund staff.
- Option #3 – Internal administration and distribution by fund staff.
- Option #4 – Mutualization: acquisition by the funds of all Wellington Management Company fund-related activities, including investment advisory services.
- Option #5 – New external investment adviser(s).
- Option #6 – New external management company for the group.
- Option #7 – Build completely new internal organization.

We quickly limited our study to the three most plausible options – #2, #3, and #4. We described these options as "the least radical" because they involved the minimum disruption of the two organizations presently in "the successive assumption of additional functions by the fund group from Wellington Management Company – first administration, next distribution, and finally investment management." While "mutualization" was explicit in Option #4, it was implicit in Option #2.

At the very outset of the "Future Structure" study, we set forth our rationale:

> This (present) structure has been the accepted norm for the mutual fund industry for fifty years. The issue we face is whether a structure so traditional, so long

accepted, so satisfactory for an infant industry as it
grew, during a time of less stringent ethical and legal
standards, is really the optimum structure for these
times and for the future – and for the Wellington
Group of Investment Companies. Or, rather, should the
Funds seek the greater control over their own destiny
so clearly implied by the word "independence"?

I favored a complete *mutualization* of the funds' operations, to be
achieved by purchasing Wellington Management's mutual fund business,
"unscrambling the egg," as it were, that I had created with that failed
1966 merger. Yes, mutualization was totally my idea, and I realized that a
mutual company would never provide me with the personal fortune that
so many denizens of Wall Street would earn. But it offered, I believed,
my last, best chance to resume my career.[7]

Innovations without precedent, however, no matter how sensible
and logical, are rarely able to win the approval of conservative directors.
Nor were they likely to gain the favor of the cautious legal counsel
whom the directors had retained, Wall Street attorney and former SEC
Commissioner Richard B. (Dick) Smith, Esq.

That initial proposal quickly died, but the board reached a compromise. It wasn't exactly the 13 colonies telling King George III to get
lost, as it were, in 1776. But fund *independence* – the right of a fund to
operate with its own leadership, in the interest of its own shareholders,
free of domination by the fund's external manager – was at its heart. But
the first small step that we would soon take was the beginning of the
full mutualization that led to the Wellington funds performing their own
activities, rather than depending on Wellington Management Company.

Achieving Independence

After the battle was more or less over, Dick Smith informed me that
he had advised the board that, whatever decision was made, it must be

---

[7] Don't forget that, at the outset, the odds against creating the new structure were
long, and that the odds in favor of building a $5 trillion colossus were essentially zero.

unanimous. So the outcome was inevitable: the board would adopt the option least disruptive to the status quo. The Wellington funds would create a new subsidiary company, with fund administration as its sole responsibility. I would continue to serve as the CEO of the funds and would also become CEO of the new subsidiary.

We defined "administration" to include fund financial affairs, shareholder recordkeeping, legal and compliance, and handling share purchases and redemptions. Most importantly, the new subsidiary was responsible for oversight of the distribution and investment advisory services provided by Wellington Management Company. "Distribution" would include control of our sales organization, advertising, and all marketing activities. "Investment advisory services" would include security analysis, stock selection, investment strategy, portfolio supervision, and handling all trading activities.

Chuck Root: The Indispensable Man

Truth told, even that positive outcome depended almost entirely on the leadership of the chairman of the fund board's independent director group, the late Charles D. Root Jr., an experienced pension firm executive. He believed in me – my character, my leadership ability, and my comprehensive knowledge of the fund industry.

Chuck Root was a man of wisdom, of passion, of conviction, and of character. Without him, the board would almost certainly have followed industry practice and allowed their adviser to dictate its choice for fund CEO. It would not have been me. Yes, Chuck Root was living proof that, as I have often observed, "even one person can make a difference."

Option #2: "Weak Tea"

To be sure, Option #2 of our "Future Structure" study, internalization of administrative functions only, was weak tea for me. The funds were barred by their own board both from engaging in marketing and distribution of fund shares and from providing the funds with investment advisory services. I knew that, if our new organization were to succeed, those walls would have to come tumbling down.

In a March 11, 1974, memorandum to the board, I was brutally honest:

> Option #2 is small in terms of people, but large in terms of dollars, and important in terms of concept. The second step — adding "internal distribution" under Option #3 — also seems particularly appropriate. But if it is not accepted now, it may well be only a matter of time, perhaps within two to three years, when it will be accepted, given the truly massive challenges to be faced in mutual fund distribution.[8]

> When that step is taken, it may well be only a matter of some more time until the fund Board will first reconsider, and then act to alter, our Group's acceptance of the traditional industry structure involving an external investment adviser.

> The reasons for that final step into a world of full independence for the Funds may relate to the control of that key function (investment advice), its organization, and its people, or to the costs involved and the performance achieved. Perhaps, then, the issue is not "whether," but only "when," the Wellington Group of Investment Companies will become completely independent.

"Fired with Enthusiasm!"

The board's initial decision echoed King Solomon's ruling in an argument between the two women who each claimed a baby as their own: "cut the baby in half." Wellington Management Company would continue as investment adviser and distributor for the funds. I would create a new firm with a new and unprecedented mutual structure. But I was left with only the narrowest of mandates, barred from undertaking any investment management or share distribution activities.

---

[8] In the "Future Structure" memorandum, I also noted "the possibility of moving to a no-load distribution system, engendering the complete elimination of all distribution revenues." No one seemed to notice.

Our crew, numbering only 28 when we began our long voyage, would be responsible only for the administration of the funds' affairs, albeit with specific responsibility for overseeing Wellington's investment and distribution activities.

Administration is but one of the three sides – and arguably the least entrepreneurial side – of the triangle that represents mutual fund activities. The other two, more critical, sides of the triangle – investment management and share distribution – were where value could be created and growth achieved. Both were to remain with my rivals at Wellington Management . . . but only for a few years.

It took no genius to realize that our destiny would be determined by the kind of funds we created, whether they could attain superior investment returns, and how – and how effectively – the funds' shares were marketed. When we were prohibited from engaging in these activities – allowed only to oversee them – I knew a rough road lay ahead. For my goal was ultimately to build a broad-based firm, and I took on my new leadership role the same way I had left my previous leadership role: "Fired with enthusiasm."

The Challenge

Despite the serious limitations that the board had placed on the firm it had created, we were confident that we could overcome those limits. With a novel structure that had never before been tried in the mutual fund industry, we would fight to make our mark.

What name should we select for a firm with such potential? It was only logical to have the name remain with the new company being formed. But the board determined that the name Wellington would remain with Wellington Management Company, although Wellington Fund would also retain its name.

I thought that decision was stupid and short-sighted, and I threatened to resign. But when lead independent director Root threw down his challenge, I decided to stay. He said, "Jack, you can call the group anything you want. And then go out and make it the finest name in the whole damn mutual fund industry!"

Ever since, that is precisely what I have strived to accomplish.

LANDMARK 2. SEPTEMBER 1974

"What's in a Name?"

With only weeks to go before our new firm's incorporation, we still had no name for the new firm. Fate, as it had done so often during my career, smiled again. Completely by coincidence, I came across a reference to HMS *Vanguard*, Lord Nelson's flagship at the Battle of the Nile in 1798.

In the late summer of 1974, a dealer in antique prints came by my office with some small engravings of the British military battles during the Napoleonic War era, illustrating the triumphant forces under the Duke of Wellington, for whom Mr. Morgan had named his first mutual fund 46 years earlier.

When I bought his prints, he offered me some companion prints of the British naval battles of the same era. Ever enticed by the sea and its timeless mystery, I bought them, too. Delighted, the dealer gave me the book from which they had been removed.

Much as I had browsed through *Fortune* in Firestone Library 25 years earlier, I browsed through the pages of *Naval Battles of Great Britain 1775–1815*, the book that had been given to me. When I turned to the saga of the historic Battle of the Nile, I was impressed. There, Lord Nelson's fleet sank almost every French fighting ship, while losing but a single English frigate, still the most complete naval victory in history. Napoleon's dreams of world conquest were over. At the close of Nelson's triumphant dispatch to the British Admiralty, it was Lord Horatio Nelson's signature, right below the name of his flagship: "HMS *Vanguard*, off the mouth of the Nile." With neither a second's hesitation nor a single consultant, I decided that "Vanguard" would be the name of the firm I would soon create.

Vanguard: The Birth of a New Flagship

The name of Nelson's flagship, the parallels to the Duke of Wellington's conquests, the proud naval traditions embodied in Lord Nelson's leadership, and the meaning of the word itself ("leader in a new trend") were more than I could resist. Incorporated on September 24, 1974, The Vanguard Group was born. The board named me chairman and chief executive, responsible for our then-27-person staff. We had defied precedent, and we had won the battle for the independence of our mutual funds to operate solely in the interests of our fund owners.

A Narrow Escape

The name that I chose for the new firm required the approval of the board of directors. (No surprise there.) But when I presented it for approval, I sensed that many, perhaps most, directors did not share my excitement for the Vanguard name. They realized, correctly, that I would be giving a nondescript firm that was charged only with the administration of the funds a name that reflected its potential to become a full-line mutual fund complex, not its humble initial activity.

Struggling for the directors' approval, I added, "The great thing about the Vanguard name is that it would leave the location of our list of fund asset values in the newspapers exactly where it was before – "V" for Vanguard abutting "W" for Wellington. Remarkably, the mood of the meeting changed, and the board quickly approved our new name. It was a narrow escape. Saving the Vanguard name was a major victory, for that name has clearly met the test of time.

The First Skirmish

As the battle began, the Wellington Fund board of directors was narrowly divided in alliances. Six board members, most based in Philadelphia with long service, were invited on the board by Mr. Morgan. Three other directors, all from Boston, had been nominated by my former partners. The three "inside directors" affiliated with Wellington Management Company – Doran, Thorndike, and I – retained our voting privileges, though we were excused from voting on the "Future Structure" proposal.

With the exception of we three principals, all of the members of the board seemed comfortable in exercising their independence in the coming battle. But it seemed clear that when it came time for a vote, the six Philadelphians (including Richard "Dick" Corroon, who practiced law in Delaware) leaned toward my position to mutualize. The three Bostonians leaned toward the Doran/Thorndike position to have the status quo prevail, to terminate me as CEO, and to get on with business.

The lead independent director, Chuck Root, a Philadelphian, clearly believed in me and favored my desire to mutualize. That was good enough for me, and I had confidence (I'm not sure just why!) that the divided board would unite, finally, and approve one of the seven options I had proposed.

Game Over?

But a potential snag quickly developed. At the next board meeting, on February 21, 1974, Chuck Root announced that James F. "Jim" Mitchell Jr. had reached age 70, the implicit age limit for service by directors. Chuck Root recommended that Jim Mitchell continue as a director until the board's final decision was made. The Boston directors strongly disagreed. Dick Corroon, whose vote I had relied upon, seemed likely to join with the Boston directors in opposing Jim's continued service on the board. It looked as though the vote would be 4–4, effectively ending Jim's service on the board and dashing my hopes of continuing to serve as the leader of the funds. I feared that the game was over.

"A Near-Run Thing"

At that moment, with the board majority that favored my confirmation about to slip away, my first thought was, "I lost." I was about to call for a recess and explain to Dick the consequences of his decision when Chuck said, "Well, we've already talked to Jim and he's agreed to stay." Dick, ever the gentleman, said, "So it would be very embarrassing to rescind that offer. He should stay." I breathed a sigh of relief.

So courtesy carried the day. Echoing the words of the Duke of Wellington after his narrow victory over Napoleon at the Battle of Waterloo, our battle, too, was "a near-run thing."

The Shareholders Approve

Vanguard commenced operations on September 18, 1974, six days before the firm was incorporated. Not until February 19, 1975, did the U.S. Securities and Exchange Commission clear our proxy statement that described the reorganization. We then mailed proxy statements to our fund shareholders, asking them to approve both the proposal to reorganize the funds and the modest reductions of some 5% in the advisory fee rates paid to Wellington Management Company.

On April 22, 1975, the shareholders of the funds overwhelmingly approved our proposals. On May 1, 1975, a new service agreement went into effect lowering the advisory fees that our funds paid to Wellington Management Company.

During the next decade, far larger fee reductions, ranging up to 90%, would follow as Vanguard moved into a position of strength. We were wise enough to propose prospective fee reductions that would only come into play after substantial growth in fund assets. (See Chapter 5.)

The formation of Vanguard largely went unnoticed by the press. Today, one searches in vain for any recognition in the financial media that a new company had been born, let alone a new company that had broken the traditional rules of mutual fund structure.

A Full-Fledged Mutual Fund Complex Emerges

My prophecy turned out to be accurate to a fault, but my time sequence proved too cautious. In September 1975, just a year after the new firm's founding, the fund directors approved Vanguard's formation of an internally administered, "unmanaged" mutual fund, the world's first index mutual fund.

Only a year and a half after that, in February 1977, the funds eliminated all sales loads and took responsibility for their own marketing and distribution. Finally, in March 1980, the funds created their own investment advisory unit to manage their bond and money market funds.

At that point, barely five years from its inception, Vanguard had become the full-fledged fund complex that I had sought at the outset.

We were ready, willing, and able – indeed eager – to make our mark by deploying our unique mutual structure and our unprecedented index strategy. That combination would lead to a remarkable wave of creative destruction that would indeed destroy the fund industry, "as we then knew it."

"A Plague on Both Your Houses?"

Later, when we did begin to attract attention, it was not kind. In a May 1975 article, *Forbes* magazine treated our new mutual structure with scorn. The headline—right out of Shakespeare's *Romeo and Juliet*—summed up the story's contempt for both Wellington Management and Vanguard: "A Plague on Both Houses?"

Decades later, then-*Forbes* editor William Baldwin issued not one but two apologies for that baneful article. The first, on February 8, 1999, said: "With the benefit of hindsight, we should not have published that snide article about The Vanguard Group." Again, in the August 26, 2010, issue, Baldwin wrote: "I'd like to officially retract a story *Forbes* published in May 1975. Bogle . . . is as vociferous as ever an evangelist for cost-cutting. I think he has done more for investors than any other financier of the past century."

Two Memorable – and Opposite – Reactions

Others in the mutual fund industry may well have felt the same way about the creation of Vanguard as did that May 1975 *Forbes* article. But they largely ignored its birth. (Little did they suspect what would lie ahead.) Indeed, I received so few comments on our new structure of fund independence that the two that meant the most to me are etched in my memory. One was that warning from Jon Lovelace, chief of the American Funds in Los Angeles, cited in the introduction to this book: our mutual structure would "destroy this industry."

The second came from Brandon Barringer, a former member of the Wellington Fund Investment Committee, and veteran investor with a reputation for deep wisdom and broad perspective. When he learned about the formation of Vanguard in 1974, he called me from his room in Pennsylvania Hospital, where he was recuperating. His words: "You have just revolutionized the mutual fund industry, Jack. Congratulations on your accomplishment." The Vanguard Experiment in Mutual Fund Governance was underway.

As it turned out, I suppose, both Mr. Lovelace and Mr. Barringer got it right.

So after the smoke had risen from the first battlefield, we had stayed the course, *Vanguard existed.* The next battle would soon begin.

Staying the Course

The guiding star of "stay the course" again proved to be an essential aspect of my ability to surmount challenges; weathering the heartaches and the disappointments of the years from 1965 to 1974 depended on my dogged determination to stay the course of my career. The battle was long and hard, but the result – Vanguard, a new star in the firmament – would one day bring a revolution to the world of mutual funds. In retrospect, I don't see how I "kept my cool" (as it is said today) under the pressures of battle. But, paraphrasing Kipling, I treated triumph and disaster – those two imposters – just the same. I knew what I wanted to accomplish and Vanguard's novel mutual structure was the key to what would come next: the world's first index mutual fund.

Chapter 4
The Index Fund Revolution
From Birth to Dominance

	12/1975	6/2018	Annual Rate of Growth
Index Assets	$11 M	$6.8 T	37.4%
Industry Assets	45.9 B	18.3 T	15.8
Index Market Share	0%	37%	
			Annual Return
S&P 500 Index	90	2,718	11.5%
Intermediate-Term U.S. Government Bond Yield	7.2%	2.1%	6.9
60% Stocks/40% Bonds	—	—	10.0

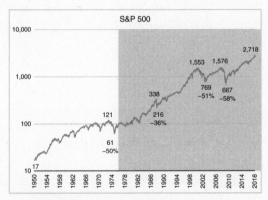

Source: Yahoo! Finance.

This index fund was Vanguard's first creation. This chart makes it clear that the index fund has not only survived, but thrived during a long-term secular rise in stock prices – an 11.5% annual return, fully 22% above the 9.6% return of the S&P 500 in the first 74 years of the index's history.

1951: The Seed Is Planted

Indexing was an idea that had first crossed my mind back in 1951 at Princeton University. In my senior thesis I wrote that mutual funds "may make no claim to superiority over the market averages." In the years that followed, my deep involvement in Wellington Fund's elusive search for some semblance of investment excellence – to say nothing of my unrequited hope that my merger partners could earn sustained superior returns – only confirmed my worst fears about active fund managers.

These firsthand experiences with active investment management taught me a lesson: *The search for winning fund managers is a tough and ultimately unrewarding strategy for the vast majority of investors.* That lesson returned to my mind when I read "Challenge to Judgment," by Nobel laureate professor Paul A. Samuelson, in the inaugural issue of *The Journal of Portfolio Management* early in October 1974. What an amazing – and happy – coincidence that I read that profound article only moments after founding the new firm![1] The timing couldn't have been more perfect.

Dr. Samuelson could find no "brute evidence" that fund managers could systematically outperform the returns of the S&P 500 Index "on a repeatable, sustained basis." In essence, he demanded that someone, somewhere, start an index fund modeled on the S&P 500. "As yet," he wrote, "there exists no convenient fund that apes the whole market, requires no load, and keeps commissions, turnover and management fees to the feasible minimum."

Motive and Opportunity

Dr. Samuelson's challenge struck me like a bolt of lightning, igniting my conviction that upstart Vanguard had a remarkable, even unique, opportunity to operate a passively managed, low-cost index fund and

---

Note: Vanguard's formation of the first index mutual fund is the seminal event in our history. I devote this entire chapter to the remarkable story of its creation.

[1] Yes, that same Dr. Samuelson whose textbook had baffled me at Princeton a quarter-century earlier.

have the market to ourselves for at least a few years. None of our competitors in the mutual fund industry wanted to start a low-cost (indeed "at-cost") mutual fund. If "strategy follows structure," a nominal-cost index fund was perfect, and singular to our new firm.

All of our peers had the *opportunity* to start an index fund; only Vanguard had both the *opportunity* and the *motive*. After all, a sponsor's objective in forming a so-called mutual fund is to increase assets under management, thereby increasing the advisory fees and thus the profits earned by the firm.[2] For better or worse in the fund business, that is "the American Way." Newly independent Vanguard, however, sought to (and later did) reduce the exorbitant fees paid to its adviser to the far lower levels prevailing for large corporate and state pension funds. The index fund was even better: it required no investment adviser, and would pay zero in advisory fees.

There were but three persons – in essence, the entire strategic team of Vanguard's tiny staff – who were in a position to develop the investment concepts and marketing plan for the index fund: myself; Jan M. Twardowski, a young graduate of Princeton and the Wharton School at the University of Pennsylvania (and later, president of Frank Russell Securities Company); and James S. Riepe, another Wharton graduate (and later, vice chairman of T. Rowe Price). We set to work to make the case for an index fund modeled on the S&P 500 Stock Index, and prepared a formal recommendation to the directors at their September meeting.

Persuading Vanguard's Directors That Costs Matter

Given the strife that had preceded Vanguard's birth, I knew that the board would question my objectivity. So I marked Dr. Samuelson's paper "EXHIBIT A" in my presentation, placed even ahead of the data that I relied on to validate my proposal.

The next exhibit presented compelling evidence that indexing would have worked effectively in the past. I tabulated the annual returns for each equity mutual fund during the 30 years from 1945 to 1975, and then calculated the simple average, comparing it to the S&P 500.

---

[2] Note the words of SEC chairman Manuel F. Cohen from 1968, cited in Chapter 2.

Result: the average annual return of the S&P 500 Index was 11.3% versus 9.7% for the average equity fund, an annual advantage of 1.6 percentage points per year for indexing. Here was hard statistical evidence – "brute evidence," if you will – of the superiority of the returns of the passive index over active funds. The data confirmed the conclusion that I had reached in my thesis 24 years earlier, then with only anecdotal evidence in support.[3]

"The Fund Is *Not* Managed"

Eager to portray this advantage for a pension account, I showed the board the data for an assumed initial investment of $1,000,000. Result: final value of the S&P 500 Index account, $25,020,000; average equity mutual fund, $16,390,000. The index fund advantage: a remarkable $8,630,000. It couldn't get much more persuasive then that.

At the board meeting in September 1975, Vanguard's directors were dubious about my index fund proposal. They reminded me that our mandate – a mandate won only after considerable struggle within our own Wellington Fund board – precluded our new company from engaging in investment advisory and marketing services.

I argued that Vanguard's operating an index fund did not violate the ban on our providing the investment advisory services to our funds.[4] It would simply own all 500 stocks in the S&P 500 Index. It would employ no investment adviser, and so would not be "managed." A public underwriting could be handled by an outside syndicate of brokerage firms.

Disingenuous or not, my argument that the index fund was not managed carried the day. With less controversy than I had expected, the board

---

[3] This spread was no mere statistical aberration. In a January 2016 paper that I wrote for the *Financial Analysts Journal*, I replicated the test for the 30-year period 1985 to 2015. Result: the annual return of the S&P 500 Index was 1.6 percentage points higher than that of the average actively managed large-cap blend fund, identical to the index advantage that I had presented to Vanguard's directors in 1975. Nearly all of both margins can be accounted for by the cost advantage of the index fund.

[4] Just five years later in 1980, that ban would be fully removed when we established Vanguard Fixed Income Group to manage our bond and money market funds, which I'll discuss further in Chapter 5.

approved my proposal by unanimous vote. (After the vote, one director decided not to serve on the board and withdrew his nomination.)

First Index Investment Trust

On December 31, 1975, we filed in Delaware the Declaration of Trust for "First Index Investment Trust"[5] – a name that reflected our determination to flaunt our primacy as the world's first index mutual fund. By April 1976, we had prepared a draft prospectus, projecting that the cost of managing an index fund would be just 0.3% per year in operating expenses and 0.2% per year in transaction costs, compared with as much as 2 to 3% for an actively managed fund (including turnover costs and amortized sales loads). "Great long-term rewards can result from small differences in cost" was my simple thesis in creating that precedent-shattering investment strategy.

Given the complexity of opening an index-tracking mutual fund, our proposed fund would break new ground. Unlike an indexed pension account or pooled trust fund, it would have to deal with federal legal requirements, daily cash flows, and the costs of handling thousands – ultimately, perhaps hundreds of thousands – of shareholder accounts.

Our initial plan described how we proposed to minimize commission costs on portfolio transactions and develop operational efficiencies that would not defeat our ability to closely match the index. In May 1976, after reviewing our responses to their questions, the directors approved the filing with the Securities and Exchange Commission of a prospectus and registration statement for First Index Investment Trust. (The name we chose withstood challenge from the SEC staff, and from a number of adversaries.)

Who Was First? Who Survived?

There is no question that First Index Investment Trust (the original name of today's Vanguard 500 Index Fund) was the first index mutual fund. I'm still sort of amazed that it fell to me to create this pioneering

---

[5] The fund is now known as Vanguard 500 Index Fund.

index mutual fund way back in 1975. How did it happen? But first, how did it *not* happen?

In the late 1960s, Wells Fargo Bank had worked from academic models to develop the principles and techniques leading to index investing. The bank constructed a $6 million index account for the pension fund of Samsonite Corporation.

Wells Fargo's initial effort failed. The bank chose as its strategy an equal-weighted index of New York Stock Exchange equities. Its execution was described as "a nightmare," and the strategy was abandoned in 1976. Their new strategy relied on the market-cap-weighted strategy of the very same S&P 500 Stock Index that we had chosen *a year earlier* for Vanguard's First Index Investment Trust. Samsonite would later face bankruptcy and abandon its pension plan.

Independently, Batterymarch Financial Management of Boston decided to pursue the idea of index investing in 1971. The idea was first pitched at a Harvard Business School seminar in 1971, but found no takers. For its efforts, Batterymarch won the "Dubious Achievement Award" from *Pensions & Investments* magazine in 1972. It was two years later, in December 1974, when the firm finally attracted its first client. But its index effort would soon die.

More Index Failures

In 1974, American National Bank in Chicago created a common trust fund modeled on the S&P 500 Index. The bank and its trust no longer exist. American Express, then new to the mutual fund industry, also sought to offer an index fund. In 1975, the firm filed a registration statement with the SEC to offer an S&P 500 index fund to pension clients (initial investment $1,000,000). But it lay fallow, and new leadership withdrew its registration early in 1976.

Not one of those fledgling efforts in indexing bore fruit. Not one of those early pilot lights ignited the flame of indexing. All of those tentative forays failed to create a single index fund that was sustainable and successful. All except one – Vanguard First Index Investment Trust.

Four decades later, the accumulated assets of the index funds formed by those early pioneers who sought to lead the indexing revolution totaled zero.

LANDMARK 3. SEPTEMBER 1975

How the First Index Investment Trust Began

Vanguard First Index Investment Trust was not a product of complex algorithms or of Modern Portfolio Theory (MPT), or the Efficient Markets Hypothesis (EMH). In 1975 I had never even heard of the now-famous (in investment history) University of Chicago's Eugene Fama and Dartmouth's Kenneth French. Later, when I came to understand the EMH, I could see that the uneven and often unpredictable efficiency of the market made the EMH an unreliable basis for indexing.

Truth told, when I decided to start our index fund, I possessed neither the training nor the talent for applied statistics. Embarrassingly (I guess!), at that time I was not familiar with either the MPT or the EMH.[6] But it didn't matter.

Nor was the first index mutual fund a product of the quantitative work done at the University of Chicago and at Wells Fargo. Indeed, when I later read Chicago's version of the origin of the index fund, I realized that, at the time I created First Index, I had never heard of a single one of those star-studded names that graced the University of Chicago article.

This list is surely a "who's who" of the biggest names in the financial academy during the 1970s and 1980s: John ("Mac") McQuown, James Vertin, William Fouse, Fischer Black, Harry Markowitz, Eugene Fama, Jeremy Grantham, Dean LeBaron, James Lorie, Merton Miller, Myron Scholes, and William Sharpe. Despite being a 1951 graduate of Princeton University with a thesis inspired by my interest in finance, I was, in a word, ignorant of what was going on at the academy and in the profession during that era.

(continued)

---

[6] I later pioneered the CMH, the Cost Matters Hypothesis that (without often being cited) is now almost universally accepted.

(continued)

No, the genesis of First Index was casual and intuitive. Jan Twardowski was one of the 28 original Vanguard crew members and the original portfolio manager of the first index fund. I'll let Jan tell the story of what happened in early 1975:

> *One day you surprised me by asking if I could run an index fund and after a couple of days' research I said yes. I wrote the index fund programs in APL on a time-sharing system, using simple cap-weighting algorithms and public databases. It was, frankly, easy, although I was quite nervous when you sold the idea to underwriters and the road show began. Actual money was going to be managed based on my little set of APL programs!*

Am I saying that one with a mere AB degree from Princeton and another with a BSEE from Princeton and an MBA from Wharton are smarter than all of those with PhDs and master's degrees who were groomed at the University of Chicago, Stanford, and Harvard? Of course not.

But I am reiterating that Vanguard 500 Index Fund is not only the first index mutual fund, but it is the only one of those early attempts at indexing, whatever the structure, that has survived the test of time. With $620 billion of assets as 2018 begins, Vanguard 500 Index Fund is one of the two largest mutual funds in the world, second only to Vanguard Total Stock Market Index Fund, with assets totaling $660 billion.

The IPO

Now it was my job to find a way for Vanguard – this new "at-cost" enterprise – to raise the capital to start an index fund, without spending money we didn't yet have on marketing and promotion. We needed to retain a group of Wall Street investment bankers to manage an initial public offering (IPO) to ensure that the new fund had the critical mass of assets needed to own hundreds of stocks.

Our objective, I brashly wrote to the board, "will be to underwrite an index fund in the $50 million to $150 million range."

In those early days, the Vanguard funds were "load funds," sold exclusively through brokers. Yet mutual fund sales, following the near 50% drop in stock prices during 1973 and 1974, had weakened dramatically. But we immediately set to work trying to enlist a top group of national brokers.

After a fair amount of persuasion, Bache Halsey Stuart (now Prudential Securities), Paine Webber Jackson & Curtis, and Reynolds Securities came aboard. They conditioned their agreement on our finding a fourth major firm to lead the underwriting. That firm turned out to be Dean Witter. Roger Wood, a leader of Dean Witter's IPO group, championed the idea of the Trust, and firmly assumed leadership of the underwriting. We had enlisted the four strongest mutual fund distributors on Wall Street.

Fortune Strikes . . . Again

Our confidence soared when *Fortune* magazine's June 1976 edition appeared with a banner headline announcing: "Index Funds – An Idea Whose Time Is Coming." In a remarkable six-page article, editor Al Ehrbar announced that "index funds now threaten to reshape the entire world of professional money management."

Focusing on pension funds, he wrote: "Their present management is terrible. Instead of doing as well as the market averages, the corporate executives charged with the responsibility for pension funds have turned the funds over to a group of experts who systematically do worse" – even, he added, "before fees are deducted." Ehrbar buttressed his position with a stream of rigorous data and a detailed exposition of index theory, and rebutted each possible objection. It was a powerful elixir for Jan Twardowski and me.

Dr. Samuelson Redux

The reception to the underwriting announcement was muted but good. But few believed what Jan and I believed – that the index fund represented the beginning of a new era for the mutual fund industry.

The most enthusiastic comments came from my former professor (and later, Nobel laureate in Economics) Paul Samuelson, who had inspired me to take that first step into indexing.

Writing in *Newsweek* in August 1976, Dr. Samuelson expressed delight that there had finally been a response to his challenge of two years earlier: "Sooner than I dared expect," he wrote, "my implicit prayer has been answered. There is coming to market, I see from a crisp new prospectus, something called the First Index Investment Trust." He conceded that the fund met only five of his six requirements:

1. That it be available to investors of modest means;
2. That it aim to match the broad-based Standard & Poor's 500 Index;
3. That it carry an annual expense charge of only 0.20%;
4. That its portfolio turnover be kept extremely low; and
5. That it provide "the broadest diversification needed to maximize mean return with minimum portfolio variance and volatility."

His sixth requirement – that it be a no-load fund – had not been met, but, as he graciously conceded, "a professor's prayers are rarely answered in full." In fact Dr. Samuelson's final prayer would be answered just six months later, when Vanguard eliminated all sales commissions and went "no-load." But until then, given our obvious need to enlist broker support for an underwriting, the Trust carried an initial sales charge (low by mutual fund standards in those days: 6% on smaller investments, tapered down to 1% on investments of $1 million or more).

The Road Shows Yield a Flop

Still, in our "road shows" in a dozen cities around the country, my second-in-command, James S. (Jim) Riepe, and I both sensed that the brokerage firms' representatives did not seem particularly smitten with the idea. An index fund, after all, implied essentially that their profession – selecting well-managed funds for their clients – was a loser's game.

When the IPO closed on August 31, 1976, it was a complete flop. It produced but $11.3 million of investor capital – not even enough to purchase 100-share lots of all 500 stocks in the S&P Index.

The apologetic underwriters suggested that we cancel the offering and return the money to the investors. "No," I recall saying to them, "we now have the world's first index fund, and this is the beginning of something big."

"Bogle's Folly"

Anyone with a new idea must expect to be greeted with skepticism, followed by condemnation and attack when the idea becomes reality. First Index Investment Trust was described as "Bogle's folly" more than once. A Midwest brokerage firm flooded Wall Street with posters, illustrated by an angry Uncle Sam using a large rubber stamp to cancel the index fund's stock certificates. Its headline screamed, "INDEX FUNDS ARE UN-AMERICAN. HELP STAMP OUT INDEX FUNDS!"

Fidelity chairman Edward C. Johnson III doubted Fidelity would soon follow Vanguard's lead. (In 1988, however, he would do exactly that.) "I can't believe," he told the press, "that the great mass of investors are [sic] going to be satisfied with just receiving average returns. The name of the game is to be the best." (Today, index funds represent fully 30% of all equity fund assets managed by Fidelity.)

Another competitor put out a flyer asking rhetorically, "Who wants to be operated on by an average surgeon, be advised by an average lawyer, be an average registered representative, or do anything no better or worse than average?" The flyer concluded with an appeal intended to be inspirational: "No one came up with a handful of dust when he reached for the stars." Most fund investors, of course, had long reached for those stars, but invested in mutual funds that came up, metaphorically speaking, with a handful of dust.

280 Stocks, Not 500

Given our optimistic $150 million underwriting target, we were less than ecstatic about the final figure. But I was ecstatic that, at last, we had our index fund! Jan Twardowski, as the fund's first portfolio manager, promptly invested the Trust's initial capital of $11 million in the stocks of the S&P 500 Index.

Given our limited assets and the transaction costs that would have been involved in buying all 500 stocks, the initial portfolio included just 280 stocks – the 200 largest (representing almost 80% of the weight of the index) plus 80 others selected to match the profile of the rest of the index. By December 31, 1976, our assets had grown to $14 million – ranking the fund 152nd in size among 211 equity funds.

"The Stone That the Builders Rejected Has Become the Chief Cornerstone"

That was just the humble beginning. By the end of 1982, the assets of First Index Investment Trust topped $100 million, ranking it No. 104 among 263 funds. We reached the $1 billion milestone in 1988, ranking No. 41 among 1,048 funds. In mid-2018, assets of Vanguard 500 Index Fund (including its sister fund designed for institutional investors, Institutional Index Fund) totaled $640 billion, second in asset size only to Vanguard Total Stock Market Index Fund ($742 billion) among 5,856 equity mutual funds.

Vanguard continues to be the dominant force in indexing. With $3.5 trillion in index mutual fund assets, Vanguard oversees some 51% of the total $6.8 trillion in U.S. index funds. Vanguard manages almost 80% of the assets in traditional index funds (TIFs) – broad market index funds designed for long-term investors. Vanguard also has a 25% market share of exchange-traded funds (ETFs) – index funds of all stripes that can be traded like stocks.

Without Vanguard, the creation of the index fund would have occurred anyway, I'm sure. But it likely would have been delayed by another decade or two. Our mutual structure, however, has yet to be copied. Still, indexing is the *major* force that is reshaping the mutual fund industry as we once knew it; indeed, it is the force that is revolutionizing the entire world of finance.

Victor Hugo got it right: "No army can resist the power of an idea whose time has come." Yes, we've seen indexing come to dominate equity investing in recent years, but it was always obvious that indexing would thrive. First Index Investment Trust took some two decades to finally gain traction with the investing public, and was assaulted by competitors from all sides. But indexing's eventual success reaffirms the moral of Psalm 118: *The stone that the builders rejected has become the chief cornerstone.*

Vanguard 500 Index Fund: Real-World Success

In mid-2018, it is clear that the promise of the Vanguard 500 Index Fund has surely been fulfilled . . . and then some. Not only because of its remarkable asset growth. Not only because it spawned a whole new proliferation of index funds and changed an entire industry in a way that placed investors, not fund managers, in the driver's seat. But because S&P 500–based index funds worked to serve the human beings who entrusted their savings to this never-before-tested concept.

To make this point, I can think of no better example than the experience of the counsel to the underwriters of that nearly failed IPO for First Index Investment Trust. (To protect his privacy, I'll refer to him simply as "counsel.") Concerned about the lack of investor purchases of the fund, he decided to purchase 1,000 shares in the initial offering.

Advance the clock to the autumn of 2011, when counsel and the leaders of the underwriting met me for dinner in New York City with two of my Vanguard colleagues. We were together to celebrate the 35th anniversary of that 1976 underwriting.

Recap: $15,000 Grows to $1,127,704

As we enjoyed our evening of fellowship, the conversation was lively and candid. Each of us told an anecdote or two, and finally counsel rose to speak: "I wanted to help out the underwriting, and bought 1,000 shares of First Index at the offering price of $15 per share, which included a 6% sales charge. I've reinvested all of my dividends in full, paying the taxes separately. Before coming to this dinner, I looked at my most recent fund statement. Here's what it shows: I now own 4,493 shares, and at today's net asset value of $250.99 per share, their current asset value is $1,127,704." [7] Then counsel sat down . . . to enthusiastic applause.

---

[7] I've updated these data to June 30, 2018.

It may seem unbelievable, but the story is true. The takeaway from this anecdote is that we must never underrate the power of compounding investment returns, and always avoid the tyranny of compounding investment costs.

Caveats

Two important caveats: (1) That 11% return on the index is measured in nominal 2018 dollars. The annual return on the index fund investment in real terms (adjusted for 4% average annual inflation) would have been 7%. The value of counsel's investment in "real" terms (adjusted for inflation) would be much lower, only (?) $256,284. (2) In the years ahead, the annual return of 11% for the S&P 500 during that period is highly unlikely to recur. In 1976, stocks had relatively cheap valuations and high dividend yields (3.9%); in 2018, valuations seem expensive and dividend yields are low (1.8%).

Vindication: *Money* Talks

In August 1995, *Money* magazine dedicated much of its issue to the success of indexing. A lead editorial by executive editor Tyler Mathisen embraced the concept, and called on readers to "make a complete reorientation of your expectations as an investor." He described the index fund's advantages – low operating costs, low transaction costs, and low exposure to capital gains taxes – as "a trio as impressive as Domingo, Pavarotti, and Carreras," the three great tenors of the era.

The headline on the editorial generously declared: "Bogle wins: Index funds should be the core of most portfolios today," and ended with a personal salute, "So here's to you, Jack. You have a right to call it the Triumph of Indexing."

Buffett and Swensen

Tyler's insightful endorsement was just the beginning. Only a year later, investment giant Warren Buffett joined the parade, writing in his

1996 letter to Berkshire Hathaway shareholders: "The best way to own common stocks is through an index fund that charges minimal fees. Those following this path are sure to beat the net results . . . delivered by the great majority of investment professionals."

In his 2016 annual report for Berkshire Hathaway, Warren put the icing on the cake. "If a statue is ever erected to honor the person who has done the most for American investors, the hands-down choice should be Jack Bogle. For decades, Jack has urged investors to invest in ultra-low-cost index funds. In his crusade . . . Jack was frequently mocked by the investment-management industry. Today, however, he has the satisfaction of knowing that he helped millions of investors realize far better returns on their savings than they otherwise would have earned. He is a hero to them and to me."

David Swensen, long-time manager of the Yale University Endowment Fund, added his own endorsement of index funds and Vanguard's mutual structure in his 2005 book *Unconventional Success*: "Investors fare best with funds managed by not-for-profit organizations, because the management firm focuses exclusively on serving investor interests. No profit motive interferes with investor returns. No outside corporate interest clashes with portfolio management choices. Not-for-profit firms place investor interests front and center. . . . Ultimately, a passive index fund managed by a not-for-profit investment management organization represents the combination most likely to satisfy investor aspirations."

Paul Samuelson Completes a New "Murderer's Row"

Add to those generous comments yet another grand endorsement by Dr. Samuelson in 2005: "I rank this Bogle invention along with the invention of the wheel, the alphabet, Gutenberg printing, and wine and cheese: a mutual fund that never made Bogle rich but elevated the long-term returns of mutual-fund investors. Something new under the sun."

It is hardly unreasonable to compare these three titans of investing – Buffett, Swensen, and Samuelson – to the famed Murderers'

Row of the 1927 New York Yankees: Babe Ruth (.356 batting average, 60 home runs), Lou Gehrig (.373, 47), and Earl Combs (.356, 6).

Why try to pitch against them?

Staying the Course

Vanguard's pioneering index fund was a double-edged tribute to staying the course. First, as a business matter, we would hold fast to a world-changing idea, and then remain patient as we dealt with the tedious delay of two full decades before finding investor acceptance. Second, investors holding fast to the simple, broadly diversified investment fund with rock-bottom costs – the S&P 500 index fund – would be rewarded with truly remarkable returns.

Chapter 5

1974–1981

A New Beginning

	9/1974	12/1981	Annual Rate of Growth
Vanguard Assets (Billions)	$1.5	$2.7	8.8%
Industry Assets (Billions)	$34.1	$241.4	32.3
Vanguard Market Share	4.4%	4.9%	—
			Annual Return
S&P 500 Index	69	123	15.0%
Intermediate-Term U.S. Government Bond Yield	8.0%	14.0%	6.6
60% Stocks/40% Bonds	—	—	11.9

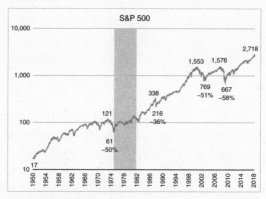

Source: Yahoo! Finance.

Starting a firm at a stock market low was no fun. Pessimism permeated the investment community. We thought things couldn't get worse. As it turned out, they didn't. During the six years following the crash, with few interruptions, the S&P 500 Index rose by 175%. But, the 80% rise in Vanguard's asset base to $2.7 billion concealed a drop in our market share to an all-time low of 1.7% of industry assets. We stayed the course.

The First Step

A "new beginning" at Vanguard started in 1975 with the board's approval of our index fund. The existence of First Index Investment Trust meant that we had made our limited entry, however tenuous, into the second side – the investment side – of the mutual-fund triangle. (Our index fund was not "managed.") The next step, in 1977, was to take responsibility for marketing and distribution; after that step was completed, the quest for the third and final side of the triangle – the right to serve as an active investment adviser to the entire range of Vanguard funds – would begin. That goal would be accomplished in 1981.

The Anomaly of Fund Share Distribution

From the outset of the struggle for Vanguard's independence, I had realized the anomaly of striving to operate at rock-bottom annual expense ratios for fund shareholders, even as we continued to be dependent on the broker-dealer community. In those days, investors who purchased shares of our mutual funds were assessed front-end sales loads of 7.5% to 8.5%. Like nearly all of our peer fund managers, Vanguard's distribution strategy was inextricably linked to stock brokers.

Immediately following the initial public offering (IPO) of our groundbreaking index fund, I decided that we must resolve that anomaly. In a letter to Vanguard's directors in the autumn of 1976, I outlined my plan to abandon the distribution system that had supported Wellington for nearly a half-century.

Under that system, Wellington Management held the exclusive right to deal with the stockbroker network that was selling shares of the Vanguard funds to their clients. Vanguard's directors had agreed not to impinge on Wellington's turf.

Once again, we devised a novel solution. I proposed to the board yet another unprecedented step: that Vanguard would terminate its distribution contract with Wellington Management Company that had been in place for nearly half a century. We would sell shares of our funds on a "no-load" basis, without sales commission, entirely eliminating the need for brokers. We would not rely on sellers to *sell* fund shares, but rather on buyers to *buy* them.

My claim to the board (again accurate, if perhaps disingenuous) was that we were not violating our pledge that precluded Vanguard's *engaging* in distribution. We were simply *eliminating* distribution.

February 1977: Control of Marketing and Distribution

Once again, a huge battle ensued. Wellington Management, still in charge of distributing shares of the Vanguard funds, asserted that such a radical move would be a "catastrophe" that would destroy both firms. While the change would surely cause some short-term disruption in our affairs, I argued that in the long-run it would bring us into the coming era of stewardship – a focus on the interests of investors, consumerism, and investor choice – rather that the existing era of salesmanship by stock brokers.

The decision – "go" or "no-go" – was made at an evening board meeting held in New York City on February 7, 1977. The discussion was heated, contentious, and political. I was reasonably confident that I could win by a one-vote "landslide," seven for, six against. It turned out that wasn't optimistic enough. When the vote was finally taken at 1 a.m. on February 8, 1977, it was eight for, five against. We announced the dramatic decision to the press and the public at 10 a.m. that morning. Victory was ours.

Just 18 months from the date our skeletal enterprise began operations with its narrow mandate, we were on our way to becoming a complete mutual fund complex. Administration and then the management of the index fund were in place, and now we were in charge of marketing and distribution.

The struggle wasn't quite over, however. The board's approval for the 1974 internalization of the *administration* of the Wellington funds had been resolved by unanimous vote with almost no public spotlight. The 1975 internalization of the *management* of the index fund was also unanimous, and the public response negative. But the decision to internalize *distribution* proved to be a bombshell. Our application to the SEC was opposed by a Wellington Fund shareholder, who called for, and received, a formal administrative hearing, held in 1978.

LANDMARK 4. 1977

The Agony of Defeat...

Our application sought permission for the Vanguard funds to spend jointly a small amount of their assets for the promotion and distribution of fund shares, subject to certain constraints. Traditionally, the SEC had successfully argued the reverse: that funds could not spend their own assets on distribution. That policy ignored the reality that fund managers were paying distribution costs out of the enormous profits they reaped in providing investment advice to the funds.

Recognizing that absurd inconsistency, we asked the commission for an exemption that would allow our funds to spend a limited amount directly on distribution. Taking into account the management fee reductions that we had negotiated in conjunction with our assuming the costs of distribution (much lower in the new "no-load" environment), a net *savings* of $800,000 per year would be generated for our fund shareholders.

The SEC regulatory hearing lasted 10 full days. During most of the sessions, I testified on the witness stand. It was said to be the longest Investment Company Act hearing since the law was enacted in 1940. Finally, in July 1978, SEC administrative law judge Max O. Regensteiner, who presided at the hearing, made his decision: *Rejection!* We were back to square one. I was furious. I seethed in the agony of defeat.

Judge Regensteiner's decision left us in limbo. While he affirmed the original SEC decision that enabled Vanguard to put its distribution plan into place immediately, pending a final determination by the SEC, he sought a revision of the plan's proposed allocation of distribution expenses among the several Vanguard funds.

So again, in a sea of uncertainty, and with the sword of Damocles hanging over us, suspended by a fragile thread, we blithely pursued our share distribution activities as before. We also addressed Judge Regensteiner's concerns by amending our application with several largely technical changes.

In 1980, we made some modest amendments to our plan, most notably that no fund's share of distribution expenses could exceed 0.20% of its net assets. (In 2017, no Vanguard fund's share exceeded 0.03% of assets.) At last, Judge Regensteiner gave his approval.

LANDMARK 5. FEBRUARY 1981

... and The Thrill of Victory

The threatening sword was finally removed on February 25, 1981, when the SEC rendered its final decision on our application. Verdict: *Victory for Vanguard*. Far better than any characterization that I could offer, the commission's words speak for themselves:

> [The Vanguard plan] is consistent with the provisions, policies, and purposes of the [Investment Company Act of 1940]. It actually furthers the Act's objectives by ensuring that the Funds' directors, with more specific information at their disposal concerning the cost and performance of each service rendered to the Funds, are better able to evaluate the quality of those services.

> [The plan] will foster improved disclosure to shareholders, enabling them to make a more informed judgment as to the Funds' operations. In addition, the plan clearly enhances the Funds' independence, permitting them to change investment advisers more readily as conditions may dictate. The plan also benefits each fund within a reasonable range of fairness.

(continued)

(continued)

Specifically, the [Vanguard] plan promotes a healthy and viable mutual fund complex within which each fund can better prosper; enables the Funds to realize substantial savings from advisory fee reductions; promotes savings from economies of scale; and provides the Funds with direct and conflict-free control over distribution functions.

Accordingly, we deem it appropriate to grant the application before us.

The decision was unanimous. Unsurprisingly, this durable "thrill of victory" monumentally outweighed our transitory "agony of defeat."

Struggling with the Index Fund

The elimination of sales commissions in February 1977 hardly reversed the disappointing early acceptance of First Index Investment Trust in the marketplace. Any sustained inflow of investor capital would have to await some seasoning and some "proof of the pudding" in the fund's performance.

In mid-1977, with the Trust's assets languishing near $17 million, I sensed an opportunity to increase them substantially. Among the other mutual funds that Vanguard administered was Exeter Fund, an exchange fund (where investors had exchanged tax-free, low-cost securities for a diversified portfolio) with assets of $58 million. Exeter could not offer new shares for sale, and it ultimately would have to be merged into another fund.

In September 1977, I presented a recommendation to merge it into First Index. After a heated debate with Wellington Management, which instead urged a merger into Windsor Fund, the board approved my proposal. The assets of First Index more than quadrupled to $75 million. At last, the fund had sufficient resources to own all 500 stocks in the index.

The 500-Index Superiority Fades

It didn't help that during the index fund's early years, the returns of the S&P 500 Index itself fell behind the returns earned by the average fund manager. After performing so sensationally from 1972 to 1976, outpacing nearly 70% of all equity funds, the index disappointingly outpaced only about one-fourth of equity mutual funds from 1977 to 1982.

This reversal of the remarkable previous superiority of the 500 Index hardly made it easier for the fund to attract additional assets. (Nearly all new fund concepts are plagued by this sort of reversal.) But we were moving toward a new decade – the 1980s – during which the index would again outperform more than half of all traditionally managed equity mutual funds.

Even after the merger of Exeter Fund, the assets of First Index didn't cross the $100 million mark until 1982. Indeed, it wasn't until 1984 that a second index mutual fund (run by Wells Fargo, also tracking the S&P 500 Index) joined the industry. By 1990, the industry had only five index funds, with total assets of $4.5 billion, still only about 2% of the assets of all equity mutual funds.

The Go-Go Era, the Nifty Fifty Era, and Their Aftermath

The stock market environment that Vanguard's index fund entered was, in a word, terrible. The mutual fund industry – including Vanguard's prehistory under Wellington Management – had jumped into the Go-Go era as if it would last forever. It didn't. (Nothing does.)

The same thing was true of the Nifty Fifty foolishness that followed. That hot air came pouring out when the bubble burst in 1973–1974. When that 50% crash in stock prices at last ended, the fund industry's reputation for "professional management" was in shreds.

From its start, the fund industry had been dominated by common stock funds, and balanced funds generally held 60% or more of their assets in equities. The industry's prospects were dependent on the stock market. But many of the once-conservative mutual fund managers had taken positions largely in speculative stocks during the Go-Go era and stocks with inflated valuations during the Nifty Fifty era, and the 1973–1974 stock market crash wreaked well-deserved havoc on the industry that had forgotten where it came from.

Even as mutual fund assets were slashed by the tumbling stock market, disappointed investors redeemed their fund shares in droves. Total mutual fund assets dropped from $58 billion at the close of 1972 to $36 billion in September 1975, a crushing loss of about 40% of industry assets.

Wellington Fund Assets Drop by 75%

Net cash flows into mutual funds turned negative in early 1972, and would remain negative well into 1978. Vanguard was hardly exempt from these trends. Despite our balanced fund bias, we did even worse. During Wellington Fund's heyday, its assets had peaked at $2 billion in 1965, only to plummet to $450 million at the stock market's 1974 low, a decline of more than 75%. (Chapter 11 provides further details about the history of the Wellington Fund.) Vanguard's market share of industry assets, just 5.8% in 1981, would soon ease further down to 5.2% in 1985, and tumble to 4.1% in 1987.

The monthly cash outflows from the Wellington funds (and then the Vanguard funds) that began in May 1971 would not end until January 1978 – 83 consecutive months of negative cash flow – a total of more than $500 million, about one-third of the initial assets of the Vanguard funds. As Vanguard director James T. Hill put it, "we are hemorrhaging." He was right. And we were not alone. It's not hyperbolic to describe the traditional mutual fund industry as facing extinction.

1971: The Money Market Fund

The industry needed a savior, and fast. We found one in a new product called the money market fund.

The first money market fund – Reserve Fund – was created in 1971 by Bruce R. Bent and Henry B. R. Brown. Its portfolio consisted of short-term money market instruments, commercial paper, and U.S. Treasury bills, and the fund would maintain (or, more accurately, strive to maintain) a net asset value of $1 per share. With bank savings accounts then limited to paying annual interest at 5.25%, and short-term paper owned by money funds yielding as high as 9%, the new fund was an immediate success. Of course it was copied virtually overnight by almost every major firm in the fund industry.

Assets of money market funds leaped from $4 billion in 1977 to $185 billion in 1981. By then, the federal interest rate limits on bank savings accounts had been removed, opening the door to new competition for money market funds. Further, interest rates would gradually tumble to historically low levels. The yield on short-term U.S. Treasury bills, which peaked at above 16% in 1981, fell to only a hair above zero from 2008 to 2015. Low interest rates could slow the money market fund train, but not stop it. In mid-2018, total assets of money market funds were $2.7 trillion.

A Late Start

We were late in starting our money fund. Whitehall Money Market Trust (now Vanguard Prime Money Market Fund) began on June 4, 1975. The fund retained Wellington Management as its investment adviser. Jumping on the money market fund bandwagon, even late, led to a major surge in our growth, as total assets of the Vanguard funds rose from $1.47 billion in 1974 to $4.11 billion in 1981.

1977: The Defined-Maturity Municipal Bond Fund

Within six months of our decision to go no-load in 1977, we came up with another transforming idea. We created a series of municipal bond funds with an unprecedented strategy. Even as I came to believe that precious few stock managers could outguess the stock market over the long-term, so I had also come to believe that precious few bond managers could accurately forecast the direction and level of interest rates and outguess the bond market.

Yet our peers offering "managed" tax-exempt bond funds were implicitly promising to do exactly that – a promise that could not be fulfilled. So we decided to depart from the crowd and form not a *single* tax-exempt bond fund, but a *three-tier* bond fund offering a *long-term* portfolio (highest yields); a *short-term* portfolio (lowest volatility);

and – you guessed it! – an *intermediate-term* portfolio (some of each). In truth, it's difficult to imagine a more banal idea. But it had never been tried before.

A Simple Innovation

Almost overnight, this simple innovation changed the way investors thought about bond fund investing, and the industry's major firms quickly adopted the concept for their own bond funds. That change helped give new life to bond mutual funds. Their assets would grow from $11 billion in 1977 to more than $1 trillion in 2001. In mid-2018, assets of bond mutual funds totaled $4.6 trillion; assets of money market mutual funds totaled another $2.7 trillion.

It was easy to envision that Vanguard's low-cost structure would provide us with a huge yield advantage, so I knew the time had come for Vanguard to take over management of our fixed income funds. In 1980, dissatisfied with the returns and costs of our municipal bond and money market funds, I proposed to the board that we terminate the contracts with their external advisers (Wellington Management and Citibank), and build our own team of fixed income professionals. The board agreed.

LANDMARK 6. 1980

Finally Completing the Triangle: Investment Management

If the simple decision to create defined-maturity bond funds could be described as "brilliant," my choice of an external manager to run the new mutual funds was quite the opposite. We selected giant Citibank, N.A. as the funds' adviser. Alas, the bank was simply not up to the task. As 1980 began, Vanguard determined to terminate the relationship.

At the same time, our large ($420 million) money market funds were paying high fees to their then-manager, Wellington Management Company. This was the moment, I thought, to recommend a giant step: having Vanguard replace Citi as manager of our municipal bond funds, and simultaneously build Vanguard's own in-house management staff to replace Wellington as manager of our money market funds, in part to reduce fees, and in part to obtain "critical mass" for gaining economies of scale.

The board meeting, held in September 1980, was contentious. On the one hand, replacing Citibank as adviser to the muni funds was a nonissue. Replacing Wellington as adviser to the money funds would generate substantial savings, largely the result of Vanguard's "at-cost" structure. But building a new staff of bond professionals at Vanguard carried its own risk. In the end, my recommendation carried, another important step in the expansion of Vanguard's responsibilities. We also determined to apply the defined-maturity concept to our new taxable bond funds, and have our in-house staff manage them.

A Curious Anomaly

The board's vote on my proposal brought a curious anomaly: as members of Vanguard's board, eight of the directors voted to create the proposed new Fixed Income Group, and, as members of the money market and municipal bond funds board, they also voted to terminate the advisory contracts. But one member, acting solely in his capacity as a Vanguard director, voted *for* the formation of Fixed Income Group ("a great opportunity for the firm"). But acting as a director of the municipal bond funds and the money market fund, he voted *against* the proposal. ("Vanguard lacks the ability to manage the funds.") Go figure. The votes were 9–0 and 8–1. The "ayes" had it. A new era had begun.

Our internal managers improved the "relative predictability" of the Vanguard bond funds at far lower costs, resulting in higher net returns to our clients. The idea of "relative predictability" was to earn returns that paralleled those of our peers before the deduction of costs. In this case, bond funds (especially defined-maturity bond funds), where prices and yields of bonds are determined largely by the level and term structure of interest rates. Vanguard's funds would almost certainly whip them over time, once costs were deducted. ("Performance comes and goes. Costs go on forever.")

It seemed obvious that Vanguard would come to dominate the fixed income field, and so we did. In 2018, we are by far the largest fixed income mutual fund manager among our competitors, responsible for 18% of the fixed income segment of the mutual fund industry. (For more on Vanguard's fixed income funds, see Chapter 15, "The Bond Funds.")

Vanguard Fixed Income Group Takes Shape

Vanguard's foray into active fund management was not only economically important but conceptually critical. While we had arguably "broken the ice" in acting as an investment adviser in 1975 when we created First Index Investment Trust, the board's 1980 decision clearly brought us into active fund management for the first time. At last, six years after Vanguard's inception, all three sides of the mutual fund triangle were in place.

With the board's approval, we began to build Vanguard's fixed income investment staff. The leader of our new Fixed Income Group was Ian A. MacKinnon, a senior manager of fixed income securities at a major Philadelphia bank. He put together a team of six professionals plus a small administrative staff. When we began to manage our municipal bond and money market funds, their combined assets came to about $1.75 billion.

New Fund Profile

During the era of our new beginning from 1974 through 1981, assets of Vanguard's traditional stock and balanced funds shrank from 98% of our asset base to just 57%, while our fixed income (bond and money market) funds had soared from 2 to 43%. (See Exhibit 5.1.) In a real sense, the money market fund brought us into a new business, one with high transaction volumes, to go along with our relatively steady long-term investment business, with much lower share turnover.

Exhibit 5.1 A Dramatic Change in Vanguard's Asset Base

| | | Percentage of Assets in Vanguard Mutual Funds | | | |
	Fund Assets (Billions)	Stock Funds	Balanced Funds	Bond Funds	Money Market Funds
1974	$1.47	42%	56%	2%	0%
1981	$4.11	42	15	8	35
Change	+$2.64	0	−41	+6	+35

1978–1993: 200-Plus Reductions in Advisory Fees

When we established Vanguard in September 1974, it was obvious that the fees paid to Wellington Management Company would have to be cut in order to take into account the administrative expenses that would be shifted to the new organization.

Further, I successfully argued that the reduction would have to include a "markup" over the actual expenses assumed by the funds to roughly reflect Wellington's profit margin in providing that service. Our board endorsed that view. The expenses assumed by Vanguard in 1974 totaled $627,000, but advisory fees were reduced by $774,000. Result: a $147,000 savings to fund shareholders in our first year. (Then, that seemed like a lot.)

In 1977, when Vanguard went no-load, the funds assumed the costs of running the distribution system, relieving Wellington of the costs it had borne in providing Vanguard with distribution and marketing services. These annual costs were estimated at $2,131,000, and (again applying the "markup") advisory fees paid to Wellington Management were cut by $2,962,000, resulting in an additional net savings of $831,000 for the year. These savings to Vanguard shareholders served to reduce the aggregate expense ratios of the Vanguard funds from 0.69% of assets to 0.65%.

Only the Beginning

Those two across-the-board fee cuts for the funds were more or less pro forma, and savings to Vanguard shareholders were small, totaling just 0.04% of fund assets. The reductions created little friction between the funds and their adviser. But after taking over distribution in 1977, the funds were able to operate independently and solely in the interests of their shareholders.

Conceptually, the Vanguard directors were now in the same position as the trustees of a pension fund. We could now negotiate with our money manager on the structure and level of advisory fees, fund by fund, or we could cancel the contracts. Negotiate we did, and we ultimately arrived at fees that were fair to our fund shareholders. It's called *fiduciary duty*.

A Wave of Fee Reductions

Following the implementation of the fee reductions entailed by Vanguard's assumption of distribution costs, we waited a year before proposing steep reductions in the advisory fees paid to Wellington Management Company, subsequently approved by shareholders in our 1977 proxy statement. Our adviser accepted these 200-plus substantial fee cuts virtually without argument, nor even complaint. How could that have happened?

First, the Vanguard funds were now in the position of power. If Wellington did not agree to the fee cuts, the firm ran the risk of cancellation of those highly profitable advisory contracts and the resultant elimination of those revenues. Second, I had the foresight to structure the reductions to be modest in the early years, with the highest rate cuts not only prospective, but also dependent on enormous increases in the assets of each fund. I believed that we would "grow into" those fee cuts. Perhaps Wellington Management did not.

LANDMARK 7. 1978

Let the Fee Reductions Begin

Happily, my strategy for reducing fees proved correct. Assets of Vanguard's actively managed funds soared from $1.5 billion in 1977 to $970 billion in mid-2018, and the average rate of fees paid to our fund managers, weighted by fund assets, fell from 0.35% to 0.09%.

Had the fee rates of 1977 still prevailed in 2018, advisory fees on Vanguard's actively managed funds would have totaled some $3.4 billion, rather than $838 million actually paid by Vanguard's fund shareholders. Result: $2.562 billion of savings for Vanguard's active funds alone. All of those negotiations paid off!

In essence, those huge reductions in fee rates simply transferred the economies of scale in fund management from the adviser to our fund shareholders. That process began in 1978, and it proved to be a priceless landmark. It was the beginning of a series of 200-plus periodic fee reductions on the Vanguard funds that would continue through 1993.

The Wellington Fund Example

The reduction in advisory fees paid by Wellington Fund to Wellington Management Company provides a fine example of growing into both the fund's fee cuts and its soaring assets. Beginning with the fee approved in the fund's 1977 proxy, the fund's fee schedule was reduced 9 times during the next 18 years through 1995, reflecting a total reduction in fee rates from 0.31% to 0.05%, a drop of fully 82% in the fee rate paid by Wellington Fund. Exhibit 5.2 presents these data.

Exhibit 5.2   Wellington Fund Fee Rate Reductions, 1977–1993

Rate	Year	Fund Assets (millions)	Effective Fee Rate	Reduction
Base Rate	1975	$776	0.31%	—
Reduction 1	1977	$706	0.23	−32%
Reduction 2	1979	$606	0.16	−30
Reduction 3	1981	$521	0.23	+40
Reduction 4	1983	$614	0.16	−30
Reduction 5	1985	$813	0.15	−19
Reduction 6	1987	$1,331	0.15	−0
Reduction 7	1989	$2,099	0.12	−20
Reduction 8	1991	$3,818	0.10	−16
Reduction 9	1993	$8,076	0.05	−50
Cumulative Reduction				−82%

By 1996, Wellington Fund assets had leaped to $8 billion, up from $706 million in 1977. In 2006, when its assets had risen to $40 billion, the fund's directors raised the advisory fee by 0.01% each year for four consecutive years, doubling the initial advisory fee of 0.04% to 0.08%. (I am unable to explain the rationale for that 100% increase.) Yes, the dollar amount of fees paid to Wellington soared from $1 million in 1978 to some $81 million in 2017. But the fees would have totaled $240 million under the original 1977 schedule, a remarkable pro forma annual reduction of almost $160 million. A victory for the adviser, yes, but also a victory for the Wellington Fund shareholders.

Across-the-Board Fee Reductions

The Wellington Fund fee reductions are but one example of the fierce fight by Vanguard to reduce the advisory fees paid to its external money managers, across the board.

Our mission to establish fair and reasonable advisory fees was broad and unremitting. The reduction would initially apply to every Vanguard fund, each of which retained Wellington Management Company as its external investment adviser, fee reductions that resulted from our funds' strong negotiating position. Exhibit 5.3 shows the enormous fee savings for the actively managed funds that constituted the original Vanguard family.

Negotiating Fees on New Vanguard Funds

Because those legacy funds accounted for 100% of Vanguard assets during the firm's early years, fee cuts played a material role in our ability to reduce the firm's aggregate expense ratio. But as we introduced new funds, the negotiations with the advisers began even before the funds were formed. Since Vanguard's imprimatur would likely bring in substantial assets, these advisers were willing to accommodate our requirements (in a few cases, reluctantly) for advisory fees far below industry norms.

Exhibit 5.3 Advisory Fees on Original Vanguard Actively Managed Funds, 1977–2018

	1977			2018		
	Assets	Advisory Fee Rate	Advisory Fee (Millions)	Assets	Advisory Fee Rate	Advisory Fee (Millions)
Wellington	$706 million	0.27	$1.91	$106 billion	0.07	$74.4
Windsor	528 million	0.43	2.27	20 billion	0.08	16.1
Wellesley Income	133 million	0.39	0.52	56 billion	0.05	28.0
Morgan Growth	81 million	0.42	0.34	13 billion	0.15	20.4
Explorer	10 million	0.48	0.05	13 billion	0.17	22.9
Long-Term Bond	49 million	0.45	0.22	16 billion	0.03	5.0
GNMA*	25 million	0.15	0.04	24 billion	0.01	2.4
Total	**$1,532 million**	**0.37%**	**$5.35**	**$248 billion**	**0.08%**	**$169.2**

*The Vanguard GNMA Fund was created in 1980.

Summary
Advisory Fees on Vanguard Fund Assets of $248 Billion, January 2018

1977 Fee Schedule	**$1.004 Million**
2018 Fee Schedule	**$226 Million**
Pro Forma Savings	**$778 Million**

Source: Vanguard.

Whatever the case, these fee rates were highly competitive in the fund marketplace. Exhibit 5.4 presents a comparison of the expense ratios of some of these subsequent Vanguard funds with their peer groups.[1] It shows the dramatic advantage offered to investors who invest in Vanguard's externally managed funds.

[1] Since our peers do not identify their advisory fees as such, we present fund all-in expense ratios, which include both advisory fees and all other fund costs.

Exhibit 5.4   Vanguard Actively Managed Funds Expense Ratios versus Peer Funds

	2017 Expense Ratios		
	Vanguard Fund*	Peer Funds	Vanguard Advantage
PRIMECAP	0.33%	1.17%	0.84%
Windsor II	0.28	1.04	0.76
Equity Income	0.19	1.15	0.96
Capital Opportunity	0.38	1.17	0.79
Health Care	0.33	1.23	0.90
Energy	0.35	1.36	1.01
Average	0.31%	1.19%	0.88%

*Weighted-average expense ratio for all Vanguard Fund share classes.

Source: Vanguard.

In 2017, the effective advisory fee rate paid by all actively managed Vanguard stock funds (including the legacy funds) averaged 0.15%, less than half of their average expense ratio of 0.31%. This figure is nearly 75% below the unweighted average 1.19% expense ratio of their actively managed mutual fund peers.

Vanguard's campaign to reduce the fees paid to its external advisers began in 1978, and by 1993 the task was close to completion. Our legacy funds (those that were in business in 1978) gained huge benefits. So did the new funds that we formed thereafter, which began their existence with low fees that were negotiated in advance of their formation.

Index Funds and Bond Funds: Still Lower Costs

Vanguard's actively managed equity funds now constitute but 10% of the firm's asset base, down from 48% as 1977 began. A major portion of our firm's huge overall cost advantage in the fund industry results from our stock index funds, now 62% of Vanguard's asset base.

These index funds receive their investment management services on an "at-cost" basis from Vanguard. Their investment expenses account for less than 0.01% of their average expense ratio of 0.07%.

The internally managed Vanguard bond funds are also low-cost and highly price competitive. In 2017, advisory fees of the funds managed by Vanguard's Fixed Income Group averaged less than 0.01% of assets, bringing their aggregate expense ratio to an average of 0.08%, only a tiny fraction of the average expense ratio of 0.77% for their peers.

Investment Expenses and Operating Expenses

The bottom line: the total investment expenses of the Vanguard funds as a group in 2018 are estimated at $838 million, representing just 0.02% of the group's total assets, a 94% reduction from the 1977 rate of 0.35%.

Vanguard's growth has also unleashed powerful economies of scale in our shareholder accounting costs and other operating costs. These costs represent the total of the "line items" in the expense ratios of the funds, excluding the costs of investment supervision. As Vanguard's asset base has risen to higher and higher levels, these operating costs have fallen from 0.25% of Vanguard assets in 1977 to 0.08% in 2018. These reductions reflect the economies of scale that have produced such benefits to our fund shareholders.

The Vanguard Total Expense Ratio

Combining the two factors just mentioned – sharply reduced advisory fee rates and extraordinary economies of scale – produces the Vanguard total expense ratio, a figure often publicized and accepted as the best measure of fund efficiency. During its long history (see Exhibit 5.5), Vanguard's weighted average expense ratio has tumbled 84%, from 0.66% of assets to 0.10% in 2018 – this huge drop came in the face of a much more modest 9% decrease in the expense ratios of our peer funds. Their expense ratios fell from 0.64% in 1977 to 0.58% in 2017 (weighted by assets).

Exhibit 5.5   Vanguard Expense Ratios, 1974–2018

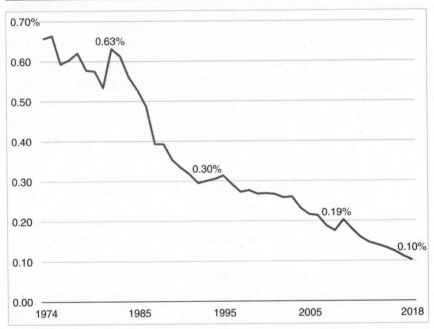

Source: Vanguard, Strategic Insight Simfund.

$217 Billion of Savings to Shareholders?

In the preceding part of this chapter, I gave you lots and lots of ratios – 0.05%, 0.85%, etc. I may have bored you with these data, but I wanted to establish a firm footing for our focus on low costs, always low costs, for our investors. Now let's have some fun and talk real dollars. The impact of Vanguard's at-cost structure translates to billions of dollars saved by investors every year.

In 2017 alone, we estimate that Vanguard's low costs saved investors $29 billion in fees and expenses.[2] If we carry this process back

---

[2] We develop this estimate by calculating the difference between the weighted-average expense ratio of the average actively managed fund and that of the average Vanguard fund, and multiplying that difference by Vanguard's total assets. For 2017, average assets of $4.5 trillion times expense ratio advantage of 0.65% equals savings of $29.5 billion.

to Vanguard's founding in 1974, the aggregate savings for Vanguard's investors – average economies of scale plus our negotiation of appropriate fee structures with our advisers – can be fairly estimated at $217 billion. I take great pride in the fact that the company I founded has been able to give so much back to its shareholders/investors. They deserve every penny of it.

Taking on the World

The fee reductions made beginning in 1978 paid off both for Vanguard and our shareholders. After Vanguard's market share of industry assets fell to a low of 4.1% in 1987, it would gradually ascend, to 8.7% in 1997, to 13.1% in 2007, and to almost 25% in mid-2018. (See Chapter 9.) Vanguard had survived, and was prepared for future growth. What's more, we had seized control of both share distribution (for all funds) and investment management (for our index funds, our money market funds, and most of our bond funds).

At last we had expanded our ambit to all three legs of the mutual fund triangle – administration, distribution and marketing, and investment management. By 1981, Vanguard had become a full-fledged mutual fund complex, ready to take on the world.

Staying the Course

The reinvention of Vanguard from its skeletal early structure to its emergence as a full-fledged fund firm that performed all of the services that mutual funds require began quickly. In 1977, barely three years after our founding, we assumed control of share distribution. To accomplish that goal, staying the course was essential, especially as an SEC law judge opposed our proposal, only to be reversed in 1981 by the Commission itself, which enthusiastically endorsed our plan.

But there was much more that we needed to do to serve our fund shareholders. Most notably, we negotiated new advisory contracts with

Wellington Management (and later with our other external advisers) that resulted in remarkable fee savings. We could even have overdone "staying the course." We continued to lower fees, negotiating future decreases in nine of the subsequent 18 years. While our fund asset base barely edged upward, we had stayed the course. We had built a solid foundation for the remarkable growth that would lie ahead.

Chapter 6

1981–1991

Setting the Stage for Future Growth

	12/1981	12/1991	Annual Asset Growth
Vanguard Assets (Billions)	$4.2	$77.0	21.5%
Industry Assets (Billions)	241.4	1,454.1	12.7
Vanguard Market Share	4.9%	6.2%	—
			Total Return
S&P 500 Index	123	417	17.6%
Intermediate-Term U.S. Government Bond Yield	14.0%	6.0%	13.1%
60% Stocks/40% Bonds	—	—	15.9

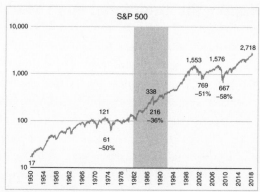

Source: Yahoo! Finance.

The 1980s was another great era for both stocks and bonds, although it will probably be best remembered for "Black Monday," October 19, 1987. On that single day, stock prices collapsed by 23%. (Few remember that for the full calendar year, the S&P 500 rose by 5.3%.)

The Happy Events of 1981

As 1982 began, we moved to capitalize on the confluence of two events. First was the SEC's final decision handed down at last in 1981, which allowed Vanguard to assume authority to control and operate all of the funds' marketing and distribution activities. That decision was essential for Vanguard's subsequent success.

Second was Vanguard's assumption of the investment supervision of our fixed income funds in 1981. In just seven years, we had achieved the independence from our external advisers that I had expressed as my central goal in that 1974 Future Structure Study.

With the SEC's tacit approval of the internalization of fund administration in 1974, followed by its formal decision to permit the internalization of fund distribution in 1981, plus our 1981 entry into providing advisory services to our funds, Vanguard had at last formally abandoned the traditional mutual fund industry structure that had defined the mission of the Wellington/Vanguard funds for nearly a half-century.

Flipping the Traditional Fund Model

The traditional model effectively put mutual funds under the control of their separately owned investment advisers. Vanguard flipped that traditional model on its head. Owned by its mutual funds, which in turn are owned by the shareholders of the funds, Vanguard had placed fund shareholders firmly in the driver's seat. Despite the enormous growth that was to follow, our new model, even four-plus decades later, remains unique in the mutual fund industry.

Surely it must have been obvious to the commissioners that, while they had just approved our unprecedented model, the rest of our industry was operating under the old model in which the advisers and underwriters – the management companies operating the funds, dominating and controlling the funds' every action – remained in the driver's seat.

Whose Interests Come First?

Our peers had placed their own financial interests first, ahead of the interests of their fund shareholders.[1] We did precisely the opposite: shareholders first. "The Vanguard Experiment" in mutual fund governance would now be tested in the marketplace.

Throughout the decade of the 1980s, I often bragged to our crew about Vanguard's spectacular asset growth, in part to maintain and build on the solid morale we had established. But in reality, our growth largely reflected the growth of the burgeoning fund industry. During that decade, mutual fund assets leaped from $241 billion to $1.45 trillion. The charge was led by money market funds, which soared from $2 billion to $570 billion, accounting for almost half of the increase.

As I mentioned in Chapter 5, investors were flocking to money market funds. With their high interest rates and relatively low risk, money market funds created a new and fast-growing asset base that may have, in fact, saved the mutual fund industry. Vanguard grew even faster.

Despite our late entry into the money market business, our asset growth in the decade from 1981 to 1991 was exhilarating – $4.2 billion to $77 billion. While our market share increased only modestly, from 4.9% to 6.2%, we stuck with these two rules: (1) Increased market share is a measure of our success in serving clients, and not an objective; and (2) market share must be earned and not bought.

Vanguard Enters the Active Management Arena . . .

Little did I realize then that our 1977 creation of the defined-maturity concept in bond funds would be the precursor to our later leap into active investment management. When it became clear that we had achieved the critical mass to establish our own Fixed Income Group (FIG) at Vanguard, we took that giant step in September 1981, bringing $350 million of bond assets under our management. The Vanguard Fixed Income Group represented our first foray into active investment management.

---

[1] I'm reminded again of the quote from SEC chairman Manuel Cohen, cited in Chapter 2, in which he clearly addressed the absence of mutuality in mutual funds.

Although Vanguard had been managing our 500 Index Fund (originally named First Index Investment Trust) since its inception in 1976, that fund merely sought to track the performance of the S&P 500 Index, and, I argued, was not managed. But as I've said many times, I've always thought of our approach to active fixed income management as "virtual indexing" because our policy was (and is) to establish market-segment-like portfolios with relative predictability.

. . . and Expands Indexing to the Bond Market

The creation of our Fixed Income Group facilitated our decision to form the industry's first bond index fund for individual investors. Vanguard had been laying the groundwork for a bond index fund during much of 1986, but the final inspiration came when *Forbes* magazine, writing about the second-rate returns and high costs of most fixed-income mutual funds, plaintively asked, "Vanguard, where are you when we need you?"

That challenge was all that I needed. With the formation of Vanguard Bond Market Fund in 1986, Vanguard was again the pioneer. The SEC would not permit the use of the name "Vanguard Bond Index Fund," since the staff of its Investment Management Division could not accept the reality that a bond index fund could own a relatively small number of individual bonds and still closely replicate the performance of a bond market index that included thousands of bonds. Without SEC objection, we would later change the name to Vanguard Total Bond Market Index Fund.

In the years that followed, our bond index fund proved to be both an artistic and commercial success, admirably tracking the (now) Bloomberg Barclays U.S. Aggregate Bond Index. By the end of its first decade, it had become one of the 10 largest bond mutual funds. By 1992, bond funds would replace money funds as our largest asset class, accounting for 33% of our then-$97 billion of assets. At the time, that seemed like a huge number. But by mid-2018, the two (virtually identical) portfolios of Vanguard Total Bond Market Index Fund totaled $356 billion, the largest component of the $1 trillion fixed income asset base overseen by Fixed Income Group.

LANDMARK 8. 1985

Eliminating Pennsylvania State Taxes

We also lowered costs for our clients in 1985 by working with the Pennsylvania legislature to substantially eliminate the Pennsylvania franchise tax paid by mutual funds. Many of our funds had been paying some 0.10% (10 basis points) of their assets annually to the Commonwealth, an unacceptable burden. If there were still such a 0.10% burden on our fund shareholders, it could have increased our present expense ratio from about 0.11 to 0.21% – a staggering increase of 10 "basis points," an annual total of $5 billion. We either had to move Vanguard's headquarters to another state or get the tax law changed. We chose the latter course.

Our lobbying efforts were led by Philadelphia lawyer Joseph E. Bright, who in turn retained former lieutenant governor Ernest Kline for support. Other Pennsylvania-based funds wanted to join the effort too, but I refused their offers. I had no interest in compromising my independent judgment in resolving the tax issue and perhaps being forced into under-the-table payments to legislators. Like other compromises that often get made in our nation's legislative process, it can be a messy process.

Both houses of the Pennsylvania legislature recognized the importance of this issue and passed a bill to eliminate this onerous tax by a unanimous vote of 450–0. Governor Dick Thornburgh signed the bill on December 19, 1985.

Two Crises

From 1981 to 1991 there were some wild periods in the bond and stock markets. Some of our innovations were responses to these external events. After being nearly overwhelmed by heavy telephone call volumes from shareholders during a crisis in the municipal bond market during April 1987, we trained virtually our entire staff to be prepared to man the phones when the inevitable next crisis would cause call volumes to surge. That next crisis came all too quickly. But with our Swiss Army, we were ready.

LANDMARK 9. 1987

The Swiss Army

The crash in the municipal bond market, momentarily tough as it was, came when rumors circulated that Congress might remove the traditional tax-exemption for municipal bond interest. Liquidity dried up, and when the markets cleared – as they always do – they cleared at much lower prices. But we were able to sell enough assets (almost always at depressed prices) to raise the cash our funds needed to meet the heavy redemptions faced by all municipal bond funds.

The crash exposed a major weakness in Vanguard's operations. Our ability to handle phone calls from our shareholders dropped sharply. Whether these shareholders sought information, or current share prices, or to redeem their shares, too many calls were delayed for extreme periods, some never answered.

We did what we could to handle the volumes, but I worried that shareholders who couldn't reach Vanguard by phone would drive to our office, possibly jamming roads, duly filmed by our local television stations and appearing on the evening news broadcasts, creating a panic.

Since it would have been totally inefficient to have a full-time staff to handle surges in volume that were rare and intermittent, I decided to have every crewmember trained to answer the phones. It is said that in Switzerland, where every citizen must be trained in military service, "the Swiss do not have an army, they are an army." And so we created our own "Swiss Army" at Vanguard.

There was a second benefit to providing training to all of
our crew members, every bit as important as preparing us for
surges in phone volumes. Doing so would remind our officers
and managers that they were part of an investor service team,
and would reinforce that those are real human beings whom
we serve, not mere numbers. Not all of those executives welcomed their new responsibility.[2]

Black Monday

On October 19, 1987 – Black Monday – stock market investors pan-
icked, and the S&P 500 fell 23% on that single day.[3] With our Swiss
Army activated, we were ready for any sudden spike in call volumes –
not perfect by a long shot, but the envy of our ill-prepared competitors.

The following year, we retained the consulting firm McKinsey
& Company to examine our technology strategy with the goal of
becoming the fund industry's leader both in client services and in firm
operations. Our seeming unwillingness to become a major user of
technology to accomplish these goals (the "we can't afford to be the
leader" mindset) was one of the "sacred cows" that I killed at a meeting
of our senior management team in 1992, described in Chapter 7. As I
told the team, "We can't afford *not* to be the leader."

32 More Mutual Funds

In 1981, with index funds still dormant and their giant resurgence still
a decade-plus away, we continued to form actively managed equity
funds. We broke new ground in creating seven equity funds managed

---

[2] I loved answering the phones. On Black Monday in 1987, I took 104 phone
calls and periodically wandered through the ranks offering appreciation and
optimism.

[3] From its high in June 1987 to its October low, the S&P 500 fell by 40%. But for
the full year, the index notched a 5% gain.

by external advisors advisers that we retained and two new equity index funds. Following the Vanguard board's decision to permit the firm to engage in traditional money management – and the subsequent formation of Vanguard's Fixed Income Group, we created 13 additional defined-maturity bond funds. Five were tax-exempt bond funds, holding long-term municipal bonds issued by specific states – California, New York, Pennsylvania, and Ohio. (New Jersey would be added later.)

We also created tax-exempt money market funds for residents of four of these states, as well as six more defined-maturity taxable bond funds, mostly holding bonds and notes issued by the U.S. Treasury.

We also broke new ground in creating nine equity funds, seven managed by new external advisers that we retained, and two new index funds to expand the still-narrow ambit of indexing, then composed entirely of S&P 500 Index funds. This surge in fund formations was a bet on the future, but also an effort to diversify our asset base and sustain Vanguard's growth until indexing inevitably came into full swing.

1981: Vanguard International Growth Fund. One of the earliest major equity funds to "go abroad," holding only stocks of non-U.S. corporations, the Vanguard International Growth Fund began as a separate portfolio of the original Ivest Fund, which was divided into a U.S. Growth Portfolio and an International Growth Portfolio. (We would later add an International Value Fund.)

In 1985, the international portfolio would stand alone, its record for all to see.[4] We chose London-based Schroders Investment Management as its portfolio manager. Richard R. Foulkes would serve with distinction until his retirement in 2005.

1986: Vanguard Quantitative Portfolios (VQP). As computer-driven stock analysis and strategies gained growing acceptance in the investment field, it was easy to see how a fund relying on quantitative techniques could play an important role in the equity fund arena. VQP would be managed by Boston's Franklin Portfolio Associates, one of the new breed of quant managers. We were able to negotiate a rock-bottom adviser fee of 0.24%, given that computers cost far less

---

[4] The asset value of non-U.S. stocks obliged, soaring skyward. Vanguard International Growth Fund rose an astonishing 96.6% during its 1986 fiscal year, a cumulative gain of 283% over its first five fiscal years.

than the full-time staff of analysts and strategists employed by traditional active funds.

Our limited advertisements for VQP headlined, "Now Vanguard Brings Relative Predictability to Every Investor." The fund held its own against the cost-free S&P 500 Index from its inception through 2005, though the edge was narrow. (Annual return 11.9% for the fund versus 11.6% for the index.) Since then, the fund's performance has slightly lagged the S&P 500 (with an annual return of 8.0% for the fund versus 8.7% for the index). In 1997, Vanguard's management decided to rename the fund Vanguard Growth and Income Fund. This struck me as changing from a brand name to a bland name.

1987: Vanguard Extended Market Index Fund. Well aware that our pioneering 500 Index Fund did not include mid- and small-cap stocks, we formed this so-called completion fund. It was designed to appeal to investors in our 500 Index Fund who wished to add the remainder of the stocks in the market in order to hold the entire market portfolio (a key characteristic on which modern portfolio theory relies). The new fund would also serve investors who believed that small- and mid-cap stocks would provide superior returns.

Since its 1987 inception, the Vanguard Extended Market Index Fund has provided an annual return of 11.0%, slightly higher than the 10.5% annual return on the S&P 500. The fund has attracted the attention of many investors. Its current asset base of $67 billion marks Extended Market Index as one of Vanguard's 20 largest funds, and ranks 27th in assets among today's 4,752 equity mutual funds.

Turning to Active Managers

Whereas Vanguard is primarily known for its index funds (78% of the firm's asset base today), fully 98% of Vanguard's assets were actively managed in 1981. In the years before indexing caught on, I placed a high premium on trusting experienced managers, focused on the long term, without excessive turnover, and operating at advisory fees that were far below the norm in the industry. While I still believe that the best solution for most investors is the broadly diversified stock market index fund, well-chosen active funds with these characteristics have the best chance of outperforming the market.

1984: Vanguard PRIMECAP Fund. In 1983, three of the most able money managers at Capital Group left that firm to start their own investment advisory firm, PRIMECAP Management Company. I was well acquainted with two of them (Howard Schow and Mitchell Milias). On a trip to California, I called on them at their office in Pasadena.

They wanted to manage money, and Vanguard wanted to organize, operate, and distribute a new mutual fund for them to run. They seemed reluctant, however, saying that managing a mutual fund was "not part of our long-term plan." But we got along famously and trusted one another, and Vanguard PRIMECAP Fund was formed on November 1, 1984. Its returns have been excellent. Since the fund's inception, its 13.8% annual return ranks near the top among all stock funds, well above the 10.5% return of the average growth fund and the 11.3% return of the S&P 500 Index. (The fund has been closed to new accounts since 2004.) PRIMECAP has proved to be among the brightest jewels in the Vanguard crown. (For more of PRIMECAP's history, see Chapter 14.)

1985: STAR Fund. The fund-of-funds structure (mutual funds whose portfolio holdings consist solely of other mutual funds) had always appealed to me. But I found the layering-on of management fees ethically distasteful and financially absurd. So we started our own Vanguard STAR Fund, charging zero fees on the fund itself. Its investors would pay only the fees on the underlying Vanguard funds.

STAR was an acronym that stood for "Special Tax-Advantaged Retirement" fund. The SEC rejected our use of that name, but the STAR name stood. It still stands. Its balanced stock/bond portfolio consists solely of 11 actively managed Vanguard funds. Its returns have paralleled those of Vanguard's other balanced funds. Its assets in mid-2018 totaled $22 billion.

A Second Windsor Fund

1985: Windsor II. The boldest move of 1985 was yet to come. In May, John B. Neff, the legendary portfolio manager of Vanguard Windsor Fund, urged me to close Windsor to new accounts. We had long agreed that the time would come for closing it. So, when that time came, we acted decisively.

At $2.3 billion, it was then the largest of all equity mutual funds and capital inflows were high.[5] John was concerned that further rapid growth would hamper his ability to produce continued superior returns. Without hesitation, I agreed. Windsor Fund was closed to new accounts on May 15, 1985.

I wasn't happy about the inevitable loss of Windsor's major contribution to Vanguard's cash flow. But I had no interest in "killing the goose that laid the golden egg." Yet we still needed to be able to offer a fund that sought undervalued stocks with above-average dividend yields. So, on June 24, 1985, we founded Windsor II Fund.

The Cynics Lose

Once the board had heard presentations from the firms that were eager to serve as the new fund's adviser, we selected Dallas-based Barrow, Hanley, Mewhinney, and Strauss. As the fund has grown over the years, additional managers were added to handle the surge in assets. Vanguard's in-house equity manager Quantitative Equity Group was added in 1991, Hotchkis and Wiley Capital Management in 2003, Lazard Asset Management in 2007, and Sanders Capital in 2010. Barrow Hanley continues to manage the largest portion of the portfolio. (For further insight into the history of Windsor Fund, see Chapter 13.)

This strategic move to create a second Windsor Fund was greeted with cynicism by the marketplace. While my goal in naming the new fund Windsor II was mainly to identify the fund as a second Vanguard value fund, I was attacked for using the Windsor name and capitalizing on John Neff's reputation. "You know that Windsor II will never do as well as Windsor" was a common criticism. The comparative annual returns over the 32-plus years since 1985: Windsor Fund with +10.1%, Windsor II Fund with +10.5%. (This is hardly the only occasion on which Vanguard's critics have been proven wrong.) In mid-2018, assets of Windsor II totaled $48 billion, compared to Windsor Fund's $20 billion.

---

[5] When Windsor Fund was closed to new investors, it represented 0.28% of the market capitalization of the S&P 500. A fund representing that share of the S&P 500 in early 2018 would be managing some $63 billion in assets.

Vanguard Specialized Portfolios

In listing our successes from 1981 to 1991, I cannot, in good conscience, ignore one of the great failures of my long career. In May 1984, I was anxious – too anxious – to compete with archrival Fidelity's hyped array of eight sector funds, including Defense & Aerospace, Leisure & Entertainment, and Technology. I decided that we needed to meet the challenge, so we formed Vanguard Specialized Portfolios with just five broad categories, a much more disciplined approach: Gold & Precious Metals (now Precious Metals & Mining), Technology, Energy, Service Economy, and Health Care.

I should have known better. In 1951, studying the fund industry for my Princeton senior thesis, I observed the performance of five "sector fund" groups: Group Securities, Diversified Investment Funds, Managed Funds, Incorporated, and Keystone Custodian Funds. They accounted for 10% of industry assets.

Group Securities, for example, offered 15 industry funds, whose assets were concentrated in steel shares and tobacco shares, which accounted for some 45% of its $100 million asset base. The managers' idea was to facilitate trading among the funds and then encourage investors to trade the 15 industries based on market trends. They soon began to founder; all 15 industry funds went out of business in 1961 and merged into other funds managed by Group Securities. With such a flawed investment premise – despite their brilliant (for a time) marketing premise – these funds ill-served their investors and fell out of the mainstream.

It occurs to me that most of the mistakes I've made during my long career came on those occasions, happily rare, when I removed my investment hat and put on a marketing hat. Two of the five original Vanguard Specialized Portfolios (Service Economy and Technology) no longer exist. While I must confess my failure, I note the irony that one of the surviving portfolios, Vanguard Health Care Fund, has likely provided the highest long-term returns for its investors in the history of the mutual fund industry.

1988: Vanguard Equity Income Fund. One way to make Vanguard's cost advantage clear is to focus on dividend yields, where there are few ways for high-cost funds seeking income to hide their disadvantage. (But you have to look!) We were confident that, because of its low expense ratio, our Equity Income Fund would give investors a premium dividend yield compared to similar funds.

Early in 2018, the average yield for its peer group was 2.0% versus 2.5% for Vanguard Equity Income Fund. But before expense ratios of 0.83% and 0.17% respectively, the gross yields were quite similar –2.7% for the Vanguard fund versus 2.6% for its average competitor. Vanguard's lower costs, however, lead directly to a 25 percentage-point yield advantage of 0.5% for more dividend income for our investors. With assets of $30 billion, it is now the largest fund in its category.

A Productive Decade

Despite the abject failure of Vanguard Specialized Portfolios, the 1980s was a decade in which Vanguard accomplished three important goals: (1) Build our asset base, with our funds launched during this period now totaling some $650 billion; (2) reinforce the strength of our bond franchise; and (3) keep us sharp, focused, and creative as we awaited the inevitable triumph of indexing. While our then-three index funds had begun to grow rapidly during the late 1980s, assets of our index funds totaled just $7 billion in 1991, only 9.1% of Vanguard's then-$77 billion asset base.

Looking Ahead

The 1990s saw the first stirrings of competition in index investing. Fidelity, despite its commitment to aggressive active management, started two stock index funds, both modeled on the S&P 500. Few other firms entered the field, and those that did so charged prices that gave Vanguard first call on the assets of investors seriously considering indexing. For example, the expense ratio on T. Rowe Price's S&P 500 Index Fund, from its launch in 1990 through 1995, remained at 0.45%.

During the next five years, we would forge ahead in our development of index funds, broadening their appeal to investors with particular goals and objectives. We created the industry's first Balanced Index Fund (1992), the first Growth Index Fund (1992), the first Value Index

Fund (1992), and the first LifeStrategy Funds (1994), precursors to our Target Retirement Funds (2003).

The decade from 1981 to 1991 paved the way for other advances in building Vanguard. Operationally, we would move in 1993 to add flexibility in allocating costs among our funds based on competitive prices as well as other factors. We would also streamline our ability to change advisers and fund fee schedules. We would also sharply lower expense ratios for our clients with larger investments via our Admiral Funds, another industry first. Our low-cost Admiral shares now dominate our asset base.

Staying the Course

Vanguard continued to stay the course as we enjoyed a near-20-fold increase in fund assets – from $4.2 billion to $77 billion. All the while, we awaited the inevitable (to me) triumph of indexing. During the 1981–1991 decade, we formed a remarkable total of 32 new mutual funds, including 13 new fixed income funds, two more index funds, and nine active mutual funds (all except one would meet with remarkable success). We continued to follow our guiding star and put the investor first, and we also prepared Vanguard for future changes in an increasingly competitive environment for mutual fund services and mutual fund distribution.

Chapter 7

1991–1996

Preparing for a New Mutual Fund Industry

	12/1991	12/1996	Annual Growth Rate
Vanguard Assets (Billions)	$77	$236	21.1%
Industry Assets (Trillions)	1.5	3.4	18.5
Vanguard Market Share	6.2%	7.0%	—
			Annual Return
S&P 500 Index	417	741	15.2%
Intermediate-Term U.S. Government Bond Yield	6.0%	6.2%	6.2
60% Stocks/40% Bonds	—	—	11.7

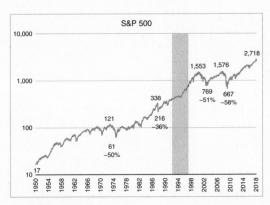

Source: Yahoo! Finance.

Any five-year period in which stock prices rise steadily without a single significant setback can't be all bad! From 1991 to 1996, stocks generated a stunning 15.2% annual return, far above the long-term average 8.6% return from 1900 to 1974. At that 15.2% annual rate, stocks doubled in value over the short period.

Beginning with a Bang

The short but productive period from 1991 through 1996 began with a bang. It was time for us to take a major step forward in indexing. Ever since 1975, we had been stubbornly unwilling to alter the original mandate of the Vanguard 500 Index Fund to encompass the entire U.S. stock market. It was already the seventh-largest equity mutual fund in the United States and accounted for 14% of Vanguard's asset base. It was beginning to grow rapidly.

While it didn't precisely replicate the entire U.S. stock market, the 500 held 85% of the broad market's capitalization and was a perfectly adequate proxy. Why alter it when we could so easily offer a sister fund that held 100% of the U.S. market's capitalization? So in 1992, we launched the Vanguard Total Stock Market Index Fund.[1] In 2013, it became the largest equity fund in the world.

In 1992, we also created the first mixed asset (bond/stock) index fund, Vanguard Balanced Index Fund, the harbinger of our LifeStrategy Funds (1994) and our Target Retirement Funds (2003). Target-date funds would quickly become the most popular investments in employee savings plans.

A major structural change in Vanguard's expense ratios came in 1993, when we gained approval to set the expense ratios of our individual funds, not entirely on their costs but also on the expense ratios charged by our competitors. Now Vanguard could be an aggressive competitor on price. But there was still much more to accomplish.

The Sacred Cows

I opened each session of our annual Vanguard management retreats, usually held in late May, with a lengthy presentation on "The State of Vanguard." Whenever possible, I liked to announce a surprise decision designed to reflect our spirit of innovation. To preserve the element of surprise, I told no one (well, almost no one) about it in advance.

---

[1] You can read more about the story of Total Stock Market Index and Vanguard's other index funds in Chapter 12, "The Index Funds."

In 1992, for example, the theme for my remarks was "sacred cows." I cited fully a dozen Vanguard policies that our management group had thought were inviolate. My major sacred cows included these three:

1. "We are not going to be a technology leader."
2. "We will not (cannot) provide custom-made investment advice and asset allocation guidance."
3. "We do not need to match the fee waivers of any of our peers."

Within a year, not one of those three presumed sacred cows remained alive.

Technology Leadership

The first of those sacred cows – not seeking technology leadership – would not last long. Yes, as I had told *Forbes* magazine earlier, "Technology is too expensive; we can't afford to be the leader." But, technology was becoming an increasingly important differentiator in fund operations, and our asset base was growing by tens of billions, month after month. So I told our managers, "We *are* going to be the technology leader . . . we can't afford *not* to."

Within months of the gathering, we began what we called our "Information Technology Voyage." It started with the recognition that we needed a consultant to do a major study of our existing technology and then draw a roadmap for our future. All of our senior officers attended a full-day session hearing proposals from a range of consultants.

When it was time to make our decision, we took a vote. All six of my colleagues favored a coalition of local technology firms that we had previously worked with in various capacities. I didn't agree. I favored a proposal from the giant consulting firm McKinsey & Company, largely because of McKinsey's size, scope, expertise, and reputation.

McKinsey won the assignment. (I think that the group understood the basis for my decision, and I heard no protests.) McKinsey's recommendations were spot-on. We followed their roadmap for technology leadership in the mutual fund industry. Much of the credit for our success goes to the late Robert A. DiStefano, whose expertise, leadership, and judgment would take us to a position of industry leadership.

(In recent years, our leadership in technology has been challenged, and dealing with our rapid growth has not been easy.)

Customized Advice

The second sacred cow – not offering custom-made investment advice to individual investors – was based on my long-held skepticism that it is largely futile (even a fool's errand) to try to pick, in advance, fund managers who could consistently outperform the market.

But index funds were finally beginning to gain traction with investors, and I was persuaded that financial advisers would increasingly focus on asset allocation rather than the selection of individual actively managed funds that would beat the market.

Within two years, we had opened our own advisory service, bringing in Richard Stevens from accounting firm Coopers & Lybrand to lead the effort. While Rich left Vanguard in 2001, Vanguard's advised asset base has grown to $100 billion in early 2018.

"A Shot Across the Bow"

The third of these sacred cows was a major theme of my 1992 address to Vanguard's senior management: competitive fund pricing. I said that we should "fire a shot across the bow" of our competitors by letting them know that there was no point in trying to undercut our expense ratios. We would find a way to selectively and creatively reduce our fund expense ratios in ways that they had not foreseen.

The Admiral Funds

At that 1992 leadership retreat, I announced to our managers that we would demonstrate our determination to compete by creating a low-cost series of four funds investing in U.S. Treasury securities (money market, short-, intermediate-, and long-term) with relatively high ($50,000) minimum initial investments. They would carry the name "Admiral," identifying them as "high ranking" in value. They would bear expense ratios of only 0.10%, less than half the expense ratios of our existing bond funds.

The new offerings bore fruit immediately, giving us valuable experience in selectively pricing our funds. In mid-2018, the assets of our four Admiral Treasury funds totaled $32 billion. Hardly a blockbuster success, but the funds provided rock-bottom expenses, higher yields, and thus higher total returns, all with only nominal credit risk, and with maturity risk held constant.

Over the years that followed, shareholder recordkeeping technology advanced. It became possible for us to create Admiral classes for our existing mutual funds. Beginning in 2000, we gradually added lower-price Admiral class options for nearly all the funds that Vanguard offers. In mid-2018, assets of our Admiral shares totaled $1.7 trillion, the largest single class of all Vanguard's funds, fully one-third of our asset base.

The Admiral concept began a revolution in Vanguard's approach to fund pricing. As a group, the huge Admiral share classes of our funds now carry an asset-weighted average expense ratio of just 0.11%, about half of the 0.20% average ratio of our Investor share classes and about 80% below the 0.63% average weighted expense ratio of our actively managed peers.

New Concepts in Indexing

During this period, Vanguard also began to rewrite the rules of the mutual fund game – to create mutual funds that, rather than simply being stock funds or bond funds or money market funds, would be shaped to meet the needs of the varying requirements of investors. Our first two new index funds represented the beginning of that strategy.

The Growth and Value Index Funds

In 1989, I gave a speech to the Philadelphia Society of Security Analysts (now the CFA Society of Philadelphia) promising that the creation of separate growth and value index funds "awaits only the development of soundly-constructed Growth Indexes and Equity Income [Value] Indexes."

Standard & Poor's Corporation introduced both indexes on May 30, 1992. We wasted little time. On November 2, 1992, we created two new index funds, separating the stocks of the S&P 500 into growth and value portfolios.

My concept for how investors should approach these two funds was simple. Investors who were accumulating assets should consider Vanguard Growth Index Fund, with a high portion of its return likely to be from long-term capital appreciation, a low portion from taxable dividend income, and with relatively higher volatility. When they reached retirement and began the distribution phase of their investment lives, investors would seek higher dividend income and lower volatility. Voilà! Vanguard Value Index Fund.

The Ideal versus the Reality

That simple, obvious idea, however, belied what would occur in the marketplace. In my annual reports to shareholders, I repeatedly warned that switching between the funds based on expectations about short-term returns of these two market segments was likely to be counterproductive. I also said that I expected the Growth Index and the Value Index to produce similar returns over the long run.

My warning fell largely on deaf ears, and my expectation, remarkably, was almost precisely confirmed. Over the quarter-century that followed their creation, the annual return on the Growth Index Fund was 8.9% and the return on the Value Index Fund was 9.4%, almost identical. But investors in both funds too often switched between the two series, and earned far lower annual returns than the funds themselves: Growth with +6.1%; Value with +7.9%. I was amazed – and more than that, a little embarrassed – that what I considered a big advance in index investing had been misused by so many of the Growth and Value Funds' investors.

The Factor-Fund Boom

Ironically, these two funds paved the way for the boom in "factor funds" that began in the mid-2000s and soon became a rapidly growing sector of the exchange-traded fund (ETF) industry. A "factor" can be described as a group of stocks with similar investment characteristics that academic financial economists have found to have been associated with market outperformance in the past. "Growth" and "value" are clearly two distinct factors. In early 2018, factor funds represented more than 20% of all ETF net cash flows over the previous five years. (As I'll note in Chapter 8, the ETF strategy has ill-served investors.)

Although they were never designed to function like their successors, Morningstar bills our Growth and Value Index Funds as the first two "strategic beta" funds. They are also the two largest funds in the field.[2] In mid-2018, assets of Growth Index Fund totaled $79 billion; Value Index Fund, $66 billion.

Bringing Lower Costs to Investors

Our philosophy in reducing the costs of investing has been diametrically opposed to that of our peers, who fight to hold the line on high fees, only grudgingly sharing the substantial economies of scale entailed by mutual fund asset growth. They prefer to introduce new funds with higher expense ratios than their existing funds. Although, as investors become increasingly cost-conscious, that strategy is getting more difficult to implement.

Ultimately, the Admiral class and its other extra-low-cost Vanguard cousins were the result of our mutual structure, maximizing the returns earned by fund shareholders rather than maximizing the returns earned by the management companies that control our peer funds.

Since individual mutual funds have always had the ability to set their own fees subject to shareholder approval, the creation of the Admiral Funds raised no regulatory issues. But it seemed obvious to me that if Vanguard were to compete on price even more aggressively, we would require even greater flexibility. The Admiral Funds were a good beginning, but our ultimate goal was to bring down prices on all of our funds. It was not easy, but we got it done.

---

[2] One might have hoped that the counterproductive investor experience of "switching" Vanguard's Value and Growth Funds would have cooled the enthusiasm of latter-day fund marketers for putting a potentially dangerous weapon in the hands of their clients. It didn't. The clients suffered.

Competing on Price . . . The 1993 Proxies

Under the terms of the original Vanguard Service Agreement, we were required to apply fairly rigid standards to the allocation of costs among our funds, such as each fund's direct costs, plus its allocation of indirect costs based primarily on its proportionate share of total Vanguard fund assets and number of shareholders – standards that largely precluded our ability to tactically allocate those costs.

We needed the ability to selectively reduce fees in discrete segments of the marketplace, particularly for investors with substantial assets. Such pricing flexibility would enable us to be an even tougher competitor.

Following clearance of our 1993 proxies by the SEC, we sought the approval of our fund shareholders to amend our service agreement to give our funds the ability to compete on price. We would continue the stern allocation methods earlier approved, but, as we wrote in our 1993 proxy statement, add a provision that would allow the Vanguard funds "to provide competitive investment services at competitive prices designed to enable Vanguard to survive and grow."

LANDMARK 10. 1993

An Attack from a Rival . . . Rebuffed

Even as our mutual structure had virtually assured our ability to compete on *cost,* the proxy provision we proposed in 1993 gave us, at last, the flexibility also to compete on *price.* This major landmark was a game changer. It threw open the doors of price competition for our actively managed funds and our passive index funds alike. Yet this important change was barely noticed. *Not a single Vanguard fund investor raised a question.* Nor did the press. Nor did any of our competitors.

Ironically, the only negative comment about our 1993 proxy proposal came on an unrelated proposal that would enable Vanguard to finance, on the most favorable financial terms, the estimated $160 million construction cost of our new campus. Our business was growing fast. We expected further growth, and we were right. As 1992 ended, our fund assets totaled $92 billion. A decade later, as 2002 ended, Vanguard's fund assets had soared to $555 billion.[3]

It was that mundane financing proposal, not the groundbreaking proposal that would enable us to compete on price as well as cost, which caught the eye of rival Fidelity. Simply put, they did not like the proposal to finance our new Vanguard campus. Fidelity took the unusual, if not unprecedented, action of requesting that the SEC hold a hearing on our proposed financing arrangement.

I was not amused. As reported in the *Wall Street Journal* on December 1, 1992, I described Fidelity's request for a hearing a "mean-spirited, arrogant interference in our internal affairs, either venal or stupid." A bitter war of words followed in the press. But when it became clear that the staff of the Commission's Division of Investment Management was reluctant to hold an inevitably tedious, costly, and time-consuming hearing, Fidelity withdrew its application.

In return, the SEC staff suggested that I refrain from further comment. The language used in that request was considerably sharper: The staff advised me to "shut the h—— up." I happily acceded to their request. (It wasn't easy!) At the fund shareholders meetings on April 12, 1993, all of our proposals were approved.

---

[3] In fairness, our 1993 fund proxies were long (30 pages or more) and complex, with as many as eight substantive proposals requiring shareholder approval, including requests to approve yet more advisory fee reductions.

Vanguard's 1993 proxy covered a lot of ground. Every bit as significant as the two proposals described earlier for financing the new Vanguard campus and the proposal to compete on price in the marketplace was a proposal to authorize each fund's board of directors "to change and select new investment advisers and enter into new investment advisory agreements rather than obtaining the approval of the shareholders of the Fund."

The root of that proposal to give the directors the authority to act in the interests of our shareholder/clients was that our mutual structure was unique. Given our internalized operations and our independence in negotiating with advisers, we believed that Vanguard should have complete independence to select and change advisers and merely report the decision to fund shareholders. Vanguard's directors faced no significant conflicts of interest in selecting our external advisers and should, we argued, be able to enjoy the same unfettered freedom to select advisers and negotiate fees as the trustees of pension plans and endowment funds.

LANDMARK 11. 1993

Freedom to Select Investment Advisers and Adjust Advisory Fees

By 1993 we had been operating for almost two decades and had implemented more than 200 fee reductions for the various Vanguard funds, each one requiring a costly shareholder's meeting. (It is no secret that 95% or more of mutual fund shareholders typically approve management proxy proposals, making the votes pro forma in nature. Our proxy proposal would eliminate the requirement for shareholder approval of fee changes, replacing it with a commitment that the funds notify their shareholders 30 days in advance of any changes in advisory fees or advisers. The proposal to leave those decisions to the board, like our other proxy proposals, was approved overwhelmingly by fund shareholders.

A Serious Blunder

As time rolled on, however, I realized that I had made a serious blunder, and I was no longer in a position to rectify my error. *If I had it to do over again, I would have made our proposal apply only to fee reductions, and would continue to require shareholder approval for any fee increases.* (In my years as CEO, I had never recommended a single fee increase, only those 200-plus decreases.)

When I approved that 1993 proxy proposal, I could not imagine the need for the future fee increases. Since 1993, however, Vanguard management has recommended few, if any, fee reductions to the board, but at least five fee increases.[4] As far as I can tell, I was the only person who noticed these increases, making my earlier blunder all the more painful.

Not coincidentally, our 1993 proxies also proposed further fee reductions for a dozen of our funds. They too were approved by shareholders. The year 1993 indeed marked a double landmark for Vanguard shareholders.

The Balanced Index Fund

Only a week after forming the Growth and Value Index Funds, we founded the industry's first balanced index fund on November 9, 1992. Since the fund's inception, its allocation has remained unchanged: 60% in the Total Stock Market Index and 40% in the Total Bond Market Index.

The fund's low costs played a major role in its superiority over peer funds, accounting for fully 1.1 percentage points of that 1.9 percentage point advantage.

---

[4] My successors at Vanguard continue to use advisory fee breakpoints, the approach I used in those early negotiations with Wellington Management. That is, as fund assets grow, the advisory fee rates paid on those additional fund assets decreases. With this approach, Vanguard's fund shareholders, not the external advisers, enjoy most of the benefits of economies of scale.

With Balanced Index Fund's broadly diversified portfolio, low costs, and moderate risk profile, it can serve as a core portfolio holding for investors with very long-term time horizons like pensions and university endowments. In fact, Balanced Index Fund holds its own when compared to even the largest and presumably most sophisticated U.S. endowment portfolios. During the decade ending June 30, 2017, the annual total return of Vanguard Balanced Index Fund has averaged 6.9%, nicely outpacing the 4.4% return of the average balanced mutual fund and the 5.0% return of the largest university endowments. Cumulative return: Balanced Index Fund, 92%; average balanced fund, 54%; largest endowments, 63%.

Spawning a Family of Balanced Funds

Vanguard Balanced Index Fund has achieved strong investment returns and parallel success in the fund marketplace. With assets in early 2018 of $38 billion, Balanced Index is the fifth largest among all 605 U.S. balanced funds.

The importance of the Balanced Index Fund to Vanguard goes far beyond its own solid history, for the fund was the precursor to two other versions of investment balance in our fund line-up. The first version was our LifeStrategy Funds; the second was our Target Retirement Funds. Target-date funds have proved to be the most powerful fund-industry-changing concept since the money market mutual fund and the index mutual fund.

The LifeStrategy Funds

The first variation from the set 60/40 stock/bond target of Balanced Index was our creation, on March 30, 1994, of four "LifeStrategy" funds with stock/bond ratios set at various levels: LifeStrategy Income, 20% stocks/80% bonds; Conservative Growth, 40/60; Moderate Growth, 60/40; and Growth, 80/20.

Alas, these funds started off on the wrong foot. (What was I thinking?) Rather than sticking with those fixed stock/bond ratios, we allocated 25% of assets in each fund to Vanguard Asset Allocation Fund, which tactically adjusted its stock/bond ratio based on its managers' expectations for future returns in the stock and bond markets.

No fund concept should be made more complicated than it needs to be. Yet I made an inexcusable "rookie error." While the Asset Allocation Fund component helped to marginally enhance returns of our LifeStrategy Funds during their early years, that edge did not continue. We abandoned that nuance in 2011.

The LifeStrategy Funds gave investors a convenient way to balance their expectations for growth against their risk tolerance, based importantly on their financial ability to assume risk and their emotional capacity to withstand risk. Lots of investors liked the idea. In mid-2018, assets of our four LifeStrategy Funds totaled $44 billion. But that was only the beginning of the remarkable expansion in role of balanced funds at Vanguard.

Target Retirement Funds

In 1994, the fund industry, led by Wells Fargo Bank, began to offer "target-date funds" (TDFs) in series, based on retirement dates specified by clients. Target-date funds rely on a "glide path," which starts with a relatively aggressive asset allocation to stocks when the investor is young, and gradually becomes more conservative as retirement approaches.

For example, in a 2035[5] retirement fund purchased in 2005, the 90/10 stock/bond balance at the outset is gradually reduced to 60/40 at retirement. The idea is that as the years remaining before retirement lessen and their assets accumulate, investors will become increasingly risk-averse.

Many fund marketers now offer a broad range of target-date funds. Each marketer of TDFs sets its own asset allocation parameters (although the differences are typically minor) according to their view of investor preferences and their assumptions regarding expected long-term returns on stocks and bonds.

---

[5] Target-date funds are now generally available for every five-year interval from 2015 to 2065.

Active versus Passive TDFs – Costs Matter

Vanguard's Target Retirement Funds, established in 2003, are no exception to this general allocation pattern, but remain almost unique. While our peers generally offer their own *actively managed* stock and bond funds, the Vanguard TDFs rely solely on stock and bond *index* funds.

That index fund structure brings with it significantly lower costs. The expense ratios of Vanguard's TDFs average 0.13%, versus an average of 0.70% for our major peers. As the investing public has become more aware of the benefits of low fund costs in creating higher long-term returns, Vanguard's Target Retirement Funds have flourished. Our assets in these funds totaled $404 billion in mid-2018, by far the largest group of TDFs in the field, with a dominant market share of 36% of TDF assets.

Introducing Other New Concepts

In 1992, we again broke new ground with the creation of Vanguard Total Stock Market Index Fund. Our second broad-market stock index fund was destined to become the world's largest. The 1994 creation of the LifeStrategy Funds was a ground-breaking adaptation of investment balance to meet the needs of investors with varying amounts of risk tolerance. Both represented major innovations in the fund industry.

But we were still not content that the range of funds and strategies that we offered to investors was sufficient to meet all of their needs. Given our traditional mission to serve investors rather than simply to attract more assets, we had to offer more options.

So we polished up our bond fund franchise. In March 1994, echoing the municipal bond strategy we pioneered in 1976, we created the industry's first taxable defined-maturity bond market index funds, with a short-, intermediate-, and long-term series.

Their reception among my colleagues at Vanguard was muted at best. After all, we already had funds focused separately on corporate bonds and on U.S. Treasury bonds and notes.[6] But I decided we should go ahead, and by mid-2018, the assets of our taxable defined-maturity bond index funds, our actively managed corporate bond funds, and our U.S. Treasury funds totaled $218 billion.

Tax-Managed Funds

In 1994, we also added the industry's first series of tax-managed mutual funds, all essentially index funds: Tax-Managed Growth and Income Fund (tracking the S&P 500); Tax-Managed Capital Appreciation Fund (the 250 S&P stocks with the lowest dividend yields); and Tax-Managed Balanced Fund (50% lowest-yielding stocks, and 50% intermediate-term tax-exempt bonds, the minimum tax-exempt allocation that would allow us to "pass through" their tax-favored treatment to fund shareholders.) In 2004, our Tax-Managed Small Cap Fund was added.

That tax-managed concept has not found much favor with investors. The main reason seems to be that the index orientation of the new funds was only slightly more tax-efficient than standard index funds held or the S&P 500. Further, to curb capital outflows that might result in the need to realize substantial capital gains that would impinge on the portfolios' tax-efficient mandate, we instituted a fee on shares redeemed by investors during the first five years following their investments. Investors did not appreciate that redemption fee. The Capital Appreciation, Balanced, and Small-Cap portfolios barely gained critical mass, with assets totaling $20 billion in mid-2018. The Growth and Income portfolio was later merged into our S&P 500 Index Fund.

Trial . . .

During that period from 1991 to 1996, we also introduced an index fund investing in real estate investment trusts (REITs), now the largest REIT fund, with $58 billion in mid-2018. We also formed a Total

---

[6] When I held my first meeting with our management to explain my reasoning for starting the new series of index bond funds, none of our senior executives attended. All sent subordinates. I cancelled the meeting on the spot. My disgust must have been obvious. At the rescheduled meeting, the entire senior staff showed up.

International Stock Index Fund, combining the shares of our emerging market and developed market index funds. Assets of Total International exceeded $340 billion as 2018 began. Strategic Equity Fund, a quantitative fund, was formed in 1995. It is internally managed by the Vanguard Quantitative Equity Group. That fund is still seeking to find its niche in the marketplace.

. . . and Error

In filling out the Vanguard menu of funds – 25 new funds in just five years – I made one really stupid error. It echoed my error in the 1985 creation of the Vanguard Specialized Portfolios. The new mistake was the Horizon Funds, introduced in mid-1995.

In a stock market which had enjoyed ever rising valuations, I intuited that our directors wanted more aggressive funds. I made the bad judgment of creating them. The Capital Opportunity, Global Equity, Strategic Equity, and Global Asset Allocation portfolios were all risky, and designed to be held by long-term investors.

The Horizon Fund Portfolios

None of the Horizon portfolios turned in acceptable results in their early years. (In 2001, the Global Asset Allocation Fund was merged into another Vanguard fund.) The one exception to lackluster success was the Capital Opportunity Fund, whose results had approached disastrous at the outset, especially because of the failure of its short-selling strategies.

In 1998, we turned its investment management over to the team at PRIMECAP. Those managers more than measured up to their new task, producing consistently superior returns. Money poured in, and we closed the fund to new accounts in 2004. As 2018 began, the assets of Vanguard Capital Opportunity Fund totaled $16 billion.

Like my foolish opportunistic move in creating Vanguard Specialized Portfolios in 1985, I was wearing my marketing hat rather than my fiduciary hat when I created the Horizon Funds. I hope that my successors and colleagues will learn from my inexcusable mistakes.[7]

Factor Funds Introduced

Early in 2018, we also introduced six actively managed factor funds designed for the ETF marketplace. The funds offer a choice among the quality factor, momentum factor, minimum volatility factor, value factor, liquidity factor, and a multifactor fund that combines these various factors into a single fund. We shall have to wait and see how they fare for their investors, and carefully assess their contribution to Vanguard's growth. I've avoided public comment on them, but the media seems to have guessed how I felt. *Bloomberg's* headline read: "Add the Hot Sauce, Hold the Bogle" (a link to the video is available on my website, www.johncbogle.com).

Staying the Course

Our work from 1991 to 1996 set the stage for Vanguard's future growth in operations, in activities, and in fund creation. It would soon begin to pay off. We stayed the course that we had set for ourselves in 1974, with serving the investor as our guiding star. We also took major steps to be even more price-competitive in the mutual fund marketplace despite a major challenge to our plan from a giant rival, the era's most powerful firm in the fund industry. We also created the first balanced index mutual fund. It was the harbinger of our LifeStrategy and Target Retirement Funds, soon to follow. In short, we built on our original balanced fund heritage established by Wellington Fund, and we stayed the course.

---

[7] So far, the evidence is mixed. In 2008, we introduced three Managed Payout Funds – offering annual payouts (from income, capital gains, and/or return of capital) of 3%, 5%, and 7%. They were unsuccessful, and in 2014, the 3% and 7% portfolios were merged into the 5% portfolio.

Chapter 8

1996–2006

The ETF Revolutionizes Indexing

	12/1996	12/2006	Annual Growth
Vanguard Assets (Billions)	$236	$1,122.7	16.9%
Industry Assets (Trillions)	3.4	10.1	11.5
Vanguard Market Share	7.8%	12.6%	—
			Annual Return
S&P 500 Index	741	1,418	8.4%
Intermediate-Term U.S. Government Bond Yield	6.2%	4.7%	5.8
60% Stocks/40% Bonds	—	—	7.9

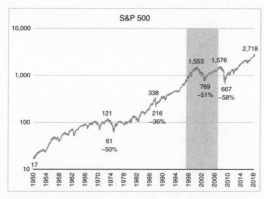

Source: Yahoo! Finance.

The bubble in stock prices that developed from 1998 to 1999 – created by the soaring prices of "New Economy" stocks – began to burst in 2000. A shocking 51% decline in the stock market quickly followed. But given the great bull market that preceded the bubble and the solid recovery that followed, stock returns generated a healthy annual return of 8.4% during the full 1996–2006 decade.

A Visit from Nathan Most

When I walked into my office at Vanguard around 7 a.m. one day in early 1992,[1] I noted that the major outside appointment on my calendar was a visit from Nathan Most, vice president of new product development at the American Stock Exchange.

He appeared on schedule, and turned out to be as fine a gentleman as I've ever met. Mr. Most had outlined his idea to me in writing a week earlier, so I knew what to expect. At our meeting, he detailed his proposal: we would partner together and create a new "product" that would allow shares of Vanguard 500 Index Fund to be traded instantaneously throughout the day, just like individual stocks.

ETFs: The Beginning

Mr. Most, who died in 2004 at age 90, was convinced that enabling, even encouraging, holders of index fund shares to trade them on the nation's stock exchanges would vastly increase the assets of our 500 Index Fund. His proposed exchange-traded fund (ETF, though that acronym wouldn't find broad usage for a decade or so) would attract a new breed of investors. Of course, it would also attract speculators, although he did not use the word.

Think of it, he said: in addition to the diversification, portfolio transparency, and low expense ratios that Vanguard already offered, an ETF would offer investors in our 500 Index Fund far greater flexibility in managing their portfolios; greater tax efficiency; lower costs; the ability to sell shares short, buy them on margin, and easily trade them on foreign exchanges; and the ETF would attract hedge funds and other institutional investors by enabling them to fine-tune their risk exposures.[2] From Vanguard's perspective, it would open new channels for distribution and expand the market for index funds. Though soft-spoken, Nathan Most was clearly a missionary for his concept.

---

[1] I can't be certain of the exact date. My datebook is not a model of clarity.
[2] As it was to happen, ETFs would also be virtually essential to the operations of electronic "robo" advisers that provide computer-driven asset allocation models.

I listened to his presentation with interest and conveyed my two reactions: (1) there were three or four flaws in the design that would have to be corrected for the idea to actually function; and (2) even if he could fix those flaws, I wasn't interested in such a partnership.

No Community of Interest

Our 500 Index Fund, I pointed out, was designed for long-horizon investors. I feared that adding all that liquidity would attract largely short-horizon speculators whose trading would ill serve the interests of the fund's long-term investors. So we found no community of interest. But we parted amicably, and enjoyed a nice friendship over the years that followed.

Were he alive today, seeing ETFs enter the mainstream of American finance, one can only wonder what Nathan Most would be thinking. Lest we forget, his relentless drive to take the ETF from idea to reality was the key to its success. His contribution has largely gone unnoticed, so I'd like to acknowledge it here, with a salute to this pioneer.

The "Spider"

As Nate Most told the story, on his train ride back to New York City he figured out how to fix the operational problems that I had found in his design. He then resumed his search for a partner, finding one at the giant firm now called State Street Global Advisers.

In January 1993, State Street introduced the Standard & Poor's Depositary Receipts. Based on the S&P 500, the "SPDR" ETF (SPY on the NYSE Arca; colloquially, "the Spider"), has dominated the ETF marketplace ever since.

Despite the amazing influx of new ETFs – there are now 2,190 in the United States alone – the Spider remains the world's largest exchange-traded fund. In mid-2018, its assets totaled $307 billion. Each day, it is the most actively traded security on the world's stock exchanges in terms of dollar volume.

Back in 1992, I had no idea that, within a decade, the ETF idea would ignite a flame that would change not only the nature of indexing, but also the entire field of investing. But in turning down Most's proposal, I stood on principle: stock trading is the enemy of the investor. Today, while I observe what I consider grossly excessive trading by many holders of ETFs, I also see an effective means to broaden the attraction of low-cost index funds to a new multitude of investors.

The ETF Catches On

The ETF was accepted in the marketplace far more quickly than was the case for its predecessor, the traditional index fund (TIF). It took only 17 years, until 2010, for ETF assets to cross the $1 trillion mark. But it took fully 35 years, until 2011, for TIFs to cross $1 trillion.

The $3.5 trillion now invested in U.S. ETFs now exceeds the $3.3 trillion invested in U.S. TIFs. (That $6.8 trillion total is surely a testament to the power of indexing.) I can unhesitatingly describe Nathan Most's visionary creation of the ETF as the most successful financial *marketing* idea so far during the twenty-first century. Whether it proves to be the most successful *investment* idea of the century remains to be seen.

The "Holy Grail" of Investing

Indeed, how could ETFs possibly outperform TIFs with any consistency? With some 2,200 ETFs in the United States alone, tracking an incredible 1,700 different indexes (!), trading ETFs offers all of the characteristics of trading stocks, only at a far more rapid rate. But in both cases, trading is a risky business, even though speculating in index funds is generally less risky than speculating in individual stocks.

It's hard for me to imagine that today's ETFs will ever become the Holy Grail of investing: that ever-sought-after secret of consistently outpacing the returns delivered by the stock market in total. Quite to the contrary.

Some ETFs offer the temptation to bet on narrow segments of the stock market, some employ exotic leveraged strategies and facilitate betting on whether the market will rise or fall on a given day, and some make betting on commodity prices relatively easy. But six-plus decades of investment experience have reinforced my basic tenet: while long-term investing is by definition a winner's game, short-term trading – yes, let's call it speculation – is by definition a loser's game.

But to be fair, nowhere near all ETF holders are speculators. ETF holders, in significant but largely unmeasurable numbers, are sensible investors, benefitting from the positive attributes of ETFs.

It can fairly be said that trading activity on ETFs is divided into two parts: (1) the Spider and (2) all other ETFs. During 2017, the Spider alone accounted for fully 22% of the average daily dollar volume of the largest 100 ETFs. Its cash flows, however, are extremely volatile. For example, in the final five months of 2007 (at the market's peak) investors added $40 billion to their holdings of the Spider; during the first five months of 2009 (near the market's low), investors withdrew $30 billion. Pouring money into the market at the top and pulling it out at the bottom does not presage investment success.

"All Day Long, in Real Time"

The early advertisements for the Spider expressed its marketing proposition bluntly: "Now you can trade the S&P 500 Index all day long, in real time." I can't help but wonder (if you'll forgive the coarse language), "What kind of a nut would do that?" Yet it's worth repeating that, day after day, the Spider lives up to its promise – invariably the most actively traded security, in terms of dollar value, on all of the world's stock markets.

In 2017 alone, its average *daily* trading volume measured 70 million shares, with an astonishing $4.3 trillion in annual trading. With the Spider's assets averaging about $245 billion for the year, that's a turnover rate of 1,786%. (The average corporate stock had a turnover of 125%. Redemptions of regular mutual funds averaged 30% of assets.) Yes, investors are indeed trading the S&P 500 Index "all day long in real time," and in unimaginable volumes.

Imitation Is the Sincerest Form of Flattery

While Nate Most would be proud that his ETF dream has been real-ized, I believe that he would be disappointed by the kinds of offbeat funds that have proliferated.

The diversity of investment options spawned by these would-be followers of the Spider now reach far beyond the boundaries of what even an innovator like Most would likely have found appropriate. "Name an exotic product – any product you can imagine – and we'll create it" is the war cry of the new breed of ETF entrepreneurs. Many, perhaps most, of these marketers are not necessarily in the game because they believe that their so-called product may be good for investors, but because they may hit the jackpot, attract a lot of assets, and make a personal fortune.

To get an idea of how ETFs differ from their TIF predecessors, consider the profiles of the major categories of each, as shown in Exhibit 8.1. Note that there are almost *five* times as many ETFs (2,169) as TIFs (472), and *seven* times as many ETFs in the "Concentrated/ Speculative" category (1,002 vs. 140).

Yes, broad-based stock and bond ETFs, used properly as long-term investments, are good for investors. But as I have often said, "ETFs are fine, just so long as you don't trade them." How could I possibly be against the idea of shares in a low-cost S&P 500 ETF being bought by an investor and held for an investment lifetime?

But the temptation for fund marketers to jump on the bandwagon of a hot new product is almost irresistible. During my career, I've seen scores of innovations, but no more than a tiny handful have served the enduring needs of long-term investors. Too many ETFs fail to meet that standard.

Exhibit 8.1   Composition of TIF Assets and ETF Assets, May 2018

Category	Assets (Billions)		Number of Funds	
	TIFs	ETFs	TIFs	ETFs
Diversified U.S. stock	$1,587	$690	69	63
Diversified non-U.S. stock	461	540	47	111
Diversified bonds	462	488	74	218
Factor/smart beta	369	1,092	142	775
Concentrated/speculative	64	724	140	1,002
Total	$2,943	$3,533	472	2,169

Source: Author's calculations using Morningstar data.

"I'm Shocked, Shocked . . ."

It seems clear there is more short-term speculation than long-term investment going on in the ETF field, not only among traders in specialty and leveraged ETFs, but in middle-of-the-road funds covering broad market segments such as the total U.S. stock market, and the total international (non-U.S.) market. The scale of that speculation is staggering. In 2017 the dollar value of trading in U.S. ETFs alone came to $17.3 trillion, 25% of all stock trading.

Those who express surprise about the huge turnover that characterizes ETFs remind me of the classic line from Claude Rains as Captain Louis Renault, the police chief in the movie *Casablanca*: "I'm shocked, shocked to find that gambling is going on in here."

Yes, much of the rapid trading in ETFs – and the Spider in particular – is done by financial institutions that use them to hedge or equitize cash reserves. But much of the activity seems to be speculation, actively trading ETFs "in real time," even trading in margin accounts. Financial institutions dominate the list of the largest holders of nearly all broad-market ETFs, and they are by far the largest traders.

No one seems to know precisely how these numbers play out, but I'd estimate that at least half of ETF assets are held by institutional investors and traded furiously, with the remaining half held by individuals. Further, I'd guess that some two-thirds of all individual holders follow trading strategies of one type or another, leaving only one-third who may do some trading, but follow more of a buy-and-hold strategy akin to that of the original TIF paradigm. That arithmetic suggests that only about one-sixth of ETF assets are held by investors with a focus largely on the long-term.

Vanguard and VIPERs

Impressed with growth and potential of ETFs, Vanguard joined the ETF parade in 2001. Gus Sauter, director of Vanguard's Equity Investment Group, led the charge. As I understand it, he was staunch in demanding that the firm offer ETFs to its present and potential clients. He then became the enthusiastic leader of its implementation. Sauter created a novel (indeed, patented) structure in which each ETF would simply be a new share class of the portfolio of one of Vanguard's existing TIFs.

To his credit, Sauter took the high road in ETF marketing, limiting our offerings to broad-market index funds and U.S. industry segments, eschewing the "lunatic fringe" of the ETF business, such as leveraged, inverse leverage, and single-country ETFs.

Vanguard's original ETFs were named "VIPERs" (Vanguard Index Participation Equity Receipts). But once you realize that a viper is a poisonous snake with long fangs (or a treacherous person), you can see that it was an odd choice of name. It was soon dropped in favor of "Vanguard ETFs."

Vanguard's decision to create ETFs was heavily influenced by its directors. Here's how Vanguard board member and Princeton professor Burton G. Malkiel described the decision to move forward with ETFs.

> *Jack Bogle . . . was very negative about the product [because of the appeal to the trading mentality of so many investors]. . . . It was Vanguard's management (not the board) that were reluctant. . . . The broker managing your account doesn't get a commission for a Vanguard fund. He can get his commission for buying you a Vanguard ETF.*[3]

Vanguard's decision to launch ETFs, then, was likely aimed largely at attracting stockbrokers to distribute the firm's ETF shares. Vanguard had eliminated distribution through stockbrokers in 1977. Ever since, the firm has been "no-load," paying no commissions to stockbrokers. However, the commissions paid on ETF transactions go directly from the investor to the broker. Our long-standing policy of not paying for distribution endures. Vanguard's considerable success in the ETF market has been earned, not bought.

After launching its first ETF, Vanguard Total Stock Market ETF in 2001, Vanguard expanded its entry into existing conventional broad-market sectors such as growth, value, large-cap, small-cap, and so forth. The firm also gradually expanded into concentrated market sectors such as energy, healthcare, and information technology; into broad

---

[3] Malkiel quoted in Joe DiStefano, "'Random Walk' Malkiel on Rates, Risk, and Why Vanguard Changed," *Philadelphia Inquirer*, January 13, 2015.

international indexes; and into a wide array of bond index ETFs. In mid-2018, about 21% of Vanguard's ETF assets were held in our S&P 500 and Total Stock Market ETFs.

Taking the High Ground

Vanguard has largely ignored the most concentrated and speculative sectors of the ETF market that encourage betting on the unknown. Nonetheless, our relatively disciplined strategy has attracted short-term speculators as well as long-term investors. The average annual turnover rates of our ETF shares are amazingly high (135%, suggesting a nine-month holding period) relative to our TIF redemption rates (18%, holding period almost six years), but only one-fourth of the 579% annual turnover rate of ETFs generally (holding period of about two months).

I applaud such marketing discipline, which is rarely rewarded in the mutual fund field. But the growth of Vanguard's ETFs belies the presumption that success in the ETF marketplace depends on marketing funds with a tiny niche or encouraging rapid trading. The firm's ETF assets have grown unremittingly, from $5.8 billion in 2004 to $885 billion in mid-2018. Vanguard's share of ETF assets has soared from just 3% in 2004 to 25%, second only to the ETF leader BlackRock (39%), and well ahead of ETF pioneer State Street Global (18%).

The Proof of the Pudding

If "the proof of the pudding is in the eating," the ETF meal has hardly proven nutritious for most of its millions of investors. The evidence continues to roll in. It shows that the returns earned by ETF investors as a group, including speculators whose collective trading volumes are extremely high, generally fall far short of the returns earned by TIF investors.

The lack of data regarding the relative investor returns of TIF owners and ETF owners has long concerned me. But, early in 2018, when I happened to examine the sources of asset growth in ETFs and TIFs, the answer jumped right out at me. Wow!

116 STAY THE COURSE

Once I did the simple arithmetic showing the relative importance of investment performance and net cash inflows to the remarkable growth in assets, I found that *two-thirds* of the growth in the assets of equity ETFs came from their success in attracting cash flow, and only *one-third* was the result of their investment return (performance).

The pattern of TIF growth was just the opposite. Almost *two-thirds* of the growth in TIFs was represented by the returns that they earned for their investors and only *one-third* by their cash inflows. In short, the growth in ETFs has been largely the result of marketing; the growth in TIFs has been largely the result of investment performance.

TIF Returns versus ETF Returns

Surprised, indeed shocked, by those data, I used them to calculate the rates of return earned by investors from 2005 to 2017 for both ETFs and TIFs (the investor return with net cash flows taken into consideration). The dramatic advantage of TIFs in cumulative investor returns lay right there before my eyes: TIFs +184%, ETFs +101%. Not only did the average TIF provide higher returns than the average ETF over the full period, but also ETF investors earned higher returns during every single one of the previous 12 years. Exhibit 8.2 presents the data. Yes, of course the returns on, say, TIFs and ETFs that track the S&P 500 will be virtually the same. But the investor returns,[4] which take into consideration the counterproductive choices made by ETF investors (high trading costs, bad bets, and poor market timing), are substantially lower for ETF holders.

Vanguard's approach to ETFs tells a very different story. The annual return on our S&P 500 ETF itself came to 8.5% during the same period, almost identical to the 8.4% return earned by its investors. So

---

[4] Investor returns represent market appreciation as a percentage of the growth in a fund's assets (net of investor cash flow) over a given period of time. While this methodology is somewhat crude, we compared the annual investor returns of TIFs and ETFs with the average fund returns reported by Morningstar, and found R-squareds of, respectively, 99.2% and 95.7%.

Exhibit 8.2   TIF and ETF Net Cash Flow and Market Appreciation, 2004–2017

	TIF	ETF
2004 Assets (billions of dollars)	$410	$185
2017 Assets ($ bil)	2,066	1,984
Net Cash Flow 2004–2017 ($ bil)	$510	$1,009
Market Appreciation 2004–2017 ($ bil)	$1,146	$790
Annualized Investor Return	8.4%	5.5%

Source: Calculations by the Bogle Financial Markets Research Center based on data from Strategic Insight Simfund.

far, my philosophical belief that great marketing ideas are rarely great investment ideas is being confirmed in the marketplace.

New Markets for ETFs Emerge

At the extreme, the contrast between TIFs and ETFs can be drawn with this example: TIFs are passive funds held by *passive* investors, and ETFs are passive funds traded by *active* investors. In this sense, ETFs, despite their apparent deficiencies in comparative investor returns cited earlier, seem to have found a sort of "sweet spot" for investors.

They respond to investors' urge to control their portfolios, their awareness that costs matter, and their proclivity to "do something." "Don't just stand there" is an intuitively satisfying philosophy, even as it has not proven to be a winning investment strategy.

ETFs also facilitate a new way of looking at diversification. The "nine box" portfolio matrix – the intersection of size (large, mid, and small) with style (growth, blend, and value) – is simple, however uncertain decisions to over- or underweight these market segments have proved to be. This nine-box segment approach has evolved into a focus on "factors" that have been associated with historical outperformance, such as value, size, momentum, quality, and volatility.

As the fee-based advisory business continues to displace the commission-based model, a new market participant has arisen: "robo advisers" now provide software-driven asset allocation services at rock-bottom fees. While these advisers rely heavily on ETFs, they rarely engage in excessive trading.

"As First ETF Turns 25, Exchange-Traded Funds Dominate the Investing World"

So reads the headline of an article on the triumph of the ETF, published in the *Wall Street Journal* on January 28, 2018. "Today, there are almost 2,200 exchange-traded products world-wide with $4.8 trillion in assets." The hyperbole was unremitting, with only a single sentence that even hinted at the failure of exchange-traded *funds* to build value for most of their *investors*. (The article concludes, "The results of all that innovation have been mixed for investors." True!)

Perhaps the reflections of "Buttonwood," a columnist for *The Economist*, are more relevant. In a May 25, 2015, article of Buttonwood's titled "Exchange-Traded Funds Become Too Specialized," the first paragraph reads: "There comes a time when every financial innovation is taken a bit too far – when, in television terms, it 'jumps the shark' and sacrifices plausibility in search of popularity. That may have happened in the exchange-traded fund (ETF) industry. The latest ETF to be launched is a fund that invests in the shares of ETF providers."

I believe that observations of *The Economist* are on point, even as I wonder how the *Wall Street Journal* headline will describe ETFs 25 years from now. The reality is that ETF investors in narrowly focused and specialized funds have fared poorly relative to TIF investors. To ignore this reality is a disservice to fund investors.

It likely will not be comparisons of past returns but actual investor experience with ETFs that will finally encourage ETF holders who are speculators to reconsider their trading strategies.

Staying the Course

While I've been deemed to be a principal detractor of ETFs (not without supporting evidence!), my views have been, and remain, far more nuanced: (1) I strongly support broadly diversified index ETFs; (2)

I don't care for narrowly focused and speculative ETFs; and (3) I believe that stock trading is ultimately the investor's enemy. I therefore conclude that only appropriate ETFs should be selected by investors. Then, they should be held for the long term.

Here's my simple recommendation for ETF investors and TIF investors alike: emphasize broad-market (e.g., S&P 500) index funds in your portfolios, and don't trade them. Whether you follow this strategy with TIFs or ETFs doesn't really matter. Either way, you're doing the right thing, as long as you stay the course.

Chapter 9

2006–2018

The Momentum Continues – Strategy Follows Structure

	12/2006	6/2018	Annual Growth
Vanguard Assets (Trillions)	$1.1	$5.0	13.6%
Industry Assets (Trillions)	10.1	21.0	6.8
Vanguard Market Share	12.6%	24.2%	—
			Total Return
S&P 500 Index	1,418	2,718	8.1%
Intermediate-Term U.S. Government Bond Yield	4.6%	2.9%	3.5
60% Stocks/40% Bonds	—	—	6.9

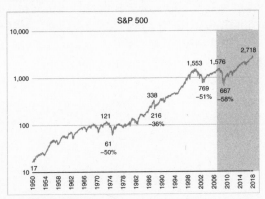

Source: Yahoo! Finance.

This long period was, on balance, a perfectly good period for both stocks and bonds. It began in 2003 after the 50% stock market crash had ended, only to be followed by another 50% crash in 2007–2009. The financial markets survived the near-failure of the world's banking system, and a new bull market began, taking stocks to valuations that were historically high in mid-2018.

The Triumph of Indexing

In 1995, to celebrate the 20th anniversary of Vanguard's pioneering first index mutual fund – originally named, appropriately enough, First Index Investment Trust – I published a monograph, largely for Vanguard's crewmembers. It was titled "The Triumph of Indexing."

I sent a copy to my lifelong friend, the late Paul F. Miller Jr., founder and senior partner of institutional money manager Miller, Anderson, & Sherrerd, and an outstanding investor. His response: "Great piece. You're too early, but you'll be proven right."

Optimism

There was some truth to Paul's insight. Even in 1995, assets of index mutual funds totaled but $54 billion, just 2.7% of total mutual fund assets, a drop in the proverbial bucket. But my optimism about the triumph of indexing was not based solely on the amount of assets that indexing had accumulated.

That optimism was – and still is – based on the fact that investors were at last beginning to understand the fundamental logic of index investing, the essential advantage of low costs, and the superior performance results that the S&P 500 Index had achieved over the long-term. After a glacially slow start, the assets of index mutual funds would soon begin to gain traction, and Vanguard's assets would grow accordingly. So of course I was optimistic about our future prospects.

It's Called *Momentum*

My 1995 forecast in "The Triumph of Indexing" turned out to be understated. Our original index fund and its successors have been the drivers of Vanguard's remarkable continued growth during the 1996–2018 period. Assets of our index funds soared from $50 billion to $3.3 trillion during that period. Our annual growth rate of 21%, driven in part by cash flows, was greatly abetted by the long bull market in stocks that characterized most of the period.

The index fund share of Vanguard's long-term (stock and bond) fund assets continued to rise unremittingly (see Exhibit 9.1). Even as the index share had more than doubled from 13% in 1991 to 31% in 1997, it more than doubled again to 74% as 2018 began. It's called *momentum*.

Exhibit 9.1   Percentage of Vanguard Assets in Index Funds, 1975–2018

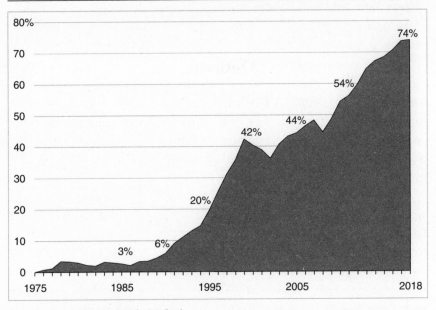

Source: Vanguard, Strategic Insight Simfund.

In today's world, "product innovation" is almost a requisite for survival. But Vanguard's first (S&P 500) index fund has remained unchanged, unenhanced since its founding in 1975.[1] It remains a major driver of Vanguard's growth in 2018, one of the industry's two largest funds. Our largest fund, Vanguard Total Stock Market Index Fund – a near twin of

---

[1] While the 500 stocks that constitute the index have changed, it remains largely a measure of the returns of the nation's 500 largest corporations by market capitalization.

the 500 Index fund[2] – has also remained unchanged in structure since its creation in 1993. Together, these two broad-market index fund siblings constitute 30% of the assets of all Vanguard long-term funds.

Exhibit 9.2 indicates that even in 2018 Vanguard remains driven by its mutual funds.

Exhibit 9.2   Over 80% of Vanguard Assets Are in Funds Launched before 1997

	Total Assets	Share
Largest Vanguard Funds (Inception)		
Total Stock Market Index Funds (1992)	$742	16%
500 Index Funds (1976)	640	14
Total Bond Market Index Funds (1986)	355	8
Total International Stock Index Fund (1996)	343	7
Wellington Fund (1929)	104	2
Top 5 Total	$2,183	47%
Other Pre-1997 Funds		
Index	$612	13%
Active	1,021	22
Total	$1,634	35%
Pre-1997 Total	$3,817	82%
Post-1997 Funds		
Index	$753	16%
Active	96	2
Total	$849	18%
Vanguard Total	**$4,666**	**100%**

The Index Revolution

Vanguard was the *de facto* leader of an index fund sector that was itself burgeoning. In 2000, just five years after my monograph was published, index fund assets had risen almost eightfold to $420 billion. By 2005, they had more than doubled to $873 billion. Index funds

---

[2] The stocks in the S&P 500 also account for 80% of the value of the Total Stock Market Index Fund.

would continue their rapid growth, reaching $1.9 trillion by 2010, and $6.8 trillion in mid-2018, accounting for an astonishing 37% of all mutual fund assets. Yes, the optimism about the future of indexing that I displayed in "The Triumph of Indexing" has proved well founded.

The growing share of industry assets represented by index funds greatly understates their role as an agent of change. During 2008–2017, net cash *inflows* into equity index funds totaled $2.2 trillion, accounting for 187% (!) of total equity mutual fund cash flows. During that decade-plus, actively managed equity funds experienced cash *outflows* of more than $1 trillion. It is hardly grandiose to describe the recent era as "the index revolution."

Vanguard's Share

Vanguard's share of index fund assets continues to dominate the mutual fund field. The firm's market share is close to 50% of all index mutual fund assets – comprising almost 80% of the $3.3 trillion in traditional index funds (TIFs), which are broad-based and designed to be held by an investor for an entire lifetime – and 25% of the $3.5 trillion in exchange-traded index funds (ETFs), which are often narrowly focused and appealing largely to the trading impulses of investors.[3]

Such dominance by a single firm, even in a field that could now be considered "mature," is truly remarkable. It is explained largely by the fact that indexing became the principal focus of Vanguard's strategy. Why? Because "strategy follows structure." It was Vanguard's proposed mutual structure that so appalled the late Jon Lovelace of American Funds, whose reaction I described in the anecdote that began this book. Jon's fear was that such a structure would "destroy the mutual fund industry" . . . as we then knew it. He was right.

---

[3] This vital distinction – essentially passive index funds held by passive investors (TIFs) versus passive index funds held by active investors (ETFs) – has been almost totally ignored by the investment community and the media.

A Revolution in Market Share

When a firm consistently dominates the fastest-growing segment of an industry, it dominates its industry by an even more impressive margin. Following its founding in 1974, Vanguard's share of total mutual fund assets had risen from less than 4% at the outset to only 5% as recently as 1991. But its share of fund assets soared to 22% in mid-2018, an all-time high. Three-quarters of that increase was accounted for by our index funds (see Exhibit 9.3). That truly remarkable momentum, too, shows few signs of slowing.

Exhibit 9.3   Vanguard Market Share of U.S. Mutual Fund Assets, 1974-2018

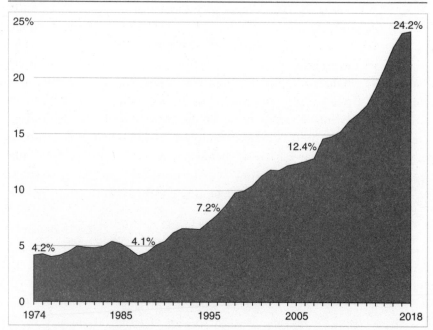

Source: Vanguard, Strategic Insight Simfund.

Yes, Vanguard had the advantage of being the first mover in the index fund revolution. But the unremitting missionary zeal of my books and speeches was, dare I say, another driving force. My first book, *Bogle on Mutual Funds: New Perspectives for the Intelligent Investor* (1993) featured index funds as one of just three major new perspectives. My sixth book, the first edition of *The Little Book of Common Sense Investing* (2007), was focused almost entirely on index funds. Together, investors have purchased 500,000 copies of these two books, suggesting a total of 1.5 million readers. The 700 comments by readers on the Amazon website rated *The Little Book of Common Sense Investing* at 4.6 stars, just a bit short of the maximum 5-star rating.[4] Yes, investors are getting the message about low-cost investing and acting accordingly.

"Uneasy Lies the Head That Wears a Crown"

Vanguard's near-25% market share of long-term (stock and bond) mutual funds is so far above historical experience that it calls for special attention.[5] During the near-century in which the U.S. mutual fund industry has existed (it began in 1924), just four firms have worn its crown of leadership. The first three achieved a top market share of about 15% of total industry assets. As shown in Exhibit 9.4 that coveted crown has been worn uneasily, held for a time by one king, then wrested away by a new king.

It's hard to imagine how both the 15% market share held by long-time leader MFS and then by Columbia could have deteriorated to today's 1% range. But that's what happened. In this context, I can't help but quote Shakespeare's warning: "uneasy lies the head that wears a crown." What succeeds in one era often turns to failure in the next.

M.I.T., then MFS

Consider first the example of Massachusetts Investors Trust (M.I.T.). During its era of leadership, its shares were marketed by a separate firm,

---

[4] After a decade of the book's sustained ranking as #1 in sales in the Amazon rankings, I brought out a 10th-anniversary edition in the autumn of 2017. It too is doing well.

[5] Vanguard's near-25% share of the assets of long-term mutual funds (stock and bond funds only) is slightly above the firm's 22% share of total mutual fund assets (including money market funds). Since money market funds did not exist during the first five decades of the fund industry's existence, we are presenting the market share of stock and bond funds for consistency in the analysis that follows.

Exhibit 9.4 Market Share of Largest Managers, 1935–2018

U.S. Stock and Bond Mutual Funds

Leader	Span	Number of Years	Assets in Peak Year	Current Assets (2018)	Market Share of U.S. Stock and Bond Funds*	
					Peak	2018
M.I.T.†	1935–1952	17	$554 Million (1952)	$228 Billion	15.3% (1950)	1.2%
IDS‡	1953–1982	29	$7.5 Billion (1972)	$154 Billion	15.8% (1964)	0.8%
Fidelity	1983–2003	10	$645 Billion (1999)	$1.5 Trillion	13.8% (1999)	8.3%
Vanguard	2004–2018	13	$4.3 Trillion (2018)	$4.3 Trillion	24.2% (2018)	24.2%

*Excludes money market funds.

†Originally Massachusetts Investors Trust, now part of Massachusetts Financial Services.

‡Known as Investors Diversified Services (IDS) during its peak years, it was founded in 1894 as Investors Syndicate. After a series of mergers, the firm's mutual funds are marketed under the Columbia Threadneedle brand today.

Source: Wiesenberger Investment Companies, Strategic Insight Simfund.

and its own trustees were directly responsible for the management of its investment portfolio.

It was the 1949 *Fortune* magazine article featuring M.I.T. that drew me, as a Princeton student, into my study of the mutual fund industry. M.I.T.'s widely diversified investment portfolio looked rather like the list of the 30 "blue chip" stocks in the Dow Jones Industrial Average. There was little room for surprise from its strategy. In today's terminology, M.I.T. was a "closet index fund," tacitly hugging the market standard and consistently providing the market's return, less costs.[6] M.I.T.'s market share peaked at 15.3% in 1950.

---

[6] Until 1969, M.I.T.'s trustees and investment management staff were paid directly by the trust. Then the trustees created a new company – Massachusetts Financial Services – to manage, distribute, and administer the Trust and its sister funds. The trustees awarded ownership and control of MFS to . . . themselves. In 1980, the trustees sold the firm to Sun Life of Canada. By curious coincidence, this metamorphosis from "at-cost" investment management to external management, and then to public ownership, was almost the polar opposite of what Wellington/Vanguard had done. Vanguard's present market share suggests that the firm made the right choice for its fund shareholders.

As the years passed, M.I.T. drew more and more competitors, generally offering the same type of conservative investment strategy. Virtually all of the mutual funds run by these firms, including the funds run by Wellington Management Company, were distributed through stockbrokers. Wellington Fund's major distinction was its policy of balance – roughly two-thirds of its assets invested in those same types of blue-chip stocks, with the remaining third represented by investment-grade bonds, a sort of "anchor to windward" for defensive purposes. For decades, it was the largest balanced fund offered by stock brokerage firms.

The growing number of fund distributors, all competitors for the attention and the business of a single group of stockbrokers, put considerable pressure on the commanding market share once held by M.I.T. Further, by the 1940s, a new type of competitor arose: the "direct distributor."

A handful of fund management companies directly employed their own dedicated sales forces to sell their fund products by calling directly on prospective investors. These firms made strong inroads into a market previously dominated by stockbrokers, who had their choice of which fund "products" to sell. With this combination of direct and indirect competition, along with the rise of the index fund, the market share of MFS has fallen from 15.3% of industry assets in 1950 to just 1.2% in mid-2018.

IDS , Now Columbia Threadneedle

By far the most powerful of these direct distributors was Investors Diversified Services (IDS), a Minneapolis-based giant whose history goes back to 1894, and whose long-time focus had been the sale of "face amount certificates" paying fixed interest rates. (That is, a saver might purchase a $10,000, 10-year certificate with an interest rate of 7% guaranteed for the full period.)

Alas, for both IDS and its clients, when interest rates plummeted during the Great Depression, the firm could no longer meet its contractual obligations to pay the interest specified on the certificates it had issued. It needed new products for its massive sales force to sell. It found two: life insurance and mutual funds.

IDS formed its first mutual fund (Investors Mutual) in 1940. It was a balanced fund, followed by a sister stock fund in 1941 (Investors Stock Fund), and then several more. Its rising assets would peak at $7.5 billion in 1972; its market share would soar to 15.8% in 1964.

IDS came from nowhere to lead the fund business for nearly a quarter of a century, but its direct-sales approach to investors faltered, even as stockbroker sales boomed. Its share of industry assets has plummeted to a mere 0.8%.

Fidelity

The rise of M.I.T. and then IDS held few, if any, parallels to that of the next leader, Fidelity Investments. When I first studied Fidelity in 1950, it was the twelfth-largest mutual fund firm. The assets of its sole fund – Fidelity Fund – totaled just $64 million, a 2% market share in a $3.1 billion industry. Fidelity Fund was a conventional blue-chip-focused equity fund. When the Go-Go era arrived a decade later, Fidelity was among the first of the traditional fund managers to join the speculative parade. It's fair to say that, for better or for worse, Fidelity brought modern marketing techniques into the fund industry.

In 1958, the firm created Fidelity Capital Fund, under the direction of portfolio manager Gerald Tsai. He became a sensation. The fund's returns "shot the lights out" (for a while). Capital was soon joined by Fidelity Trend Fund, managed by young Edward C. Johnson III, son of Fidelity's founder and CEO, Edward C. Johnson Jr. It too produced specular returns. Until it didn't.

In the bull market of that era, both funds grew by large orders of magnitude. Together their assets totaled $2.2 billion at the 1967 peak, a 5% market share of fund industry assets – representing almost two-thirds of Fidelity's total share of 8%. But in the bear market that followed, both funds collapsed, and disappointed shareholders abandoned them in droves. Nonetheless, Fidelity had made a name for itself among stock brokerage firms. Their implicit motto: "Don't accept the stock market's return. We can do better."

Magellan Fund

The Go-Go era ended with a bang, but Fidelity's reputation survived. (Apparently brokers' memories are short.) In 1963, Fidelity launched a new fund named Magellan that rewrote the industry's rulebook. It outpaced the S&P 500 by an astonishing 22.5 percentage points *per year* from 1975 to 1983, mostly before the tiny fund's shares were offered to the public.

Magellan continued to perform well for another decade, although not nearly as well as in its years of incubation. From 1984 until 1993, it outpaced the S&P 500 Index by 3.5 percentage points a year. Shortly after star portfolio manager Peter Lynch retired in 1990 (when the fund's assets had exploded to more than $100 billion), Magellan began to fall behind the index, lagging by almost two percentage points per year for the next 24 years. During that near-quarter-century, the cumulative return on Magellan Fund totaled 539%, a shortfall of 266 percentage points behind the cumulative 805% return of the S&P 500.

Depending on the success of a few hot funds in the Go-Go era – and then on a single hot fund through the 1980s – proved a risky strategy for Fidelity. Magellan Fund's assets grew from an initial $100,000 to more than $100 billion, peaking at $110 billion in 2000. But the fund's bubble inevitably burst.

By 2018, the assets of Magellan Fund had plummeted to $17 billion, an astonishing decline of $93 *billion* as it failed to meet the heady expectations of its shareholders. Fidelity's market share tumbled accordingly, from its high of 13.8% of the total assets of all stock and bond mutual funds in 1999 to 8.2% in 2018. Lesson: "He who lives by the sword shall die by the sword."[7]

Vanguard

Will Vanguard's experience be any different from the experience of those firms that previously held the crown of market leadership in the

---

[7] By early 2018, Fidelity's market share had stabilized, largely because of the growth of its index fund business. Index funds now account for 25% of Fidelity's equity fund assets.

mutual fund field? Even with a 24% share of the assets of all stock and bond mutual funds – a record market share, more than half-again larger than its predecessors as industry leaders – should Vanguard be uneasy? *Of course we should be uneasy!* Complacency is the enemy of any firm that flies too close to the bright sun of success.[8] But Vanguard's unique mutual structure and our low-cost, index-focused strategy suggest that our reign will be far more sustainable than those of the three earlier leaders of the fund industry.

- M.I.T.'s problem was that the broker-dealer sales network is fickle, fraught with competition and plagued with conflicts. Vanguard's direct-distribution "no-load" approach relies on serving clients, not on supporting agents. M.I.T.'s conversion from a quasi-mutual structure to MFS, and then that firm's subsequent acquisition by a Canadian life insurance company surely didn't help.

- IDS learned the hard way that while having a controlled sales force may well be the best way to ensure success in distribution, it carries the disadvantage of offering a narrow and relatively inflexible line of proprietary funds, often requiring a "hard sell" that may lead to dissatisfied investors.

- Fidelity did well by betting on the market's whims and the "hot hands" of its money managers. While that can pay off in the short-run for fund managers (though rarely for fund investors), it has *never* paid off in the long-run. Fidelity seemed to have ignored the timeless principle of "reversion to the mean" in fund performance – strong- and weak-performing funds alike tend to revert to the mean returns of their peers and then above or below it. Given its focus on funds with relative predictability, Vanguard should be little impacted were one of its active managers' formerly hot hands to go cold.

Strategy Follows Structure

In short, the record is clear that Vanguard's strategy and structure represent an entirely different approach to serving investors than any of

---

[8] I'm reminded of the story of Icarus, whose waxen wings melted when he flew too close to the sun. He then plummeted to his death in the ocean far below.

those of the three predecessors that have previously worn the crown of leadership during the 94-year history of the mutual fund industry.

Each of our predecessors focused on offering their funds through a sales network, and ultimately on providing competitive compensation for the distribution force. Their overriding goal, as SEC chairman Cohen suggested in that quotation in Chapter 2, was to build the earnings of the advisory firm. The goal of our low-cost mutual structure, on the other hand, is to build the earnings of our fund investors, rather than for a separate external adviser or for a sales force, dealer-based or direct.

The Low-Cost Structure

Vanguard's mutual structure dictates a focus largely on funds in which the value of low costs can be easily measured. Such a structure leads to a strategy favoring three fund types:

1. Index funds. All well-run S&P 500 Index funds earn the same gross return before costs. Hence, the lowest-cost index provider earns the highest net returns for its investors.
2. Bond funds. Vanguard's low costs allow us to emphasize higher-quality (lower-risk) issues in our portfolios, while still offering higher-than-competitive yields.
3. Money market funds, which, under SEC regulations, are required to hold short-term paper that meets certain high-quality standards. As a result, money market fund portfolio quality tends to be high and uniform. Lower-cost money market funds, therefore, are almost bound to provide higher yields than their peers.

In the arena of actively managed equity funds, low-cost index funds also normally hold a sustainable long-term advantage. Broad-based funds like those tracking the S&P 500 capture the market's return – no more, no less. For active equity funds, performance comes and goes, and the public tends to invest in them *after* they've done well. When they falter, as they inevitably do, expectations are dashed, and investors desert their ill-timed original choices. Investors are too often their own worst enemies.

To avoid the powerful negative of chasing past short-term returns by fund investors, I emphasized to Vanguard's senior staff the importance of "relative predictability" even before we began to operate our first index fund. That philosophy has been a major factor in the success of many of our equity funds that are managed by the external investment advisers that we retain.

"Relative Predictability" in Practice

It has sometimes been said that the key to Vanguard's remarkable growth is not the fact that we are the leader in index funds, but that we hold the position as the lowest-cost firm in the field. I beg to differ. The truth is just the reverse. Our low-cost structure *demands* our index fund strategy.

To be sure, while the returns on Vanguard's actively managed funds clearly gain a significant edge from their combination of low expense ratios and (generally) low portfolio turnover, many of them have also been deliberately structured as multi-manager funds to provide returns that closely track the returns of competitive peer groups and the appropriate stock market segments. In 1987, one of Vanguard's actively managed funds began to use such a multimanager approach. Now five of our equity funds do so. Why? Because when the portfolios of several managers with similar strategies are combined into a single fund, the fund's performance is highly likely to be similar to that of its benchmark.

The Benefits of Relative Predictability

Given Vanguard's position as the low-cost provider, the beauty of relative predictability is that funds with similar objectives and strategies tend to earn similar *gross* returns. Therefore, the funds with the lowest costs are likely to earn higher *net* returns. A fund with an advantage of some 1.5% in total annual costs (including expense ratios, turnover costs, and sales loads) would provide a 20% advantage in return over its peers during a full decade, *without assuming any additional risk*.

Where It All Began: HMS *Vanguard* Leads Historic 1798 Sea Victory. Flagship of Fleet Under Command of Admiral Horatio Nelson.

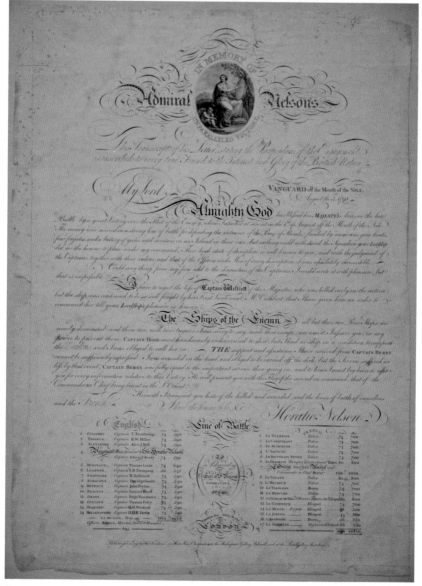

This antique print, circa 1820, was presented to John C. Bogle, Blair Academy, Class of 1947, by J. Brooks Hoffman, MD, Blair, Class of 1936, on December 14, 1993.

"Vanguard" through History

A portrait depicting the only meeting of the Duke of Wellington (left) and Lord Horatio Nelson, 1805.

A portrait of John C. Bogle dressed as Admiral Nelson, by Roberto Parada, from *American Way* magazine, April 1, 2010.

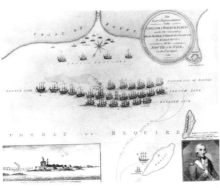

Battle line of the French fleet (center) and the British fleet (upper and lower lines) at the Battle of the Nile, August 1, 1798.

The author chose the name **"Vanguard"** for his new firm immediately upon reading these words describing the great victory over Napoleon's fleet in Aboukir Bay, Egypt, August 1, 1798.

Nothing could withstand the squadron under my command. The judgment of the captains, together with the valor. . . of the officers and men of every description was absolutely irresistible.

Vanguard, off the Nile,
Horatio Nelson
August 3, 1798

The Bogle Family

William Yates Bogle Jr.
First Leftennant, Royal Flying
Corps of Great Britian, 1917.

Josephine Lorraine Hipkins
Bogle, 1921.

The Three Bogle Boys

John Clifton, David Caldwell, and William Yates Bogle III, 1935.

Two JCB Commencements

Blair Academy   Princeton University

John C. Bogle, '47, cum laude.   John C. Bogle, '51, magna cum laude.

Two Princeton Entrepreneurs

Jeffrey P. Bezos, '86.   John C. Bogle, '51.

Photographs of two of the most disruptive entrepreneurs of the modern age hang next to each other on the "Wall of Fame" of the Yankee Doodle Taproom in the Nassau Inn, Princeton, New Jersey.

Two JCB Degrees

Receiving his AB degree in Economics from Princeton University, 1951.

Receiving his honorary Doctor of Laws degree from Princeton University, 2005.

Blair and Princeton

Bogle Hall (1989) is dedicated to Josephine Hipkins Bogle and William Y. Bogle Jr. by their three sons: William Y. Bogle III, B'45, and David C. and John C. Bogle, B'47.

Armstrong-Hipkins Center for the Arts (1999) is dedicated to the memory of Effie Armstrong Hipkins and John Clifton Hipkins by their three Bogle grandsons.

Some 52 years after the completion of his senior thesis at Princeton, John Bogle '51 met again with his thesis adviser Philip W. Bell AB '46, PhD '56. Dr. Bell enjoyed a distinguished career as a professor of economics at various universities.

Without These Three Men, No Vanguard

Walter L. Morgan and John C. Bogle.

Charles D. Root.

Mr. Morgan, founder of Wellington Management Company, served as chairman from 1928 until April 1967, when he turned the firm's leadership over to Mr. Bogle. At first, Mr. Morgan applauded his firm's merger with a group of young money managers. Later, he was disturbed by their performance failure. He strongly supported the "Future Structure Study" that Mr. Bogle presented to the directors of the Wellington Funds in 1974.

Mr. Root, chairman of the independent directors of the Wellington funds, provided support for the mutualization proposed in the Future Structure Study. His backing proved essential to the creation of the new firm. Mr. Root continued in that role on the Vanguard board until 1989.

Growing Older

1959

1970

1986

2004 *Time* magazine names John Bogle one of the "100 most influential people in the world" (foreground, Dickens; background, *Blue Chip*).

The Merger That Failed, June 6, 1966–January 23, 1974

Reprinted with permission of *The Institutional Investor* 2018.

Barron's: Don't Bet on It
Could these be the perfect new jobs for the fund-industry legend?

By Joe Queenan

When word got out that the Vanguard Group's founder and senior chairman was going to be forced to step down because of a rule mandating that its board members retire at 70, it quickly became obvious that John Bogle was not quite ready to be put out to pasture. Since Bogle clearly believes—probably quite rightly—that he can still make a useful contribution to society, the question presents itself: What types of jobs are best suited to the skills of a septuagenarian legend who has spent virtually his entire adult life in the mutual-fund industry?

The perfect job for a man who radiates such immense personal charisma and who has built such an enviable rapport with the general public is obvious: an official greeter at a major Atlantic City casino . . . it's even possible to imagine the former fund chief commuting to his new job every day, wearing the tuxedo and ever-present smile needed in this line of work.

The only problem with this scenario is Bogle's penchant for criticizing his company's products. For years, Bogle preached the gospel of index funds to the masses, insisting that portfolio managers, as a group, were incapable of consistently outperforming a basket of diversified, inactively managed stocks . . . it's hard to imagine Bogle refraining from criticizing the products marketed by any of his employers. Integrity, after all, isn't something you put on and take off like a greeter's tux.

Which means that as soon as the first limo pulls up in front of the casino and the first high roller steps out, Bogle just might start bending his ear about the terrible long-term odds at the poker or roulette tables. If Bogle were as outspoken in his capacity as a greeter as he has been as a mutual-fund manager, one can easily imagine his new employer also forcing him to take a hike.

Especially if his new employer were named Trump.

What other job openings remain for a man like John Bogle? . . . [He would be] credible as a consumer advocate. Bogle actually sounds convincing when he uses numbers. . . . he sounds a lot like John Wayne.

Another role Bogle would fill admirably is commissioner of baseball. Bear in mind, it wasn't all that long ago that the person charged with charting the fortunes of the national pastime was Bart Giamatti, a former Yale president who could effortlessly quote Socrates and Santayana and Aesop, just as John Bogle can.

Clearly, these are not the only shoes the mature, sagacious Bogle would fill. His refinement and acumen would seem to give him the inside track on any number of academic positions: provost, dean, university president, Bursar.

His intimate familiarity with the workings of the financial markets also would seem to make him an obvious candidate to replace Fed Chairman Alan Greenspan, especially since both are given to discursions on the excessive emotionalism that often characterizes investors' decisions.

But what if none of these happy scenarios comes to pass? What if, six months down the line, a hale and hearty John Bogle is still looking for new worlds to conquer, but no new employer has yet beaten a path to his door?

In that case, he should go back and re-examine his beginnings. Over the years, Bogle has often said that he got into the mutual-fund business only because of a "wonderful accident." Back in 1949, while seeking a subject for his senior thesis at Princeton, Bogle happened to open a copy of Fortune magazine to an article about mutual funds. From that point on, he was hooked.

But . . . suppose it hadn't been Fortune magazine that he rifled through that fateful day, but say, Garment Industry News . . . he might have ended up writing his senior thesis on the rag trade, and spent the next 50 years in and around Seventh Avenue. Had he only selected the path not taken, then today, at the ripe old age of 70, he wouldn't have to worry about getting bounced out on his ear by an ungrateful company that he actually founded. Proving, once again, that if you're searching for inspiration in the business world, Fortune magazine is the wrong place to be looking. *Excerpted from Barron's, October 11, 1999.*

Sorry, Joe Queenan: no casino greeter, no Commissioner of Baseball, no Federal Reserve Chairman, no rag trade.

JOHN C. BOGLE
LEGACY FORUM

In February 2000, following his departure from the Vanguard board, John Bogle formed Vanguard's Bogle Financial Markets Research Center. The Center continues to provide a strong voice for reform in the mutual fund industry, and a demand to place the interests of fund investors first.

The all-day Legacy Forum on January 31, 2012, was held at the Museum of American Finance in New York City. It celebrated Bogle's completion of 60 years in the mutual fund industry. The list of the Forum's leaders represented a "who's who" of the investment community.

Co-Chairs: Paul Volcker (Chairman, Federal Reserve, 1979-1987) and Arthur Levitt (Chairman, U.S. Securities and Exchange Commission, 1993-2001)

Host Committee: From Yale, Professor Roger Ibbotson and endowment fund manager David Swensen; from Princeton, Professors Burton Malkiel and Alan Blinder, and endowment fund manager Andrew Golden; U.S. Senator Peter Fitzgerald; former TIAA CEO John Biggs; former FDIC Chair Sheila Blair; former SEC Chairman and NYSE Chairman William Donaldson

Principal Organizer: Institute for the Fiduciary Standard, Knut A. Rostad, President

John C. Bogle and Paul A. Volcker

Yale's David Swensen (right) and Vanguard's Gus Sauter.

The Three Bogle Boys, 2012 version.

Photos: © Johnson Sarkissian 2018.

The Bogle Issue, March/April 2012

Journal of Indexes

www.journalofindexes.com

the bogle issue

March / April 2012

The Economic Role Of The Investment Company
John Bogle

The Bogle Impact: A Roundtable
Featuring Gus Sauter, William Bernstein, Burton Malkiel, Don Phillips, Ted Aronson and more!

Lessons From SPIVA
Srikant Dash

The Case For Indexing
Christopher Philips

Plus an excerpt from Bogle's forthcoming book and an interview with the man himself,
as well as thoughts on Indexes and Investing from Agather and Blitzer

Among Many Awards . . .

Bogle receives the CME Group Melamed-Arditti Innovation Award, November 14, 2017. From left, Nobel laureates Robert C. Merton, MIT, and Myron S. Scholes, Stanford; and John P. Gould, University of Chicago.

Bogle receives the Gold Medal for Distinguished Achievement from the Pennsylvania Society, December 10, 2016.

The Bogle Financial Markets Research Center

The crew members of the Bogle Financial Markets Research Center: Founder John C. Bogle, veterans Emily A. Snyder (33 years at Vanguard), Michael W. Nolan Jr. (17 years), and Kathleen M. Younker (16 years, left). Paraphrasing Winston Churchill, "seldom has so much been done for so many by so few."

Crowd at the Waldorf Astoria during the 2016 Pennsylvania Society Gold Medal ceremony. Bogle's acceptance speech focused on the "Acres of Diamonds" that he discovered ever since he first moved to Philadelphia in 1949.

With Two Presidents – #42 and #1

President William J. Clinton and John Bogle, Chairman of the National Constitution Center, at its grand opening on July 4, 2003.

Bogle in June 2002 with an actor portraying President George Washington and a statue of President Washington from Founder's Hall of the Constitution Center.

From *The Economist*

Voice in the Wilderness

An illustration of Bogle as a professor by Satoshi Kambayashi from *The Economist*, September 15, 2012. Used with permission 2018.

"Jack Bogle ploughs an increasing lonely furrow. . . . In Mr. Bogle's words, 'investors need to understand not only the magic of compounding long-term returns, but the tyranny of compounding costs.' . . .

"Through [Vanguard's] index funds, investors can own a diversified portfolio for a fee that is a fraction of a percentage point a year. . . .

"A further problem is that investors overlook fundamentals. Mr. Bogle distinguishes what he calls 'investment return' from equities, which is the initial dividend yield plus earnings growth, from the market return to shareholders, driven by the change in valuation (which Mr. Bogle dubs the 'speculative return')." —*Buttonwood*, September 15, 2012

THE WALL STREET JOURNAL.

Some of the Wisest Words Ever Spoken About Investing

Thanksgiving dinner hosted by journalist Jason Zweig, *WSJ*, November 25, 2016. (Illustration by Christophe Vorlet. Used with permission 2018.)

Tens of thousands of investment pilgrims hang on Warren Buffett's every word at the Berkshire Hathaway annual meeting. "Just buy an index fund," he tells them.

From *Grant's Interest Rate Observer.*

Clockwise from front Left: **Jason Zweig** **Benjamin Franklin, Benjamin Graham** **Sir Isaac Newton, Nobel Laureat** **Daniel Kahneman, Aristotle, Berkshir** **Hathaway's Charles Munger and Warre** **Buffett, and Vanguard founder John Bogl** Seated with these tablemates—even hypothet cally—is as fine a legacy as I could imagine.

"Investors shouldn't let Thanksgiving pass witl out making sure to count their blessings. . Be thankful for the low costs of investing. . Sir Isaac Newton wrote, 'If I have seen furth it is by standing on ye sholders of Giants.' . Individual investors have no greater advanta; over professionals than the ability and freedo to think for themselves, rather than having follow the herd."

Wellington Fund's returns clearly demonstrate this relative predictability.[9] The fund's combined stock/bond benchmark explained fully
98% of the variations in Wellington's monthly returns over the past
decade. (This figure is known as the R-squared, an awkward phrase
that is now in common use.[10]) A pure index fund composed of these
two indexes would have an R-squared of 100 percent.) Arguably, the
fund's adviser has been responsible for only 2% of the sources of the
fund's return.

The close link between the returns earned by Wellington
Fund and its benchmark is hardly unique to Wellington Fund
among Vanguard's actively managed funds. Exhibit 9.5 offers a few
examples:

Exhibit 9.5   R-Squared of Selected Vanguard Funds, 2018

Fund	R^2
Wellington Fund	0.98
Explorer Fund	0.99
Intermediate-Term Tax-Exempt Bond	0.97
Windsor Fund	0.95
PRIMECAP Fund	0.93
Capital Opportunity Fund	0.92
Average Vanguard Equity Fund	0.96
Average of Peer Actively Managed Equity Funds	0.88

Vanguard's Actively Managed Funds

Despite the obvious benefits of high relative predictability, that characteristic is not a Procrustean bed into which all of our actively managed funds need to fit. First, if clients chose an active Vanguard fund,

---

[9] Wellington Fund pays an extra incentive fee to its adviser when its performance
exceeds its benchmark, and a symmetrical penalty fee applies when its performance lags. The fund's benchmark is a portfolio composed of 65% S&P 500
Index and 35% Bloomberg Barclay's U.S. Credit A or Better Bond Index.

[10] R-squared represents the percentage of the variation in a mutual fund's return
that is explained by the variation in returns of the appropriate market index. It is
the square of correlation, and therefore an even more rigorous standard.

it is reasonable to conclude that they did not wish to own a passive Vanguard index fund. (When we began in 1974, we managed only active funds.)

So when a rare — very rare — star is born, we treasure that star. Think Windsor's John Neff, of course; Barrow Hanley's Jim Barrow; PRIMECAP's Howard Schow and Mitch Milias. When they depart, we observe the aptitudes of their successors and decide whether to retain the firm and/or to bring in a new external manager to supplement the existing manager (I have always given the firm the benefit of the doubt).

Closing Funds to New Investors . . . When Appropriate

Yes, RTM (reversion to the mean) has been a universal rule in mutual fund returns. But when a fund's asset base grows large, we're finally left with a judgment call. One major way of protecting the long-term interests of fund shareholders is to be conscious of the debilitating impact of giant asset size in producing superior returns.

As a fund's assets grow due to cash inflows, the managers are forced to invest additional cash into their best investment ideas — presumably at higher prices — or into their next-best investment ideas, then their third-best ideas, and so on. In general, heavy cash inflows make it harder for active managers to achieve their investment goals. So there are times when it becomes imperative for fund managers to close their funds to new investors.

In 1985, in order to stem rising cash flows and burgeoning asset growth in Windsor Fund, Vanguard became only the second fund firm to close a fund. Over the past 30 years, we've closed our funds to new investors more than 30 times in order to limit cash inflows that could impair their managers' ability to successfully achieve their performance goals. Thanks (again!) to our mutual structure, we need not be hesitant to use this tactic.

Finally, of course — let's face it — without maintaining our legacy funds (Wellington and Windsor) and creating all those new active funds (Windsor II, PRIMECAP, International Growth, etc.), Vanguard could not have survived the two-decade wait for indexing to flourish.

Vanguard's Mutual Structure

The low costs engendered by Vanguard's mutual structure essentially arise from our at-cost model. Rather than following the industry's practice of charging mutual fund shareholders high fees and passing the profits along to management company stockholders, our low costs mean essentially that Vanguard returns its potential "profits" to the funds themselves.

The mutual structure that accomplishes this goal is logical and straightforward, and has now proved itself over some 44 years. The cost-savings of Vanguard owners as a group are the principal reason our fund shareholders have earned significantly higher returns than the aggregate of peer fund shareholders as a group.[11]

Fees versus Rates

While we take pride in our rock-bottom costs, it's important to avoid confusing advisory *fees* with advisory fee *rates*. Yes, Vanguard has been a tough negotiator in setting the fee structures for the funds managed by our external advisers. But no, our advisers hardly need take vows of poverty when they manage Vanguard funds. Under Vanguard's aegis, fund assets typically grow quite large, and the dollar amount of fees is substantial.

"Vanguard Is Not . . . Different" Really?

It is precisely Vanguard's structure and strategy that have led to the "triumph of indexing" that I foresaw way back in 1995. I believe that those two factors will endure and continue to constitute our bedrock foundation. Accordingly, I expect the crown of fund leadership to remain with Vanguard during the coming era.

Yes, others have denied that our structure is a value creator for our firm and its investors. Indeed, some well-credentialed observers deny that our structure makes any difference whatsoever. Writing in the *Yale*

---

[11] Perhaps the most impressive measure of Vanguard's success is Morningstar's award of "gold" analyst ratings to mutual funds representing the top choices available to investors. In early 2018, 48 Vanguard funds boasted gold ratings, more than the total of 43 for our next four peers *combined*.

Law Journal (March 2014), Professor John Morley almost sneeringly derides the role played by mutuality in shaping Vanguard's rock-bottom cost structure, its strategy, and its remarkable rise to preeminence in the mutual fund field:

> *Vanguard's founder, Jack Bogle, is a vigorous critic of separation of funds and managers. ... In economic reality ... Vanguard investors are not truly the "owners" of the management company. ... In reality, Vanguard is not meaningfully different from any other mutual fund management company.*

To Professor Morley, I can only say, "Let's look at the record."

Nothing Succeeds (or Fails?) Like Success . . .

The remarkable growth that Vanguard has enjoyed during 2006–2018 has been largely built on the momentum – and the mutual funds – created decades earlier. While I made (similarly foolish) judgments in 1985, at least one of our individual Specialized Portfolios (Health Care Fund) emerged as one of the best-performing mutual funds of all time. We were also stumbling when we formed our Horizon Funds in 1987. But the dominant remainder of our fund assets has nonetheless flourished and the asset growth that began in earnest in 1987, when Vanguard's fund assets were at $27 billion, has continued, indeed accelerated, ever since.

Yes, it's nice to affirm the old axiom, "nothing succeeds like success." There's lots of truth to that. But there's also the opposite axiom: "nothing fails like success." That axiom is all too evident in the falls from grace of the three previous holders of the crown of fund industry leadership.

Even as each of these previous wearers of the mutual fund crown – M.I.T./MFS, IDS/Columbia, and Fidelity – was doubtless caught by surprise when its long reign began to recede, Vanguard must not be complacent. History has a way of making fools of us all.

Only if we deal successfully with the many unknowns we shall face in the future – new and different challenges than those I faced in starting and building Vanguard – will we continue to hold that crown.[12]

---

[12] I'll discuss some of Vanguard's future challenges in more depth in Part III, "The Future of Investment Management."

. . . but Trees Don't Grow to the Sky

One of those major challenges is that Vanguard's funds are now massive and powerful in their potential impact on corporate governance. Vanguard funds now hold some 8% of all U.S. stocks, a number that increases each day. In my view, we will have to participate even more actively, even more thoroughly, in corporate governance issues. We can be confident that Congress and our regulators will not ignore the issues surrounding the concentration of corporate ownership engendered largely by the three major index fund managers now holding fully 20% of the voting stock of all U.S. corporations.

All of the heads that have worn the mutual fund crown were greatly favored by strong stock markets, Vanguard most of all. But trees don't grow to the sky, and today's stock valuations (measured by price-earnings multiples) are close to record highs, with dividend yields near record lows.

The S&P 500 has turned in remarkable annual nominal returns averaging 12.1% during Vanguard's long history, doubling in value every six years. That return is far above the 8.7% average nominal return (before adjusting for inflation) of the previous half-century. Today's consensus view suggests that future returns on stocks will not come close to that level, and might well be as low as 3% to 5% per year during the coming decade. (At a rate of return of 4%, stocks would double every 18 years.) No one can know what returns the future holds in store for investors, but caution would seem called for.

Challenges to the Index Fund

Just three index fund managers – Vanguard, BlackRock, and State Street – are responsible for 80% of all index mutual fund assets. Their low fees are the result of competition among these firms. That puts downward pressure on the fees charged by other large mutual fund firms. Given the 2018 introduction of Fidelity's "zero cost" index funds, fees can hardly fall much further. The concentration of stock holdings among such a small number of managers will raise issues about control of large corporations, competition, and fiduciary duty. Our government will surely be paying attention. (In Part III, "The Future of Investment Management," I'll discuss this issue in greater depth.)

Past experience tells us that, during market declines, the S&P 500 Index Fund has fallen in about the same dimension as the average mutual fund. Given that net cash flow into index funds has been unprecedented in recent years – largely at market valuations close to record highs – it may turn out that index investors will overreact during the inevitable next bear market, selling their shares near market lows after buying them near market highs.

Especially during those times of uncertainty, I encouraged investors to "stay the course." During Vanguard's long history, that advice has worked magnificently. But in the stock market, the past is not prologue, and only time will tell if investors will continue to heed that advice in the years ahead.

An Organization That Cares

Finally, large size has often led to organizational sclerosis, complacency, self-indulgence, and losing sight of the firm's original mission. Should Vanguard's leadership (see Appendix I at the end of this chapter) ever forget where we came from and slide away from our mission to serve investors, Vanguard's crown could easily move to another head. (Although I confess that I have no idea what firm that might be.) These are merely some of the major "known unknowns" that face Vanguard. The "unknown unknowns" may be an even larger challenge.

But through it all, one fact is surely known: the strength of the Vanguard crew, laced with veterans (15 years or more of service), a crew that is properly motivated, completely trusted, and has a clear understanding of our mission. We need only be sure that we make the caring that has fostered that character – caring for one another, caring for those human beings who are our client/owners, caring for the institution that we know as Vanguard – continue to be the central element of managing our rapidly growing firm.

Staying the Course

By 2004, Vanguard had become the fourth firm to hold the crown of leadership in the mutual fund industry since its inception in 1924. At some point in their lives, our predecessors were all powerful firms, but somewhere along the way, they lost their bearings and proved unable to deal with changes in the investment environment, investor preferences, and the industry's distribution systems.

Vanguard is different. We began following our guiding star of "shareholders first" 30 years before our rise to preeminence in 2004, and we have continued to follow that star. Staying the course with our mutual structure and our index strategy should assure Vanguard's leadership for decades to come.

But we must take care to avoid complacency and continue to stay the course that we established all those years ago, lest some new challenges arise to topple from Vanguard's head the hard-earned crown of leadership.

Appendix I

My Successors

On January 31, 1996, I relinquished my role as Vanguard's CEO, remaining as chairman of the board of directors. While I thought that it was only fair to turn the management over to a younger team, my decision was precipitated by my failing health. I had been plagued by heart problems since my first heart attack in 1960 at age 31. Over the next 36 years, I struggled with periodic complications. But after a seemingly interminable waiting period of 128 days in Philadelphia's Hahnemann Hospital, I received a heart transplant on February 21, 1996. (Now there's one unforgettable landmark!) More than 22 years later, I'm doing fine, thank you.

In those two-plus decades since the transplant, I've remained active – even hyperactive – in my work at Vanguard as president of the Bogle Financial Markets Research Center. There we conduct research in finance, largely focused on the mutual fund industry. I'm in my office at Vanguard every day. It is here that my director of research, Michael Nolan, and my prized assistants, Emily Snyder and Kathy Younker, produce the results of that research and analysis that form the foundation of my speeches and books (including this one).

I continue to work with a variety of fellow Vanguard crewmembers, celebrate their anniversaries and retirements, and observe with pride and pleasure the continued momentum in Vanguard's growth, based as it is on index funds in general, and in particular the basic traditional index fund that I created way back in 1975.

John Brennan

The person I chose to succeed me was John J. Brennan, who had joined Vanguard as my staff assistant in 1982, his second career step following his graduation from Harvard Business School. We developed a remarkably close relationship (including regular squash matches), and he moved up in the ranks quickly. Beginning in 1985, he served with competence as chief financial officer, where he quickly earned a reputation as a tough manager. Of all the people I've ever worked with, no one possessed Brennan's ability to get what he wanted.

He became Vanguard's CEO on January 31, 1996. Some of his accomplishments in that role include bringing marketing into a far more prominent place in the Vanguard spectrum, as well as instituting firm-wide data-driven performance management.

Brennan also made the final decision to create Vanguard's exchange-traded funds (ETFs), and was ultimately responsible for building an organization to support them. While my decision to bring Vanguard into the international business had been timid, he initiated a broader approach to our foray into the world's markets. However, Brennan was skeptical of aggressive international expansion. Our major expansion into Europe, Asia, and the Americas came during the tenure of his successor, William McNabb.

F. William (Bill) McNabb

Brennan stepped down in 2008, after 12 years of service as CEO. His choice of successor surprised no one. Bill McNabb, a Wharton School MBA, had joined Vanguard from Chase Manhattan Bank in 1986, and had moved up rapidly. In 1995, he became the head of our Institutional Marketing group.

Bill is what we call "a people person." He engaged with the crew, even as he built our institutional business into (in my informed opinion) the strongest unit in our industry. While that may not quite qualify as a landmark, his returning Vanguard to my vision of a more personal, human place for our burgeoning crew to serve certainly does.

Surely Bill's bold decision to have Vanguard offer an advisory service to individual investors in 2015 also reaches landmark status. This was a gutsy strategic move that placed the firm in direct competition with the registered investment advisers (RIAs) who were offering shares of the Vanguard funds to their clients.

While some RIAs and other brokers were not amused by the new competition, this issue has gradually receded. Vanguard's entry into the growing "robo advice" market – essentially low-fee computer-driven asset allocation strategies for individuals – proved to be a timely decision, drawing assets of $100 billion by mid-2018. (Much of that total came from Vanguard's existing clients.)

I particularly applaud Bill's aggressive (in the best sense) move to strengthen our growing role as a major shareholder in just about every publicly held corporation in the nation. In 2018, Vanguard now owns more than 8% of every public corporation in the United States. To me, our role in corporate governance has always been to ensure – as best we can – that corporations are managed with the interests of their shareholders as their highest priority. Bill's bold moves in this area delighted me.

Mortimer J. (Tim) Buckley

Bill stepped down as CEO on December 31, 2017, continuing as board chairman. His successor as CEO is Tim Buckley, who first joined Vanguard in 1991 as my assistant. Two years later, Tim entered Harvard Business School, where he was awarded his MBA degree before returning to Vanguard.

I found Tim to be a remarkably poised and intelligent young man, and over the 19 years that followed, he moved into leadership roles in our individual investor group, our technology group, and finally our investment group. Tim's broad leadership experience at Vanguard prepared him well to take on the role of CEO. Our clients should be in good hands.

Tim faces great challenges in managing a $5 trillion enterprise. They include: maintaining shareholder privacy and information security in an age of hackers; eschewing the hucksterism that pervades today's fund industry; joining the coming revolution in data management; determining the implications of artificial intelligence; and dealing with the public policy implications of the ownership and control of our nation's giant publicly held corporations by index funds and other large institutional investors.

How different from the challenges I faced! While my task was to start from close to ground zero, develop a strategy for a new firm to survive, preside over its implementation, and to lead the new firm to success, Tim leads a firm that has enormous momentum. But dealing with massive size and the industry dominance that Vanguard has achieved are no mean challenges. I wish him well.

Appendix II

❦

Vanguard by the Numbers

Year	Total Assets* (Year-End) (millions)	Market Share of Long-Term Assets	Total Cost (millions)	Expense Ratio†	Market Appreciation (millions)	Net Cash Flow (millions)	Cash Flow Percent of Assets 5-yr Moving Avg.	Number of Funds (incl. ETFs)	Number of Crew Members	Crew/$Billion of Assets	Index Fund Share of L-T Assets
1974	$1,457	4.3%	$10	0.66%	–	-$52		6	28	19	–
1975	1,758	4.16	11	0.66	$360	-60		8	47	27	–
1976	2,035	4.26	11	0.59	411	-133		10	97	48	0.8%
1977	1,831	4.02	12	0.60	-105	-99		13	99	54	1.4
1978	1,919	4.15	12	0.62	105	-17	-4.4%	13	106	55	4.1
1979	2,380	4.48	12	0.58	315	146	-2.0	15	133	56	4.1
1980	3,326	4.97	16	0.58	840	106	-0.3	18	167	50	4.3
1981	4,161	4.86	20	0.53	781	54	1.6	20	272	65	3.9
1982	5,660	4.82	31	0.63	913	586	5.4	21	360	64	3.4
1983	7,316	4.95	40	0.61	306	1,350	10.3	24	431	59	4.8
1984	9,877	5.40	48	0.56	821	1,739	13.6	32	663	67	4.4
1985	16,408	5.19	69	0.53	2,222	4,308	21.4	37	886	54	2.9
1986	24,961	4.73	101	0.49	2,736	5,817	28.2	44	1,124	45	2.5
1987	27,007	4.13	102	0.39	1,874	173	25.5	48	1,497	55	4.5
1988	34,172	4.42	120	0.39	6,942	222	20.9	53	1,588	46	5.1
1989	47,562	5.07	145	0.35	9,080	4,311	18.6	53	1,873	39	6.8
1990	55,711	5.40	172	0.33	3,792	4,357	11.7	57	2,230	40	9.7
1991	77,027	6.19	211	0.32	8,198	13,117	9.4	57	2,631	34	12.8

(continued)

Year	Total Assets* (Year-End) (millions)	Market Share of Long-Term Assets	Total Cost (millions)	Expense Ratio†	Market Appreciation (millions)	Net Cash Flow (millions)	Cash Flow Percent of Assets 5-yr Moving Avg.	Number of Funds (incl. ETFs)	Number of Crew Members	Crew/$Billion of Assets	Index Fund Share of L-T Assets
1992	$97,412	6.56%	$258	0.30%	$4,821	$15,564	13.3%	68	3,112	32	14.4%
1993	125,755	6.53	336	0.30	11,303	17,040	16.6	69	3,520	28	16.1
1994	130,743	6.49	392	0.31	2,853	2,135	14.4	79	3,545	27	18.8
1995	178,317	7.15	485	0.31	32,957	14,617	14.8	83	3,927	22	24.2
1996	236,006	7.82	606	0.29	31,498	26,191	13.1	87	4,798	20	31.0
1997	322,441	8.69	762	0.27	50,844	35,590	12.0	87	6,400	20	36.6
1998	431,693	9.77	1,044	0.28	63,087	46,165	11.4	92	8,113	19	41.5
1999	537,405	9.94	1,299	0.27	62,313	43,399	13.1	94	9,886	18	48.8
2000	561,236	10.42	1,479	0.27	4,183	19,649	11.6	99	10,129	18	47.2
2001	577,942	11.26	1,521	0.27	-18,604	35,310	9.9	96	11,200	19	46.5
2002	555,789	11.80	1,466	0.26	-59,473	37,320	8.2	115	10,495	19	44.0
2003	689,980	11.77	1,623	0.26	100,170	34,021	6.5	121	10,007	15	47.2
2004	818,513	12.20	1,753	0.23	72,999	55,534	6.1	132	10,251	13	49.3
2005	928,862	12.37	1,888	0.22	63,062	47,287	6.5	133	11,205	12	50.5
2006	1,122,722	12.58	2,187	0.21	145,238	48,621	6.3	148	12,000	11	53.4
2007	1,304,606	12.86	2,280	0.19	101,388	80,496	6.5	154	11,944	9	56.2
2008	1,045,935	14.62	2,060	0.18	-331,385	72,714	6.4	157	12,534	12	55.0
2009	1,336,082	14.82	2,409	0.20	167,843	122,304	7.1	165	12,587	9	56.3
2010	1,563,797	15.25	2,594	0.18	137,260	90,454	7.3	181	12,483	8.0	60.7

Year	Total Assets* (Year-End) (millions)	Market Share of Long-Term Assets	Total Cost (millions)	Expense Ratio†	Market Appreciation (millions)	Net Cash Flow (millions)	Cash Flow Percent of Assets 5-yr Moving Avg.	Number of Funds (incl. ETFs)	Number of Crew Members	Crew/ $Billion of Assets	Index Fund Share of L-T Assets
2011	$1,649,177	16.21%	$2,551	0.16%	$8,087	$77,294	7.2%	180	12,872	7.8	62.3%
2012	1,973,503	16.85	2,643	0.15	184,861	139,465	7.5	180	13,500	6.8	65.2
2013	2,441,655	17.62	3,091	0.14	338,693	129,459	7.7	182	14,000	5.7	69.7
2014	2,848,111	19.13	3,513	0.13	187,680	218,776	7.1	177	14,200	5.0	71.6
2015	3,073,030	20.91	3,671	0.12	-5,189	230,107	7.4	194	14,000	4.6	72.7
2016	3,612,844	22.80	3,738	0.11	263,776	276,039	8.2	198	15,000	4.2	75.0
2017	4,547,219	24.06	4,174	0.10	591,101	343,274	8.4	210	17,000	3.7	77.4
6/2018	4,671,986	24.23	4,610	0.10	43,175	81,593	7.8	217	17,000	3.6	77.9

*U.S. domiciled mutual fund assets. Non-U.S. domiciled assets total $400 billion.

†Costs as a percentage of average assets, including management fees paid to external advisors.

148

Chapter 10

Caring

The Founder's Legacy

T he previous nine chapters of this book focused on the basic structure and the development of the strategy that together formed Vanguard's original foundation. Simply because they were good ideas – and, as history has proven, they surely were good ideas – these innovations have been the wellspring of Vanguard's remarkable growth. They have also changed the fundamental nature of investing. But as I have said over and over again, "Ideas are a dime a dozen. Implementation is everything."

So in this final chapter of Part I, I want to describe my efforts to make sure that our implementers at Vanguard – our crewmembers – were capable, fairly treated, well-trained, fully informed, committed to our mission, and inspired by the values that I hold high. If the firm that I founded could do that properly, the vigorous and disciplined implementation of our strategy would follow.

To a considerable extent, the firm's founding values reflect my own personal values. They are actually pretty conventional values: respect for each human being – from the highest to the humblest – whom we meet along the road of life; fair dealing; commitment to one's colleagues and one's career; trusting and being trusted; personal integrity; passion and energy; and service to our client/owners, our communities, and our society.

The Founder's Mentality

Our founding heritage goes back less than five decades, to our firm's inception in 1974. But I believe that Vanguard's heritage continues to drive the firm and its now 17,000-person crew. Nothing could describe my legacy as Vanguard's founder better than these few paragraphs from *The Founder's Mentality*[1]:

> *Most companies that achieve sustainable growth share a common set of motivating attitudes and behaviors that can usually be traced back to a bold, ambitious founder who got it right the first time around. The companies that have grown profitably to scale . . . often consider themselves insurgents, waging war on their industry and its standards on behalf of an underserved customer, or creating an entirely new industry altogether.*

> *Such companies possess a clear sense of mission and focus that everyone in the company can understand and relate to . . . what the company stands for. Companies run in this way have the special ability to foster employees' deep feelings of personal responsibility. . . .*

> *[Founders] abhor complexity, bureaucracy, and anything that gets in the way of the clean execution of strategy. They are obsessed with the details of the business and celebrate the employees at the front line, who deal directly with customers. Together, these attitudes and behaviors constitute a frame of mind that is one of the great and most undervalued secrets of business success.*

> *The founder's mentality consists of three main traits: an insurgent's mission, an owner's mindset, and an obsession with the front line. In their purest expression, these traits can be found in companies . . . where the clear influence of the founder still remains in the principles, norms, and values that guide employees' day-to-day decisions and behaviors.*

Wow! "A bold, ambitious founder . . . insurgents, waging war on their industry . . . creating an entirely new industry altogether . . . a clear sense of mission . . . employees' deep feelings of personal

---

[1] Chris Zook and James Allen, *The Founder's Mentality* (Boston: Harvard Business School Press, 2017).

responsibility . . . abhor complexity [and] bureaucracy . . . celebrate employees at the front line."

I repeat these phrases so that readers will not quickly overlook their parallel to the Vanguard story. Truth told, these phrases are a perfect thumbnail sketch of what I did my best to create. And, by and large, that spirit endures to this day with Vanguard's current 17,000-person crew.

Great Leaders of History

I have never thought that I possessed a charismatic leadership profile, one that comes right out of central casting. But I have always been inspired by the great leaders of history: America's Founding Fathers, especially Alexander Hamilton, Abraham Lincoln, Theodore Roosevelt, Winston Churchill. When I chose the name "Vanguard" for our firm in 1974, I was inspired by yet another hero, Lord Horatio Nelson. As I studied *Naval Battles of Great Britain 1730–1815*, I learned a great deal about Lord Nelson, whose leadership in the Royal Navy was legendary.

Lord Nelson: "An Infectious Trust in People"

On October 23, 2005 – the 200th anniversary of Lord Nelson's death at the Battle of Trafalgar – my wife Eve and I, as honored guests of the British admiralty, were seated in London's magnificent St. Paul's Cathedral. We were awed by the words of the Right Reverend and Right Honourable Richard Chartres, the Bishop of London, in his sermon celebrating the great day:

> *It is true that Nelson was a consummate professional and a hard-working manager . . . but at times of decision, leaders need to make contact with foundational convictions and with a sense of calling which comes from going deep within oneself. This is the source of healthy self-confidence and the ability to master fear and to encourage people in the most extreme circumstances. Any education system which*

hopes to produce effective leaders and followers must take the formation of these foundational convictions very seriously.

Yet we live at a strange time when the periodic table and anything that can be quantified and reduced to a mathematical truth is regarded as an accurate description of reality, but the Beatitudes and the teachings of the world's wisdom traditions are seen as little more than the debatable opinions of dead sages.

Nelson's sense of personal and individual call was developed within a tradition which also understands growth in the spiritual life as growth in love of neighbour. Nelson spared no pains to stand by and serve his shipmates. He exhibited an infectious trust in people which called out the best in them and engaged them in the cause in which he believed . . . a faith that people are to be trusted in a way that helps them to be trust-worthy.[2]

Having heard those inspiring words focused on foundational convictions 200 years after Nelson's death, I was thunderstruck by how much of Nelson's philosophy I had emulated when I founded Vanguard in 1974. A philosophy that would endure, even in an era of large corporations, "big data" and robots, and the gradual – and unfortunate – change in the values of finance from moral absolutism to moral relativism.

The Vanguard Award for Excellence

Building a new firm is always a challenge. When a firm is born under the dire circumstances that Vanguard faced at the outset, the challenge is monumental. Yes, much of my focus was on strategy and the creation of new funds, and that was working well. But I remained – and still remain – deeply involved in maintaining the character and morale of our Vanguard crew, even by 1983 only 430 strong.

We also continued to innovate internally, positioning our small but growing firm for the long term. In 1984, we created the Vanguard

---

[2] The text of the speech by Reverend Chartres was printed in a program that was given to the attendees of the ceremony. The text of the speech has been reprinted at www.leadershipnow.com/leadingblog/2008/12/out_of_context_the_ leadership.html.

Award for Excellence (AFE) to recognize outstanding members of our crew, chosen by their peers. The idea was simple: the award was designed to be a public manifestation of my conviction that, to provide valuable services for our clients, we need the human beings who serve on our crew to uphold our values, to maintain our corporate character, and to capitalize on our spirit. In a word, to *care*.

Loyalty Is a Two-Way Street

It takes little genius to realize that if we are to ask those who work at Vanguard to care about our institution – and to care about the honest-to-God, down-to-earth human beings whom we serve as our owner/clients – we must in turn care about our crew. Loyalty, after all, is a two-way street. We would manifest our high regard for the human beings who dedicate their careers to Vanguard by treating each individual – again, from the highest to the humblest – with the respect they deserve.

An important part of this policy is that we should minimize the advantages that "higher-ups" in some firms often take for granted. Hence, our "no perquisite" rule: no leased cars, no reserved parking places, no first-class flying, and no executive dining room.

If we expect our crewmembers to trust our management, our management must trust our crewmembers. We should all be rolling up our sleeves every day and working as equals. My firm-wide standard of conduct, applied universally to officers and crew alike: "Do what's right. If you're not sure, ask your boss."

The idea was to introduce a regular ritual that would honor those who embodied "the Vanguard spirit." During the 34 years since its creation, quarter after quarter, the AFE has been awarded to more than 500 crewmembers.

"Even One Person Can Make a Difference"

What makes earning the Award for Excellence especially meaningful is that the candidates for the award are nominated by their peers. As CEO, I personally presented the awards to the winners at a celebration among their colleagues. At each award luncheon, we quoted from the glowing nominations submitted by fellow crewmembers. In an organization that serves human beings, who in turn are served by other human beings, the AFE is a tribute to individual effort, teamwork, and professionalism.

Yes, "I believe that even one person can make a difference." These words are inscribed on the plaque that each winner of the AFE receives. And so each person can – and does – make a difference at Vanguard, even as our asset base has grown, no matter the size of our crew or our fleet. Even in 2018, to emphasize my continuing support of our founding principles, I continue to meet one-on-one for an hour with each recipient of the award. Our crewmembers know that I still care – about them and about Vanguard.

Caring About the Institution

In speaking with Vanguard's crew, I've often used this quotation from Howard M. Johnson, president of the Massachusetts Institute of Technology from 1966 to 1971. By 1986, when I first cited his words, our crew had grown to 1,100 members:

> *We need people who care about the institution. [It] must be the object of intense human care and cultivation: even when it errs and stumbles, it must be cared for, and the burden must be borne by all who work for it, all who own it, all who are served by it, all who govern it.*

> *Caring, we know, is an exacting and demanding business. It requires not only interest and compassion and concern; it demands self-sacrifice, wisdom and tough-mindedness, and discipline. Every responsible person must care, and care deeply, about the institutions that touch his or her life.*

Caring. That one word summed up my attitude toward our crew and our clients alike. But how to make it real and tangible? Words can take an idea only so far. Deeds make words tangible.

The Vanguard Partnership Plan: Another Landmark

Early in our history, in my periodic speeches to our crew as we crossed various asset milestones, I bragged about how we were driving our expense ratios down. Our goal: to be the world's lowest cost provider of mutual funds. To put it bluntly, however, I sensed considerable unease among some crewmembers. They were concerned that their compensation was being held down by our cost discipline.

The solution was not very complicated: create a bonus system in which crewmembers would share in the savings we generated for our shareholder/owners. Under extreme cost pressure during the firm's early years, that would be no more than an idea. But by 1984, our assets were burgeoning, our expense ratios were tumbling, and our cash inflows had soared to record levels. It was time to implement my idea – the Vanguard Partnership Plan.

So late in 1984, we did something tangible, and more unconventional than the Award for Excellence. We brought every crew member in our organization "on board," giving each person a share of the firm's "earnings." The Vanguard Partnership Plan (VPP) was designed to recognize the collective efforts of our crew in creating value for our shareholders and our institution.

Cash on the Line

VPP would pay substantial annual cash distributions to each and every crew member. The payouts were based on the cost savings to our clients and the investment performance of our funds relative to their peers. On their first day on the job, without investing one cent of their own capital in the Vanguard Group, each crewmember became a partner in Vanguard and shared in the rewards of the Partnership Plan.

The "Landmark" features that I cited in earlier chapters of this book denoted each of the major hurdles that Vanguard had to leap in order to build the shell that was Vanguard at its inception into the full-fledged empire it is today. The Vanguard Partnership Plan may be the most important landmark of all, for it was designed to solidify the community of interest between our crewmembers and the shareholders that they serve . . . to care about one another and to care about our investors.

LANDMARK 12. 1984

The Vanguard Partnership Plan: How and Why

The Vanguard Partnership Plan was created to build a bridge that joined the interests of our crew – the implementers of our founding structure and innovative strategy – with our success in serving our clients with lower costs than those of our peers and higher investment returns. The results have been phenomenal: earnings per unit of the VPP have grown steadily over the years, from $3.43 in 1984 to $248.45 in 2017, a compound annual rate of 13.9%.

Because Vanguard is a truly "mutual" mutual fund family, effectively owned by the shareholders of its mutual funds rather than by an external management company, we could not formally calculate earnings for our firm. Rather, we defined our earnings as a combination of the value added to our shareholders' returns in the following two ways:

1. The difference between Vanguard's fund expense ratios and the expense ratios of our largest competitors. We apply that difference to Vanguard's fund assets under management.
2. The extra returns (net of any shortfalls) earned for shareholders by the superior investment performance of our funds.

Together, these are the two elements of the savings pool, a modest portion of which is allocated to the Vanguard Partnership Plan.

As I mentioned in Chapter 9, our expense ratio advantage came to 0.65% of total assets in 2017. Multiplied by our average assets of $4.5 trillion, our net savings/earnings for the year came to $29.5 billion. The percentage of these annual savings to be shared among our crewmembers is set by management. (As former CEO, I am no longer involved in setting this percentage.)

The cost of the Vanguard Partnership Plan, I'm confident, has been repaid many-fold to our owners/investors by the commitment of our crew, our operational effectiveness, our efficiency, and our productivity.[3]

In the early years of the VPP, we distributed the partnership checks at our annual Vanguard Partnership picnic in June. The checks could equal as much as 30% of a veteran crewmember's annual base salary, leaving little reason to wonder why thousands of crewmembers seemed so enthusiastic about gathering under a huge tent in our Valley Forge parking lot. There I delivered some informative and (I hope!) inspirational comments about Vanguard's corporate values and business prospects. (My annual VPP talks and many other speeches on special occasions have been called "sermons," but I'm not sure that word was used in a complimentary sense!)

I repeat: *loyalty must be a two-way street.* Woe to any firm that does not pledge – and reward – loyalty to those on the front line who are doing the hard work. Yes, money talks. But it delivers the message that I wanted to deliver to our crew. *We're all in this together.*

Our Nautical Heritage

While I believed deeply in acknowledging the value of both individual recognition and partnership participation, I also believed that we needed something more to tie us all together. So, during my 23 years as Vanguard's CEO, I regularly reminded the crew that we were engaged in an important pursuit, that of serving the community of our owner/ shareholders, and that the efforts of each individual human being who serves on the crew of HMS *Vanguard* made a difference.

---

[3] The plan provisions that I've described are those that were largely in effect during my tenure as CEO. Since 2000, when my own participation was terminated, I have had no involvement in the operations of Vanguard Partnership Plan. Happily, it remains in existence.

Since the chain of any anchor is no stronger than its weakest link, we did our best to ensure that all of our links – each of our divisions, each of our crewmembers – were strong (all the while recognizing that this is a perfection that we rarely find here on Earth). That sense of participating together in a worthy human enterprise is evident in the hundreds of wonderful letters I have received – and still receive – from current and former crewmembers.

What's in a Name?

The choice of the name "Vanguard" proved to have durable resonance. Our nautical heritage has permeated the very fabric of Vanguard. As that program for financing and building our new campus in the suburbs of Philadelphia (described in Chapter 7) was being completed, we decided to name each building in honor of one of the ships of the line in Nelson's fleet at the Battle of the Nile in 1798. Most had wonderful, evocative names.

Here we go! On the original central campus: HMS *Victory, Goliath, Majestic, Audacious, Zealous,* and *Swiftsure.* On our east campus: HMS *Alexander, Leander,* and *Theseus.* On our new west campus (so far): HMS *Orion* and *Defense.*

Years earlier, when we celebrated crossing the $10 billion mark in assets in February 1985, I drew on the meanings of some of the names of those warships to describe our firm's values:

We are Zealous – "devoted and diligent."

We are Audacious – "bold, reckless, and defying convention."

We are Swift – "capable of moving with great speed" and Sure, "confident."

Finally, at our best, we can be Majestic[4] – "of imposing aspect, grand." . . . Without any sense of majesty in the sense of "stately

---

[4] In 1999, the Majestic building, the center of our original campus, was renamed "Morgan" by my successor, in honor of my mentor and friend, Walter L. Morgan, founder of Wellington Fund. A later building named "Majestic" now houses Vanguard's extensive training facilities.

dignity," we have become one of the proudest names – one of the most majestic names, if you will – in our industry.[5]

Two Complementary Views

Let me close this chapter with two complementary views about what "caring" means. The first is an anecdote about our initial foray into establishing a personnel department at Vanguard, back in 1976. The second is a famous excerpt from *Devotions Upon Emergent Occasions*, a book of prose meditations written in 1620 by the English poet John Donne.

Nice People

As Vanguard began to grow from that original crew of 28 in 1974 (reaching 167 as 1980 ended), it occurred to me that we should establish a personnel department (now "Human Resources"). Then we were still struggling financially, and striving to keep our expenses down.

So I decided that we could not afford to add a new crewmember to take charge of personnel. Rather, after a casual search, I came upon Eleanor Zentgraf, an assistant to Raymond Kaplinsky Esq., our sole attorney in those ancient days. A lovely woman, she was smart, hard-working, kind, and professional. I asked Eleanor to take on the responsibility. Eleanor immediately agreed –"Whatever you want, Mr. Bogle" – and left my office.

Moments later, she returned and asked, "But just what is it that you want me to do?" I thought about her question a moment and responded: "I'm not sure exactly what I want you to do. But I am sure of one thing: I want you to hire people who are nice and caring, and then make sure that they hire people who are nice and caring."

---

[5] You may recall from Chapter 2 that as we emerged from the crisis of 1974, the goal "Go out and make [Vanguard] the finest name in the whole damn mutual fund industry" was set by Charles D. Root Jr., the late leader of our independent directors.

As I look at the throng of nice, caring human beings who now populate our 17,000-person crew today, I can only say to Eleanor Zentgraf, "Well done!"

"No Man Is an Island"

The poet John Donne's stirring passage pulls together, I think, many of the threads of the fabric of this chapter. He reminds me of the critical role played by our crewmembers, especially our thousands of veterans who have served for 15 years or more. Yet almost as swiftly as they come and serve, they ultimately depart.

I care – and care deeply – about the fine human beings who have helped me to build Vanguard. The departure of even one veteran crewmember has always been hard for me to accept, for it diminishes our enterprise. Donne's words remind me, too, that while I have done my best for Vanguard during my long life and exciting career, neither will they go on forever.

> *No man is an island entire of itself;*
> *every man is a piece of the continent,*
> *a part of the main; if a clod be*
> *washed away by the sea, Europe is*
> *the less, as well if a promontory*
> *were, as well as any manner of thy*
> *friends or of thine own were; any*
> *man's death diminishes me, because*
> *I am involved in mankind. And*
> *therefore never send to know for*
> *whom the bell tolls; it tolls for thee.*

Until that day comes, my memories of a thrilling career remain. My boosters in our shareholder base – most notably "the Bogleheads" of the nation's most popular financial website – continue to write to me almost daily. My 11 books (prior to this one) continue to resonate with enthusiastic readers. My joys in working with so many wonderful crewmembers endure. My confidence remains strong that the firm that I founded all those years ago will carry on and uphold the caring values that I did my best to establish.

Staying the Course

The unique mutual structure and pioneering index fund strategy that we created at Vanguard's founding are the two dimensions that have together changed the mutual fund industry. These two innovative dimensions of Vanguard continue to drive our firm, even as they largely continued to do so even after I stepped down as CEO of Vanguard in 1996 and chairman in 2000. But we have also thrived importantly because of yet a third dimension.

That dimension is the human dimension – building a crew of dedicated human beings who care deeply about Vanguard and our values. I've done my best to ensure that the members of our now-huge crew of 17,000 also care about our institution. Of this I am sure: times change; industries change; and markets change. But fundamental values do not. The Vanguard crew has developed that caring attitude about one another, and about our clients. Holding high these values and staying that course will be essential to Vanguard's ability to maintain our industry leadership.

When I founded Vanguard, I never sought to leave a legacy as such. My goal was to create only an enterprise that was of the shareholder, by the shareholder, and for the shareholder. While I have yet to consider retirement, I remain confident that, even generations from now, Vanguard will continue to "stay the course," continuing the endeavor that I threw myself into with such abandon and delight.

Part II
The Vanguard Funds

In Part I, my focus was almost entirely on the history of Vanguard, the firm's founding structure, and the index strategy demanded by that structure. The six chapters in Part II look closely at the mutual funds operated by Vanguard. These funds have brought Vanguard to its dominant leadership position. The final chapter of Part II evaluates a few Vanguard funds that at first lived up to their promise, only to falter and fail years, sometimes decades, later.

In Chapter 11, I'll discuss Wellington Fund, the foundation upon which Vanguard was built. Chapter 12 focuses on Vanguard's index funds. Vanguard is almost synonymous with indexing, and index funds now account for some three-quarters of our total assets.

The next two chapters focus on some of our most successful actively managed equity funds. Chapter 13, the Windsor funds. Windsor Fund was the first equity fund offered by Wellington Management Company, Vanguard's predecessor firm.

By the mid-1980s, Windsor was a runaway success, but its growth necessitated the fund's closure to new investors. Closing that door opened the door for the creation of Windsor II, which has proven equally successful. Chapter 14 tells the story of PRIMECAP, an actively managed fund with a superb record that shares some of the best traits of indexing – low costs and low turnover.

Chapter 15 is focused on Vanguard's bond funds. Our first attempt at active management was the Vanguard Fixed Income Group, and (of course!) Vanguard was the pioneer of bond index funds.

Finally, in Chapter 16, I'll highlight the two new funds that I launched that enjoyed remarkable success in their early decades, Vanguard U.S. Growth and Vanguard Asset Allocation, only to falter and fail. I'll close the chapter by discussing Vanguard Growth Equity Fund, a New Economy fund that seemed ill-starred from its beginning. It too would finally fail.

Chapter 11
Wellington Fund
Vanguard's Alpha and Omega

The Alpha

Wellington Fund (now Vanguard Wellington Fund[1]), founded in 1928, is the alpha of the Vanguard Group of Investment Companies, not only our first fund, but the balanced fund that helped set the standards that would establish Vanguard's character.

During the half-century that followed the fund's formation, Wellington was the only fund managed by Wellington Management Company. Today, with assets of $104 billion, it ranks among Vanguard's largest funds, and is again one of the two largest balanced funds in the industry.

Wellington Fund remains the prototypical balanced fund – by convention, a fund that typically invests some 35% of its portfolio in investment-grade bonds and the remaining 65% in blue-chip stocks.

Providing some downside protection during market declines, with commensurate upside limits in market advances, Wellington truly has been "a fund for all seasons." As the slogan we used for many years stated, "A complete investment program in one security."

---

[1] In 1980, when all of our funds assumed the Vanguard name, the fund's formal name was changed to "Vanguard Wellington Fund." For a more complete and detailed history of Wellington Fund, please see Chapter 8 of my book *The Clash of the Cultures* (Hoboken, NJ: Wiley, 2012), titled "Wellington Fund: The Rise, the Fall, the Renaissance."

The Founding Objectives

Ever since its founding, Wellington has sought to achieve three objectives: (1) conservation of capital, (2) reasonable current income, and (3) profits without undue risk. While these stated objectives have been in place throughout the fund's long history, their implementation has not always been appropriate.

During its first four decades, Wellington's portfolio had been composed largely of investment-grade bonds and blue-chip stocks held for the long-term. Then, in 1966, a new group of investment strategists, my partners in that year's merger of the fund's investment adviser, took over. They appointed a new portfolio manager who sought to earn higher returns through an aggressive strategy. Heavily laden with speculative elements, that strategy proved an abject failure over the decade that followed.

Walter L. Morgan, Founder and Mentor

When I joined the fund's adviser, Wellington Management Company, on July 9, 1951, Wellington Fund was our sole mutual fund, not an unusual situation for the fund managers of the day. Founded by mutual fund pioneer Walter L. Morgan in 1928, this balanced mutual fund then supervised assets of just $174 million, the eighth-largest fund in the then-$3.1-billion mutual fund industry. Mr. Morgan became my mentor and the architect of my career.

I have now been associated with Wellington Fund for 67 years of its nearly 89-year history. It fell to me to be the key decision-maker at two crucial turning points in its history. The first occurred in 1966, when, in the search to improve the fund's lagging performance, we brought in yet another new portfolio manager. Alas, he moved the fund away from its traditional focus on conservative investment policies to a far more aggressive and riskier profile. Over the next decade, that strategy failed.

While I played no role in Wellington's remarkable rise to prominence during the years from 1928 to 1960, I served as a member of its Investment Committee during the 1960–1965 era. I share a heavy responsibility for the failure that followed. But it taught me the error of my ways.

In 1978, when the second turning point arrived, I was ready. It took some wisdom and determination, and some respect for tradition, to force a return to the fund's original long-term standards – a balanced portfolio focused on stocks and bonds of good quality, current income, risk control, minimal advisory fees and other operating costs, and competitive investment returns. I took the initiative of returning Wellington Fund to its traditional investment roots. During the decades that followed, that strategy succeeded.

The Fall: Wellington Fund's Nadir (1965–1978)

When the 1966 merger was completed, our aggressive new managers "couldn't wait to get our hands" on Wellington Fund. They quickly set out to "modernize" its investment portfolio. Inappropriate as it may seem in retrospect, the conservative fund joined the new speculative parade. In 1967, they named Walter M. Cabot as the fund's portfolio manager.

Cabot had left the Putnam fund organization to join Wellington Management. Acting quickly, he raised the fund's target equity ratio of 62 to 72%. Here's how Cabot described his philosophy in the Wellington Fund 1967 Annual Report:

> *Obviously, times change. We decided we too should change to bring the portfolio more into line with modern concepts and opportunities. We have chosen "dynamic conservatism" as our philosophy, with emphasis on companies that demonstrate the ability to meet, shape, and profit from change. . . . A conservative investment fund is one that aggressively seeks rewards . . . [one that] demands imagination, creativity, and flexibility. . . . Dynamic and conservative investing is not, then, a contradiction in terms. A strong offense is the best defense.*

Encouraged by our firm's new partner/managers, Cabot was taking an aggressive stance without precedent in the fund's long history. By 1972, he had raised the equity ratio to an all-time high of 81%, just as the great bull market peaked, and a great bear market began.

"Dynamic Conservatism?"

In the bear market, the S&P 500 Index fell by 48% from its earlier high. Wellington's asset value fell by 40% – nearly 80% of the decline in the index, a shocking excess relative to the "downside protection" that had characterized the fund's long history. It would take until 1983, 11 long years later, to finally recoup that loss.

Cabot's "strong offense" proved no "defense" at all. We had brought in new managers as partners to improve the lagging performance that Wellington had delivered during the early 1960s, but had succeeded only in making it worse. (There is, of course, a profound lesson here!)

The balanced "blue-chip" Wellington Fund had departed from its conservative roots. It had increased both its equity position and its risk exposure far beyond their traditional levels. It had increased its exposure to speculative stocks of dubious quality, stocks of less-seasoned companies, and stocks selling at historically high market valuations.

March 1972: A Warning About Speculation

That change in the fund's character alarmed me. On March 10, 1972, I wrote a sharply worded memorandum to our investment executives, warning them about both the excessive risks and their all too likely unhappy consequences. A few excerpts follow:

> *Wellington Fund, at the moment, can barely be considered a "balanced fund." . . . The fund's equity ratio is now 81 percent. I have grave doubts as to whether we are meeting the investment policy test specified in the fund's prospectus.*

> *Wellington Fund is the foundation upon which our company is built. In Wellington Fund, to a major extent, lies the value and goodwill of the very name that we at Wellington Management Company apply to almost everything we do.*

Cabot responded promptly. He didn't agree with me, nor did he accept my conclusions. Here are excerpts from his reply:

> *This, in my opinion, is a marketing problem and really has very little to do with the investment objectives or strategy for Wellington*

Fund. . . . I would not return it to its traditional investment posture. . . .
The balanced concept is outmoded.

I found his response totally unsatisfactory. Even worse, he was dead wrong.

Abject Failure

Under Cabot's management, accentuated by the new and risky strategy, Wellington was hard-hit by the decline. From 1966 to 1979, Wellington's *total* return was *minus* 6.3%, a far cry from the average return of *plus* 14.4% earned by our balanced-fund peers, and flat-out last during Cabot's 10-year tenure. Even when the market recovery came, Wellington continued to lag compared to its peers.[2]

As the ghastly combination of poor performance and terrible market conditions took their toll, the fund's asset base continued to tumble. From its year-end peak of $2.0 billion in 1965, Wellington's assets were on their way to a modern low of $470 million, reached in June 1982. The situation was dire. There seemed no way out.

For a moment, I entertained the idea that we should simply merge Wellington Fund, that Grand Old Lady, once the paradigm of our high standing in the industry, into another of our funds, and get on with our business. But I couldn't do it. It was not only loyalty to Wellington Fund founder Walter Morgan that drove my decision, but my conviction that the fund's balanced concept remained fundamentally sound.

I had failed, however unintentionally, to live up to Mr. Morgan's confidence. He had hired me, trusted my judgment, and in the spring of 1965 named me to lead the company. I owed everything to my marvelous mentor. I could not let him down. I was confident that in Wellington's original three sound objectives – (1) conservation of capital, (2) reasonable current income, and (3) profits without undue risk – lay the solution to its problems.

I was determined to do whatever was necessary to restore Wellington to her former grandeur. However deeply disguised, it was

---

[2] Cabot went on to become the president of Harvard Management Company and the manager of the Harvard University endowment fund.

the opportunity of a lifetime. How to accomplish my goal? I used my power as chairman and president of Wellington Fund and the other Vanguard funds, a position of surprising strength.

1978–2018: The Renaissance

As Wellington Fund's chairman, one of my responsibilities was to evaluate the returns earned by each of the now-Vanguard funds. My fellow directors were every bit as concerned as I was about the blot on Wellington Fund's once-proud reputation. Even so, restructuring Wellington Fund would be no easy task. However, with the support of Princeton professor Burton Malkiel, who had joined the Wellington Fund board in 1977, we got the job done.

In 1978, the board agreed to adopt my three policy recommendations: (1) hold the equity ratio firmly within a range of 60% to 70% of assets; (2) emphasize seasoned dividend-paying blue-chip stocks, with less reliance on low-yielding growth stocks; and (3) sharply increase the fund's dividend income.

We directed Wellington Management Company to implement the restructuring, spelled out in my memorandum to the board:

> *What kind of current and future income might we be able to generate? Here are the projections, assuming a balance of 65 percent stock and 35 percent bonds. . . . Such a change (implemented gradually) could increase the Fund's income dividends from $0.54 per share in 1978 to $0.91 in 1983 (an increase of 70%).*[3]

A 70% Dividend Increase

Here's how I announced these changes in Wellington Fund's 1978 Annual Report:

> *Your Board of Directors has approved a change in investment approach which will increase the amount of dividends earned on the fund's*

---

[3] To aid Wellington Management in its task, I presented the firm with a model stock portfolio of 50 stocks that met the standards that I had outlined. The list was compiled from financial data published in the Value Line Investment Survey.

common stock investments. This goal . . . should be accomplished with-
out any material sacrifice of "total return" potential (income plus capi-
tal appreciation). We launched a vigorous program for increasing current
income in the closing months of 1978, and plan to further increase the
emphasis on income in 1979.

When I gave these marching orders – especially our insistence in
raising the fund's income dividend by fully 70% over the next five
years – Wellington Management was not pleased. The partners believed
that growth stocks were the optimal choice, and that the emphasis on
higher-yielding stocks would harm performance.

Nonetheless, when the client speaks, the wise manager listens.
While Wellington Management reluctantly signed on to the new strategy, Vincent Bajakian, Cabot's replacement as portfolio manager, implemented it with excellence. The fund's annual income dividend began
a steady increase. In fact, the dividend of $.91 per share targeted in
1978 for 1983 was exceeded – $.92 per share. It looks easy, but only in
retrospect.

Strategy + Implementation – Cost = Fund Return

Nor was the recovery in the fund's returns easy to accomplish. But,
once completed, Wellington's founding character was restored and the
fund's record over the past half-century-plus improved to a near-insur-
mountable edge over its average balanced fund peer.

From 1965 to 1982, that edge had been negative. Wellington Fund
earned an average annual return of just 5.8%, versus 8.0% for its peer
group. But the fund's powerful recovery followed, and Wellington
earned an average annual return of 11.0% during 1982 to 2017, overwhelming the earlier shortfall. (See Exhibit 11.1.)

For the full period 1965–2017, Wellington Fund's annual rate of
return came to 9.3%, fully 1.2 percentage points over the 8.1% average of its peers. Result: for investors who stayed the course through
the years of travail, an initial investment of $10,000 in Wellington
Fund in 1965 would have grown to $1,005,734 as 2018 began (see
Exhibit 11.1). During that same period, a comparable investment in

Exhibit 11.1   Wellington Fund: Growth of an Initial Investment
of $10,000, 1965–2018

Bad Era: 1965–1982			
Initial Investment 1965	Terminal Value 1982	Annual Return	Average Balanced Fund
$10,000	$25,996	5.8%	8.0%

Good Era: 1982–2017			
Initial Investment 1982	Terminal Value 2017	Annual Return	Average Balanced Fund
$25,996	$1,005,734	11.0%	8.1%

Modern Era Total: 1965–2017			
Initial Investment 1965	Terminal Value 2017	Annual Return	Average Balanced Fund
$10,000	$1,005,734	9.3%	8.1%

Source: Vanguard.

the average balanced fund would have grown to $566,955. *The magic of compounding returns writ large.*

To use a favorite metaphor of mine: the long-term *magic* of compounding *returns* can be easily overwhelmed by the long-term *tyranny* of compounding *costs*. *Costs matter!* Given Vanguard's mutual structure, Wellington Fund, uniquely among its peers, has minimized the tyranny of compounding costs, and its shareholders have prospered from the eternal magic of compounding returns.

Exhibit 11.2   Wellington's Long-Term Performance Tops Its Peers'

	Returns and Costs 1965–2017		
	Gross Return before Costs	Expense Ratio	Net Return after Costs
Wellington Fund	9.58%	0.39%	9.20%
Average Balanced Fund	9.32	1.10	8.21
Wellington Advantage	0.26	−0.71	0.99

Source: Wiesenberger Investment Companies, Vanguard.

The Cost Advantage

Unarguably, it has been Wellington Fund's substantial cost advantage vis-à-vis its peers that has been the mainspring of its comparative advantage – its superior record. Wellington's cost advantage over its balanced fund peers – an average long-term expense ratio of 0.39% versus 1.10% – simply adds a non-trivial 0.71% *directly* to the fund's net return (see Exhibit 11.2). That remarkable margin has enabled the fund's cumulative return to explode over that long span.

In fact, as Exhibit 11.2 shows, the lion's share of Wellington's 0.99% annual edge over its peers – nearly 1 percentage point per year – has resulted largely from that huge annual cost advantage of 71 basis points. The other 26 basis points – encompassing both the good times described in this chapter and the bad times that preceded them – resulted from Wellington's conservative investment strategy, ably implemented by Edward P. Bousa, the portfolio manager appointed by Wellington Management Company in 2000, still on the job in 2018.

Wellington Fund has yet another cost advantage over its peer group – lower turnover of its portfolio holdings. Wellington Fund's focus on long-term investing leads to less trading by its portfolio managers, which results in lower transaction costs for the fund. Over the long-term, Wellington's annual turnover rate has averaged 31%, while the average balanced fund's turnover has been 87%. Less frequent trading translates directly into lower costs and higher returns for fund shareholders, and appears to be a durable advantage. In yet a second instance of comparative advantage, Wellington has achieved a commanding advantage over its peers.

Summing Up

As 1966 began, Wellington Fund was the largest balanced mutual fund served by the then-dominant brokerage community. Assets had soared to an all-time high of $2.1 billion, only to plummet by 70% to a low of $470 million in 1982, and then, at last, returned to a long-term path of growth that by 1989 had carried assets past its previous high of $2.1 billion. (See Exhibit 11.3.)

Exhibit 11.3   Wellington Fund Assets, 1965–2018

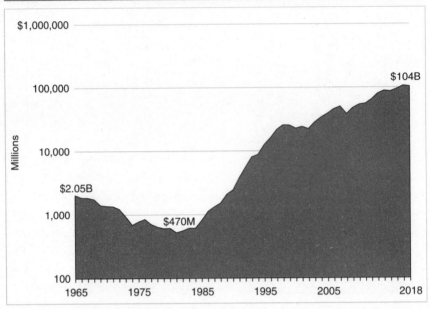

Source: Vanguard, Strategic Insight Simfund.

It got even better. In mid-2018, Wellington Fund's assets totaled $104 billion, a 50-fold increase over those earlier highs. Solid returns in the financial markets were at the core of this increase. But net cash inflow from investors also played a major role. From 1985 through 2014, Wellington Fund enjoyed its most positive net cash flow in 25 years.[4]

The Omega

Almost 90 years after its founding in 1928, Wellington Fund remains the alpha of the Vanguard Group – our first fund and our only fund – for a half-century. (Vanguard now operates 180 mutual funds in the

---

[4] Since 2013, as its assets have burgeoned, Wellington Fund has been largely closed to cash flows from new investors. As a result, the fund has experienced modest net cash outflows in each of the past three years.

United States alone.) But Wellington Fund continues to play a vital role as the custodian and exemplar of Vanguard's conservative investment traditions.

Wellington Fund, then, is both the alpha and the omega of Vanguard. Its balanced credo still prevails, and, I believe, always will prevail. Think of the fund's target balance of 65% stocks and 35% bonds. Then realize how similar that ratio is to that of the aggregate asset base of the Vanguard funds today: 71% stocks and 29% bonds. Balanced investing, once largely achieved in a single mutual fund, but now represented by a portfolio of funds, will never go out of style. *Plus ça change, plus c'est la même chose.*

Chapter 12
The Index Funds

For decades, Vanguard's surprising creation of the world's first index mutual fund in 1975 – First Index Investment Trust (since 1981, Vanguard 500 Index Fund) – created but a small rivulet flowing into the mutual fund river. It took until the mid-1990s before the index fund concept became a stream. By 2000, index funds had become a river. And in 2018, index funds have become a torrent, almost untamed.

In Chapter 5, I focused on the struggles to form that first index fund. Lots of luck and fortuitous timing were involved. But so were the early enthusiasm, the determination, and finally the disappointment that followed. Using a different metaphor, the young acorn seemed destined never to grow into the giant oak that it would finally become.

In this chapter, we'll go beyond that single fund and consider the index empire that it has spawned at Vanguard. During the early twenty-first century, indexing has been the dominant force in building our firm. Index funds now account for $3.5 trillion, or 77% of our $5 trillion asset base.

Our Index Fund Is Copied . . . and Praised

The 500 Index set the standard for the index funds that followed Vanguard's innovation, first at Wells Fargo (1984), then at Colonial (born 1986; died 1993, R.I.P.), and then at Fidelity (1988). The first exchange-traded index fund (ETF), the now-famous SPDR (or "Spider") formed in 1993, also tracks the S&P 500 Index.

If more adulation were needed, Warren Buffett is among the most enthusiastic proponents of the Vanguard 500 Index Fund. He continues to make our 500 Index Fund his major – indeed his almost universal –

recommendation to investors seeking guidance. He's been doing so for at least two decades. Here's what he wrote in the 1996 Annual Report of Berkshire Hathaway Corporation:

> *Most investors, both institutional and individual, will find that the best way to own common stocks is through an index fund that charges minimal fees. Those following this path are sure to beat the net results (after fees and expenses) delivered by the great majority of investment professionals.*

Yet from the beginning we realized that the S&P 500 Index, while was not a perfect reflection of the U.S. stock market, was a fine proxy for the total stock market index. (In those days, the Wilshire 5000 was the accepted index of the total U.S. stock market.) Over the long term, the differences between the S&P 500 and the total U.S. stock market index have been trivial.

Since S&P data were first published in 1926, the annual return on the S&P 500 has averaged 10.1%, compared to 9.9% for the Total Stock Market Index. Since 1930, the returns have been identical—9.7% annually for the S&P 500 and 9.7% for the total market. The record shows that the returns of the Wilshire 5000 explain more than 99% of the variation in the returns of the S&P 500.

Betting on the 500 Index Fund

Even when we chose the S&P 500 as the target for our firms' index fund, we were aware that in the ideal, the Total Stock Market Index would be the most pristine means for capturing the market's returns. So in 1987 we created our second equity index fund, Vanguard Extended Market Index Fund. This was a "completion fund," holding the mid- and small-cap stocks that were not included in the S&P 500.

Vanguard investors who wanted to hold the entire stock market could simply allocate roughly 80% of their investment to Vanguard 500 Index Fund and the remaining 20% to Vanguard Extended Market Index Fund. While Extended Market was used for that purpose by some investors, its principal use came from investors who believed that mid- and small-cap stocks would earn higher long-term returns than their large-cap cousins.

Whatever the case, Vanguard Extended Market Index Fund has earned a strong place in the index fund pantheon, with assets of $68 billion in mid-2018. It has provided investors with thier full share of the returns earned by its 2018 portfolio of 3,270 non–S&P 500 stocks.

As the 1990s began and the evidence poured in about the success of index investing, we continued to seek to broaden Vanguard's lineup of index funds. The broad U.S. stock market was already covered by our 500 Index Fund (1975) and Extended Market Index Fund (1987). Bonds were covered by our Total Bond Market Index Fund[1] (1986). The next logical step was to offer index funds that tracked stocks beyond the borders of the United States.

International Stock Index Funds

In 1990, we considered offering an index fund tracking the MSCI EAFE (Europe, Australasia, and Far East) Index, which would encompass stocks from all major non-U.S. developed markets. But I had serious concerns about the Japanese stock market at the time.[2] I didn't want to force investors seeking broad international exposure to risk fully 67% of their non-U.S. capital in the Pacific region. So in June 1990, we launched not one, but two international index funds – one investing in European stocks, the other in Pacific stocks. This innovation was, once again, without precedent.

With the 1994 launch of Vanguard Emerging Markets Index Fund – also the first of its kind – we continued to innovate in the international arena. This fund gave investors a broadly diversified exposure to stocks of the so-called developing markets of the world.

---

[1] I'll discuss the 1986 creation of our second index fund, Vanguard Total Bond Market Index, in Chapter 15.

[2] As its peak in 1989, with the Nikkei Index at a high of 38,900, the price/earnings ratio of the Nikkei Index had risen to nearly 70. By 2003, the Nikkei would plummet to a low of less than 8,000. By 2010, the market capitalization of the Japanese stock market had fallen from 45% of global equities to 7%.

Vanguard's innovation in international investing didn't stop there. Today, Vanguard offers 11 international stock index funds – covering everything from the Total World Index (including U.S. stocks) to international high-yield stocks to small-cap stocks – as well as two international bond index funds. In total, Vanguard now manages over $700 billion in international index funds.

Enter the Total Stock Market Index Fund

Early in 1992, we took another big step. Our "completion fund" approach to holding the total U.S. stock market portfolio was proving unsatisfactory. The need for investors to invest in two index funds – 500 and Extended – in order to hold the entire U.S. stock market seemed unnecessarily complicated and complex. Why make all-market indexing more difficult and convoluted than it needed to be?

So we made the obvious decision. Vanguard created a simple all-U.S.-stock market portfolio – arguably the optimal investment strategy – one that would be readily accessible to investors at low cost. On April 27, 1992–probably belatedly–some 17 years after our creation of that pioneering first index fund based on the S&P 500 Index, we formed Vanguard Total Stock Market Index Fund. Total Stock Market has been a runaway success. With more than $740 billion in total assets[3] in mid-2018, it is the largest mutual fund in the world.

Growth and Value Index Funds

Only months later, in November 1992, we further refined the concept of indexing by adding a Growth Index Fund and a Value Index Fund, based on the Growth and Value Indexes that had been introduced by S&P in 1991. These indexes were based, simply enough, on each stock's market price relative to its book value (low book-to-market=growth;

---

[3] Including the assets of its sister fund designed for institutional investors.

high book-to-market=value),[4] and then divided all 500 stocks into two groups so that one-half of the market was capitalization of the Index categorized as "growth" and the other one-half as "value." At the outset, the growth index comprised 190 stocks, the value index 310 stocks. In 2018, with the funds now tracking CRSP indexes, the respective totals are 300 growth stocks and 337 value stocks.

Success for the Funds, Failure for Their Investors

Our Growth and Value Index Funds have succeeded in one way, but failed in another. With assets in mid-2018 of $79 billion and $66 billion respectively, they remain the two oldest and largest funds categorized by Morningstar as "Strategic Beta" funds. Often called "Smart Beta" funds or "factor" funds, strategic beta funds generally seek to enhance returns or minimize risk relative to the broad market by holding stocks with particular characteristics such as value, small-cap, and even stock price momentum.

But, as I discussed in Chapter 7, during their 25-plus years of existence, the 9% annual returns earned by each *fund* dwarfed the returns earned by each fund's *investors* – a staggering annual shortfall of −2.7% for investors in Growth Index Fund and −1.4% for Value. I had designed our Growth and Value Index Funds to be held for the long-term, and regularly warned investors *not* to use them to "time" the markets.

Investors seem to have largely ignored my advice. Both our Growth and our Value Index Funds have been used predominately by short-term traders, apparently convinced that they know which factor will provide the higher return, and for how long. Call the history of our Growth and Value Index Funds "the law of unintended consequences."

---

[4] This may seem a crude matrix. It is. But 97% of the returns of the S&P Growth and Value Indexes has been explained by the returns of their respective counterparts in the more sophisticated Russell 1000 (large-cap) Growth and Value Indexes (R-squared). In 2003, the Vanguard Growth and Value Index Funds changed their benchmarks to the MSCI U.S. Prime Market Growth and Value Indexes, then in 2013 to the CRSP U.S. Large-Cap Growth and Value Indexes.

More Index Funds

Immediately following the creation of the Growth and Value Index Funds in November 1992, we created the industry's first Balanced Index Fund. In April 1996, we combined our European, Pacific, and Emerging Markets index funds into a single Vanguard Total International Stock Index Fund. (In 2018, its portfolio consists of the stocks that constitute the FTSE Global All-Cap Ex-U.S. Index.) With assets of $343 billion in mid-2018, Total International has become Vanguard's fourth-largest index fund.

Vanguard's leadership in index innovation – the "first mover" – has played a major role in our dominance. Since 1996, Vanguard has launched 59 index funds for U.S. investors, and now offers index funds to investors in Europe, Asia, Canada, and Latin America. Today, Vanguard offers index funds covering all of the "nine-box" segments of the U.S. stock market (large-, mid-, and small-cap; growth, blend, and value), sector index funds, index funds covering U.S. Treasury and corporate bonds, and a municipal bond index fund, just to name a few. Our "veteran" index funds, all formed before 2000, account for fully $2.9 trillion, equal to 86% of Vanguard's index fund asset base. Exhibit 12.1 lists the major groups of Vanguard's 75 index funds, their 2018 assets, and their dates of formation.

Market Indexes Have Outpaced 91% of Actively Managed Funds

In the spring of 2018, Standard & Poor's Corporation produced its annual comparison of the 15-year returns on all major classes of actively managed funds and compared them to the returns achieved by the S&P index in each category. The report is titled "Standard & Poor's Index Versus Active," commonly referred to as the "SPIVA Scorecard."

The across-the-board superiority of the indexes reflected in the SPIVA Scorecard is astonishing. (See Exhibit 12.2.) The S&P indexes outperformed some 93% (!) of actively managed funds in the U.S. large-, mid-, and small-cap categories, from a low of 86% of small-cap value, to a high of 99% of small-cap growth funds. The S&P 500,

Exhibit 12.1 Assets and Expense Ratios of Vanguard Index Funds by Inception Date, December 31, 2018

Fund Name	Inception	Total Assets ($Bil)	Expense Ratio (Admiral/ETF)
500 Index	1976	$640	0.04%
Total Bond Market Index	1986	355	0.05
Extended Market Index	1987	67	0.08
Large-, Mid-, and Small-Cap Index Funds	1989–2006	296	0.07
European and Pacific Index Funds	1990	33	0.10
Total Stock Market Index	1992	742	0.04
Growth and Value Index Funds	1992	145	0.06
Balanced Index	1992	38	0.07
Bond Index Funds	1994	94	0.07
Emerging Markets Index	1994	89	0.14
Total International Stock Index	1996	343	0.11
REIT Index	1996–2017	64	0.10
Developed Markets Index	1999	110	0.07
FTSE Social Index	2000	4	0.20
Sector Index Funds	2004	63	0.10
Dividend Index Funds	2006	64	0.08
Other Non-U.S. Stock Index Funds	2007–2009	61	0.11
Corporate, Treasury, MBS Bond Index Funds	2009	64	0.07
Short-Term TIPS Index	2012	25	0.06
Total International Bond Index	2013	107	0.11
Other	2007–2017	48	0.17
Total		$3,451	0.09%

Source: Vanguard.

the best-known of the indexes, outperformed 92% of all active large-cap funds. The SPIVA Scorecard offers overwhelming evidence that indexing strategies have given investors their best chance at investment success.[5]

---

[5] The SPIVA data account for "survivorship bias." Only about *40%* of the mutual funds that began the 15-year period still existed at the end.

Exhibit 12.2   Percentage of U.S. Equity Funds Outperformed by Benchmarks, 2017

Category	Benchmark	% Outperformed by Benchmark over the Previous 15 Years
Large-Cap	**S&P 500**	**92%**
Growth	S&P 500 Growth	94
Core	S&P 500	95
Value	S&P 500 Value	86
Mid-Cap	**S&P MidCap 400**	**95%**
Growth	S&P MidCap 400 Growth	95
Core	S&P MidCap 400	97
Value	S&P MidCap 400 Value	89
Small-Cap	**S&P SmallCap 600**	**96%**
Growth	S&P SmallCap 600 Growth	99
Core	S&P SmallCap 600	97
Value	S&P SmallCap 600 Value	90
Average		**94%**
Other		
Real Estate	S&P U.S. REIT	81
Global	S&P Global 1200	83
International (Non-U.S.)	S&P International 700	92
International Small-Cap (Non-U.S.)	S&P Developed Ex-U.S. Small Cap	78
Emerging Markets	S&P/IFCI Composite	95
All Funds	**All Indexes**	**91%**

Source: S&P SPIVA, year-end 2017.

Index Funds Dominate

From the fortuitous creation of First Index Investment Trust in 1975 – the world's first index mutual fund – to today's portfolio of 75 index funds in the United States alone, Vanguard has been the leader in the burgeoning index fund sector of the mutual fund industry. As shown in Exhibit 12.3, the index fund share of the assets of all U.S. equity funds has soared from a market share of 4% of assets in 1985 to 43% in mid-2018. Yes, we have seen the triumph of indexing, and it isn't over yet.

Exhibit 12.3 Index Share of Equity Mutual Fund Assets, 1976–2018

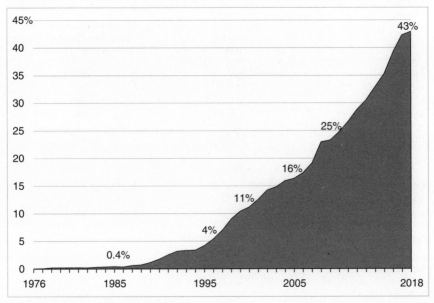

Source: Vanguard, Strategic Insight Simfund.

Vanguard's traditional index funds now account for almost 80% of the TIF category and our exchange-traded funds represent 25% of the ETF category. Together, Vanguard funds represent approximately one-half of the assets of all U.S. index mutual funds.

The continuation of Vanguard's leadership depends upon our deserving it: earning the confidence of the investors who have entrusted their savings to Vanguard, and meeting their long-term expectations for the efficient and economical administration of their accounts. Such leadership also depends in part on growing investor recognition of the demonstrably higher value to investors provided by TIFs relative to their ETF cousins (see Exhibit 12.4).

Exhibit 12.4 Vanguard Share of Total Index Fund Assets, 2018

	Traditional Index Funds	Exchange-Traded Funds	Total Index Funds
Vanguard Index Assets	$2.6 trillion	$885 billion	$3.5 trillion
Industry Index Assets	$3.3 trillion	$3.5 trillion	$6.8 trillion
Vanguard Share	78%	25%	51%

We know that index funds that are focused on broad diversification in the major market sectors, bought and held for the long term, have proved to be the optimal strategy for investment success. My bet is that the vast majority of investors, informed by their own experience, will come to favor TIFs over ETFs. Time will tell.

*   *   *

The remarkable success of index funds has attracted trillions of dollars from millions of investors. But I repeat that we'd best be careful that the old adage "Nothing *succeeds* like success" doesn't morph into "Nothing *fails* like success." Some of the challenges to the growth of index funds that lie ahead are described in Part III, "The Future of Investment Management."

Chapter 13
The Windsor Funds

From 1928 until 1958, Wellington Fund was the only mutual fund in what would become The Vanguard Group of Investment Companies. The firm's sole focus on a conservative balanced fund helped Wellington dominate the balanced mutual fund category almost ever since the fund's founding. To use the common saying of the day, Wellington had "carved out a niche" that few peers – most of them focused on stock funds – sought to challenge.

But in the late 1950s, the competition to attract the attention (and favor) of the stockbrokers who were offering mutual funds to their clients was getting more and more intense. Our team of wholesalers was getting restless for the lack of an equity fund to offer investors under Wellington Management's aegis.

I was probably the most restless of all. I even wrote a strongly worded memorandum to Joseph E. Welch, the fine but cautious man who, as president of the firm, reported to chairman and CEO Walter Morgan. My message: *We need to create and offer an equity fund. Now is the time, and time is of the essence.*[1]

So, persuaded in part by that logic, plus the fact that a successful stock offering would immediately be profitable for his then-solely owned Wellington Management Company, Mr. Morgan gave the "go" signal.

Given the small size of our staff, the opportunity to create a new mutual fund from scratch and prepare its IPO prospectus came to me. It was by far the most exciting project of my young career.

---

[1] Two new equity funds had been created earlier in 1958. Lehman Brothers' One William Street Fund and Lazard Freres' Lazard Fund. The former raised $198 million (about $1.7 billion in 2018 dollars) in its initial public offering (IPO), the latter $118 million ($1.0 billion) – astonishing numbers in a year when the total net cash inflows into all mutual funds came in at just $1.1 billion.

We chose Kidder Peabody as the lead manager of the IPO and Bache & Company as the co-manager. Both firms employed highly competent investment bankers, and both had long been active in the distribution of Wellington Fund shares to investors. For weeks we sat with our lawyers around a large table in Mr. Morgan's office and thrashed out the details – fund objectives, policies, administrative procedures, and the choice of the fund's directors (the same as Wellington Fund's). We chose the name Wellington Equity Fund. (That was my advice, as it happens. I thought that it had a better "ring" than "Wellington Stock Fund.")

What's in a Name?

The name for the new fund turned out not to matter. We were soon struck by a disaster of sorts. A dissatisfied shareholder of Wellington Fund, aided by a member of the plaintiff's bar, argued that the name "Wellington" was the sole property of Wellington Fund, and that Wellington Equity Fund was improperly capitalizing on it.

The case was complicated, and we thought it was absurd. But the plaintiff's position prevailed in the Delaware District Court, and then in the Delaware Supreme Court. The Supreme Court of the United States refused to consider it. We had lost.

Obviously, we needed a new name for the fund. My choice was Windsor Fund. And so the "British W" strategy began. We would later offer Wellesley Income Fund, Westminster Bond Fund, Whitehall Money Market Fund, Warwick Municipal Bond Fund, and even W. L. Morgan Growth Fund. Those names lasted only until 1980, when we dropped them in favor of a unified "branding" policy: all Vanguard funds would henceforth begin with the name "Vanguard."

Modest IPO, Weak Returns

Alas, when our underwriting took place in October, the barrel of money available for mutual fund IPOs was close to empty. But we succeeded in raising $38.4 million. Wellington Equity Fund began investing on October 23, 1958. While we were prepared to operate and distribute the fund, however, we seemed less prepared to manage its investments.

Windsor's returns thrashed around in the early years, its managers uncertain on what direction to take. We were riding a rising bull market: +11% annually for the S&P 500 from 1958 to 1964; yet Wellington Equity Fund lagged at only +7.7%. The fund's assets crossed the $75 million threshold by mid-1963. Then help arrived. And remarkable help it was! The fund's record improved almost immediately.

Enter John B. Neff

John B. Neff, retained as the new portfolio manager, had been searching for a new career opportunity. He had spent eight years in the trust department of the National City Bank in Cleveland. He was ready for a new challenge.

Neff found his challenge in the (by then renamed) Windsor Fund. He assumed his duties as portfolio manager in the summer of 1964. He felt right at home, and we immediately began a friendship that would last for the rest of our lives.

Here's how John described the start of our friendship: "We had an immediate kinship because there was something about me that he liked that he couldn't put his finger on. I know exactly what it was, though. We both had crew-cuts then."

It took a while for Neff's value philosophy to materialize into improved returns for Windsor. Under Neff's aegis, Windsor had become at once conservative and aggressive: conservative in the sense of his "prudent man" approach to value investing, emphasizing carefully analyzed stocks with depressed market prices and usually generous yields, an approach designed to limit downside risk.

But his approach was also aggressive, in the sense that the portfolio was highly concentrated in Neff's favorite issues, meaning that the fund's returns over the short-term would be less predictable relative to the returns of more broadly diversified competitors. However difficult it was to articulate, the Windsor story finally got across.

Strong Fund Returns, Strong Cash Flows

By 1965, the performance of Windsor was turning upward. Its annual return averaged 12.6% through 1970 compared to just 4.8% for the S&P 500. Of course Windsor lagged the 500 during the "Nifty Fifty" growth stock madness from 1970 to 1973. But its annual returns surged in 1974–1979: Windsor 16.8%, S&P 6.6%. (Cumulative returns for 1965–1979, +359% for Windsor, +126% for the S&P 500).

In the mutual fund world, such remarkable performance draws the attention – and the money – of watchful investors and opportunistic stockbrokers. In Windsor's case, it worked out for better as Neff continued to shine. In the case of most of Windsor's successful peers, for worse; "hot" funds are doomed to turn cold.

At the start of 1981, Windsor Fund's assets totaled less than $1 billion. As the huge cash inflows from investors into our money market funds returned to more modest levels, Windsor picked up the slack – and then some. From 1981 to 1984, net cash flows into Windsor totaled $965 million, fully 17% of our firm's total fund cash flows. By the close of 1985, Windsor's assets totaled more than $4 billion – the largest equity fund in the nation.

That seemingly inevitable devil of reversion to the mean (discussed further in Chapter 16) in equity fund returns seemed to ignore Windsor, and John Neff pressed on. Despite a surprising shortfall in 1989–1990, the fund's annual return averaged a remarkable 17.2% from 1980 through 1992, well ahead of the return of the S&P 500 by 1.2 percentage points per year.

"The Time Has Come"

Even as Windsor Fund replaced Wellington Fund as the flagship of the Vanguard fleet, John Neff and I both realized that, well, "trees don't grow to the sky." Painful as it might be for Vanguard, we agreed in principle that the day would come when we would have to close the fund. The failure to do so could cause Windsor to become so big that sheer size would impinge on the investment flexibility that had become Neff's hallmark.

In May 1985, John came into my office, sat down, and said, "The time has come to close down cash flow into Windsor Fund." Almost before the words were out of his mouth, I agreed. I had no more an interest than he did, as I put it, in "killing the goose that laid the golden egg."[2]

The closing of Windsor to new investors was almost without precedent in the mutual fund industry. Conventionally structured fund managers would sooner die than cut off cash inflows into their flagship funds and squelch the soaring management fees they received from their meal-ticket funds. But Vanguard's mutual structure had happily removed that issue from my consideration. I didn't care about gathering assets and maximizing advisory fee revenues.

What to Do?

I was certain that Vanguard needed to continue to offer a value-oriented fund to our growing family of fund investors. My logic told me to start a second value fund, with its own independent portfolio manager, not advised by Wellington Management. No controversy there. But when I decided to name the sister fund Windsor II, I was subjected to scathing criticism. "You are capitalizing on Windsor Fund's name and John Neff's stellar record, because you know that Windsor II will *never* succeed in living up to the returns that Windsor Fund will generate."[3] The doubters were proved wrong.

For the Doubters, a Surprising Outcome

During the spring of 1985, we interviewed half a dozen money managers with solid credentials as value investors. My choice was Barrow,

---

[2] When Windsor Fund closed in May 1985, its assets were $3.6 billion, about 0.3% of the total market capitalization of the S&P 500. Today, 0.3% of the S&P 500 would be about $63 billion.

[3] During the 1964–1995 Neff era, Windsor outpaced the S&P Index by 3.4 percentage points annually. I believe that this accomplishment is without precedent in the history of the mutual fund industry. Hail, John B. Neff.

Hanley, Mewhinney & Strauss, an established money manager head-quartered in Dallas, Texas. The firm was run by experienced principals. Their leader, James P. (Jim) Barrow, seemed trustworthy and likely to be a good partner for Vanguard, and our board of directors agreed.

On May 15, 1985, the decision to close Windsor was announced and immediately implemented. Advance notice would have surely created a rush of cash flow into Windsor, precisely what we were trying to avoid. The offering of shares of Windsor II began a month later.

In retrospect, our choice of Barrow, Hanley, Mewhinney & Strauss seems inspired. In 2018, 33 years later, the firm remains the manager of the largest portion of Windsor II's assets. The fund has not only held its own with its esteemed forebear, but has actually provided a slightly higher rate of annual return: Windsor Fund 10.1%; Windsor II, 10.5%. Give most of the credit for that accomplishment to Jim Barrow's stewardship.[4]

The Multi-Manager Concept

In the interest of ensuring the "relative predictability" of the returns on Windsor II, I decided that, as the assets of Windsor II continued to grow, we needed to further diversify the fund's portfolio. In 1989, as the fund's assets crossed $2 billion, we retained a second manager, INVESCO of Atlanta. This firm assumed responsibility for $250 million of the fund's assets.

This move was Vanguard's first foray into using multiple managers for a single fund. The idea – as I had expressed it back in 1974 – was to offer funds with relative predictability of performance. If a fund could merely emulate the gross returns earned by its peers, it would win based solely on its low costs. That philosophy has worked effectively for Vanguard's investors.

What we knew in theory, we confirmed in practice with the Windsor Funds: two independent sets of portfolio managers, both with a confirmed philosophy of value (vs. growth) investing, both with experienced and proven leaders, should produce similar returns

---

[4] Jim Barrow is a wonderful character whose wit conceals his gift for investment strategy. When one of the Vanguard directors asked Jim if we were worried about a market correction, he quickly responded: "No. Because the fat lady ain't sung yet."

over time, and carry similar risk profiles. So it would be. Since 1985, the volatility of Windsor Fund has been 17.2%, of Windsor II, 16.0% (slightly less than the 16.5% volatility of the S&P 500).

Led by Jim Barrow, the fund's lead manager from 1985 through 2015, Windsor II returns were fully competitive. The fund's return outpaced the average value fund by 1.4 percentage points per year through 1989.

From 1995 to 1998, immediately following Neff's retirement, his successors, named by Wellington Management Company, struggled. Windsor's annual return was 19.2%, while Windsor II delivered 27.7%. But reversion to the mean struck again – as it almost always does – and the tables were turned from 1999 to 2007: Windsor, 8.0% annually; Windsor II, 6.5%. Since 2007 ended, the returns of these two Vanguard value funds have been virtually identical: Windsor, 7.2%; Windsor II, 6.7%.

Exhibit 13.1 charts the relative cumulative returns of Windsor and Windsor II. When the line is moving up, Windsor Fund is outperforming, and when the line moves down, Windsor II is winning. Despite some ups and downs over the years, the returns over the long-term have been quite similar, with only a small advantage to Windsor.

Exhibit 13.1 Windsor/Windsor II Relative Cumulative Return, 1985–2018

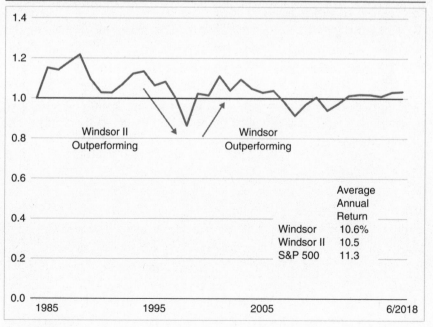

Source: Vanguard.

The Lessons of History

So what's to be learned from the history of the Windsor Funds? First, be sure and begin with an outstanding portfolio manager. We were lucky here, of course. But "once you have found him," as it were, "never let him go." While he's now been retired for 23 years, my friendship with John Neff endures, and will forever.

Second, realize that time flies. Portfolio managers have finite lives, and finite periods in which they excel. One good way to be prepared is to rely on several managers from several different firms – both operating under the same mandates (as in Windsor II's case). There's no magic in setting a limit on the number of managers.

Third, hold fund costs to a minimum. (*Performance comes and goes, but costs go on forever.*) Of course that means a fee structure that favors the fund shareholders. But it also means an appropriately low turnover level for the fund's portfolio holdings. Stock trading is expensive, and is ultimately a loser's game for investors as a group.

Fourth, candor is the central tenet of all communications to investors, the media, and the public. It's important to explain the sources of the returns of an actively managed mutual fund. No fund is immune to the vagaries of performance.

I did my best to honor these principles, never more than in the Windsor Fund Annual Report for 1990, after a fiscal year in which the Windsor return was −27.9% and the return on the S&P 500 was −7.5%. Here's how I began my letter to shareholders, "I've been writing to you for 25 years now, and this is the most difficult letter I've ever had to write." The story of the Windsor Funds is, above all, about the wisdom of staying the course.

Chapter 14

The PRIMECAP Funds

Way back in the summer of 1984, something wonderful – if sort of random – happened. It would become a highlight in Vanguard's history. I was in California interviewing prospective managers for a new growth fund that I believed we needed to balance out our value-oriented fund lineup, dominated by Windsor Fund.

By the early 1980s, Windsor – led by its peerless portfolio manager John B. Neff – came to represent fully one-half of our equity oriented fund asset base. By 1985, with assets of $4 billion and rising fast, Windsor was the nation's largest equity fund. My experience warned me that times change and styles go in and out of favor. I wanted to be prepared to act before Windsor's rapid rate of asset growth inevitably declined.

In the aftermath of the Go-Go era of the 1960s and the stock market crash of 1972–1974 that followed, many growth fund managers had faltered and then failed. I knew about that firsthand, from the catastrophic merger that I described in Chapter 2. Among the survivors, we "rounded up the usual suspects."

I visited four of them, but no obvious candidate emerged. Along the way, I learned that Mitchell J. (Mitch) Milias was working on a plan to start a new asset management firm. I had worked fairly closely with Mitch when he managed money for us at Wellington Management Company during 1969 and 1970. He then moved on, joining the giant American Funds Group in Los Angeles. When we met in mid-1984, I again found him to be a fine person, one that I could trust, and an excellent investment professional with high values.

PRIMECAP Management Is Formed

Uncomfortable with Capital's growing size, Mitch and Howard B. Schow, his co-manager of the firm's new AMCAP fund, were frustrated by Capital's process for allocating transactions among its then-huge equity funds (even larger today) and the tiny but growing AMCAP. They decided to leave Capital and, along with their colleague Theo A. Kolokotrones, start their own firm. American was startled, for their professionals *never* leave. (Or never left until then.)

The new partners named their firm PRIMECAP Management Company. On September 15, 1983, they opened an office in nearby Pasadena. PRIMECAP had gradually attracted a blue-chip list of pension clients. When I dropped in a year later, I renewed my friendship with Mitch and my acquaintance with Howie. We got along famously, and they seemed to resonate to my tentative proposal. Essentially, this was my message:

> *Vanguard understands the mutual fund business, its operations, its regulations, and its distribution requirements. We aren't interested in managing money. You understand the stock market and have proven yourselves as professional money managers. But you aren't interested in those peripheral – albeit essential – business activities. So let's start a fund together. We'll do the operations and distribution. As the fund's adviser, you'll do the investing. We'll bear all of the costs of forming and operating the fund, and it won't cost you a penny.*

They liked the idea, but wanted time to consider my offer. While Mitch was eager to do the deal, Howie was concerned that such an affiliation "was not in our business plan." He then changed his mind and told Mitch that he was on board, "only if we can trust Jack." After those earlier years on the Wellington team together, Mitch told Howie that he and I had a bond of trust that he was certain would not break. And so, without a single lawyer on either side, or a single word in writing, we made the deal.

Vanguard PRIMECAP Fund Is Formed

Vanguard PRIMECAP Fund was incorporated on August 20, 1984, with the same officers and directors as the other Vanguard funds. (Our firm's total fund assets were then $8.8 billion.) The new fund began with $100,000 of seed capital, which in those days I had to personally provide. (Legal issues precluded Vanguard's ownership of its own funds.

Wasn't I lucky!) After we had finally inked our signatures on the requisite investment advisory contract, PRIMECAP commenced investment operations on November 1, 1984.

Let's Look at the Record

PRIMECAP Fund performed well during its early years (see Exhibit 14.1). In 1984–1986, it outpaced the S&P 500's return by about 16 percentage points. Then, in 1987–1989, it faltered, underperforming the index by 25 percentage points, and leaving the fund's performance during its first seven years slightly below par. Perhaps I hadn't adequately schooled my fellow Vanguard fund directors about the inevitable ebb and flow of fund performance, for several of them urged me to terminate the advisory contract. Of course I refused to do so. (And got away with it!)

Exhibit 14.1 PRIMECAP/S&P 500 Relative Cumulative Return, 1984-2018

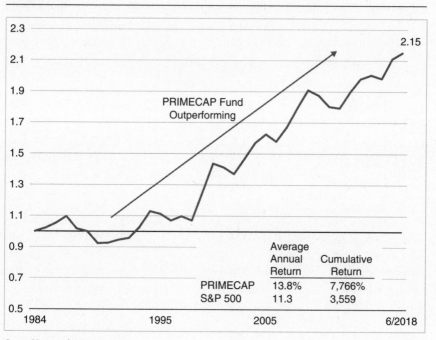

	Average Annual Return	Cumulative Return
PRIMECAP	13.8%	7,766%
S&P 500	11.3	3,559

Source: Vanguard, Morningstar.

The rest is history. During the 27-plus years that followed, these ebbs and flows of performance continued – in our profession, an inevitability. While PRIMECAP outpaced the S&P 500 in 17 of those years, it marginally lagged the S&P in the other 10 years, notably in 1996 and in 2001 and 2002, when the "New Economy" bubble burst, giving way to a major bear market. But during the fund's recovery, PRIMECAP has outpaced the S&P 500 by a remarkable margin – 17.4% annual return for the fund, 12.8% for the index.

Low Costs Account for Much of PRIMECAP's Advantage in Annual Return

The fund's low costs proved to be an advantage that has had a major impact on the fund's success. PRIMECAP's expense ratio of 0.33% in 2017 is a full percentage point below the 1.33% ratio of its peer large-cap growth funds. Vanguard's cost advantage, back then, accounted for about 40% of the annual 3.3 percentage point edge that the fund's lifetime annual return of 13.8% reflects over its peer funds (10.5%). (Almost one-half of the fund's expenses reflect Vanguard's operations efficiencies and economies; the other one-half is due to the relatively low ratio of advisory fees to the fund's assets.)[1] The magic of low-costs and long-term compounding writ large!

It took a while for the fund to attract the attention of investors. Assets didn't top $500 million until 1992. (Then, we thought that was pretty good!) Assets crossed $1 billion in 1994, and gradually grew to $22 billion in early 2001. Despite the fact that the fund has been closed to new investors since 2004,[2] thanks to good markets and good performance,

---

[1] PRIMECAP Fund's growth has resulted in a sharply declining expense ratio. Since 1990, it has fallen by one-half; from 0.75% to 0.33% in 2018. Vanguard's operating costs have fallen from 0.24% to 0.14%; PRIMECAP Management's advisory fees have fallen from 0.51% to 0.19%. While the fee *rate* may be low, the fee *dollars* are large. The advisory fees paid to PRIMECAP management for PRIMECAP, Capital Opportunity, and PRIMECAP Core funds totaled more than $191 million in 2017 alone.

[2] PRIMECAP Fund initially closed to new investors in March 1995, reopened in October 1996, and then was closed again from April 1998 through April 2001.

PRIMECAP begins its fourth decade with $65 billion of assets. Its "gold" rating from Morningstar commemorates the fund's achievement.

Vanguard's "Four Ps" in Evaluating Fund Managers

Our selection of PRIMECAP to manage Vanguard's new growth fund was more than sheer luck. PRIMECAP met my standards for selecting new advisers, which I outlined in my 1985 Chairman's Letter in the fund's first annual report and paraphrase here:

> *Developing working relationships with the principals of PRIMECAP has been an important and enjoyable part of our first year in business together. Our selection of the firm was based on these "four Ps."*
>
> 1. ***People.*** *Who are the managers of the fund? The people of PRIMECAP are outstanding investment professionals with sterling reputations borne from a total of 85 years of experience in money management.*
>
> 2. ***Philosophy.*** *What are they seeking to accomplish? The implementation of an investment philosophy with a growth orientation. [I also loved the managers' focus on the long term from 2009 to 2017. The fund's annual portfolio turnover averaged just 7% per year.]*
>
> 3. ***Portfolio.*** *How do they go about implementing their philosophy? The pension portfolios managed by PRIMECAP include a mix of blue-chip stocks, some with a growth orientation, some with generous yields, some companies deemed possible subjects of take-over bids, and some in businesses deemed interest-sensitive.*
>
> 4. ***Performance.*** *What has their record been? "Past performance" was not our first criterion, but our last. Important, yes, but only in the context of the other three factors. [I warned that there would surely be periods when PRIMECAP outpaced its peers – and periods when it did not. An obvious insight rather than a brilliant forecast!] The goal: to earn competitive long-term returns.*

These four Ps, it seems to me, have met the test of time.

PRIMECAP in Retrospect

My role as director of the fund ended on January 31, 2000. But in the years that followed, I have kept the promise that I made in the fund's 1999 Annual Report: *"I will remain vigorous and active in a newly created Vanguard unit . . . [and] will continue to keep an eagle eye on your interests as PRIMECAP Fund shareholders."*

That's what I have done, and I'm delighted – personally as a shareholder and professionally as a researcher of fund returns – that the fund's results since then have remained outstanding. In PRIMECAP's now-34-year history, the fund has outpaced the S&P 500 in 21 years and lagged in 13 years. Let these ups and downs serve as a reminder that even the best managers cannot beat the market every year. Good enough? The fund's lifetime record speaks for itself.

PRIMECAP and Vanguard Capital Opportunity Fund

In 1994, in the midst of a strong bull market, Vanguard's board encouraged me to form new equity funds with more aggressive profiles and lower relative predictability than our existing funds. I went along with that strategy; a *marketing* decision, not an *investment* decision. (I repeat: hard experience had warned me about the lack of wisdom in such a trade-off.) So in 1995, we formed Vanguard Horizon Funds, four funds with strategies whose outcomes were relatively unpredictable. Among those funds was Vanguard Capital Opportunity Fund.[3]

I selected (I cannot blame anyone but myself!) an aggressive manager, California's Husic Capital Management Company, already running a segment of Vanguard's Morgan Growth Fund, to manage the portfolio of Capital Opportunity. Husic would have a more flexible

---

[3] Capital Opportunity was one of the three Horizon Funds that survived, along with Global Equity and Strategic Equity. The fourth fund, Global Asset Allocation, went out of existence in 2001.

mandate, including the ability to sell stocks short (i.e., betting that their prices would decline). His implementation of the strategy failed. In 1997, with the S&P 500 return *plus* 33% for the year, the total return on Capital Opportunity Fund was *minus* 8%. Incredible! We terminated our relationship with Husic, and PRIMECAP accepted our offer to take over as the fund's investment adviser.[4]

The turnaround in the performance of Capital Opportunity was dramatic. During the fund's early years under Husic, its annual return of 5.4% fell well short of the 28.1% annual return of the S&P 500. Over the 20 years that have followed since PRIMECAP Management took over: Capital Opportunity, 14.1%; S&P 500, 7.1%. (Exhibit 14.2.)

Exhibit 14.2   Capital Opportunity/S&P 500 Relative Cumulative Return, 1995–2018

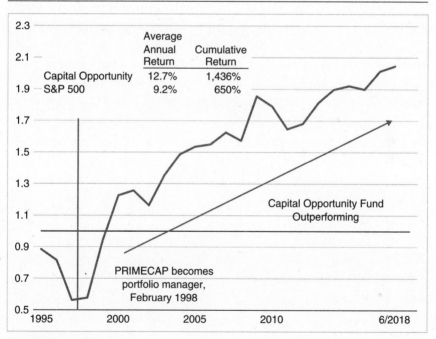

Source: Vanguard, Morningstar.

---

[4]The decision by my successor to select PRIMECAP Management delighted me.

What's to be said? Again, the four Ps paid off, earning a "gold" rating from Morningstar. When it came under the supervision of PRIMECAP management in 1997, the fund's assets were just $63 million; the assets of Capital Opportunity Fund now exceed $17 billion.

The PRIMECAP Funds Today

The three original portfolio managers of PRIMECAP Fund were Howie (now gone), Mitch (who retired as senior manager of Capital Opportunity at year-end 2013), and Theo Kolokotrones, still one of PRIMECAP's leaders. Now-seasoned investment professionals steeped in PRIMECAP's sturdy investment values were also added to the staff, including Joel Fried, Al Mordecai, and Mo Ansari. Each manages parts of both Vanguard funds. All have contributed to the success that is evident in their funds' continuing strong records.

In addition to the PRIMECAP and Capital Opportunity Funds, PRIMECAP Management also advises the Vanguard PRIMECAP Core Fund. Founded in 2004, PRIMECAP Core is yet another testament to its adviser's abilities. Since inception, the fund's annual return of 10.6% has easily outpaced the 8.4% return of the broad U.S. stock market. With just under $11 billion in assets, the fund has been closed to new investors since mid-2009.

Summing Up

As Vanguard's assets have grown – from some $9 billion when PRIMECAP first came on board in 1984 to $5 trillion today, much has changed. But it is no accident that the PRIMECAP funds have remained relatively modest in assets. By mutual agreement, we closed both PRIMECAP and Capital Opportunity to new investors, essentially eliminating inflows of additional assets to manage. Once again, as in Windsor Fund's earlier case, "why kill the goose that laid the golden egg?" Better to control asset size and preserve the flexibility of the portfolio managers who are responsible for the two PRIMECAP portfolios.

Beginning in those ancient days, we operated on strict principles of fiduciary duty to our shareholders – who represent our sole responsibility – and made our commitments with a bond of trust. Among the best parts of those "good old days" is exemplified by Vanguard PRIMECAP Fund and, later on, Vanguard Capital Opportunity Fund.

The partners who became trusted friends in that unlikely 1984 venture have surely prospered. PRIMECAP Management – a relatively small and manageable unit in a giant fund complex – has well earned its subsequent advisory fees by producing the extraordinary returns that these funds have delivered to the shareholders who placed their trust in us. The firm has added luster to Vanguard's reputation in actively managed funds.

Of course, Vanguard has changed. So has PRIMECAP. But lest I commit the apparent sin of "nostalgia," so has the investment profession changed; so has the financial system; so has the nation; so has the world and almost everything that's in it. But as long as we honor our proud past and continue to maintain our investment strategy and human values, Vanguard will continue to stand tallest among our peers for as far ahead as we can imagine.

Chapter 15

The Bond Funds

D uring its formative years, the mutual fund industry was virtually bereft of bond funds. But almost from my first day on the job at Wellington in July 1951, I was indoctrinated in the Wellington Fund philosophy of balance: bonds for income and risk reduction, stocks for capital appreciation. I totally bought into it.

In those days, bond funds were but a tiny factor in the fund industry. In 1960, there were but 12 bond funds among the industry's 161 mutual funds, representing just 6% of total fund assets. And by 1970, there was no longer a category for bond funds in the Wiesenberger Investment Companies annual publication, then the primary source of mutual fund data. But I was a contrarian, and when I became CEO of Wellington Management Company in 1965, I couldn't shake the idea of adding a bond fund to Wellington's conservative menu.

As a contrarian, my conviction was reinforced when a sassy new magazine, *Institutional Investor*, ran a story in May 1969 slamming bonds. It was a cover story, illustrated with a drawing of enormous dinosaurs. The title: "Can the Bond Market Survive?" It would be hard to miss the message!

Yet my conservative bent was hardly in evidence with my 1966 decision to merge industry giant Wellington Management Company with a small new Boston investment adviser, Thorndike, Doran, Paine, & Lewis, Inc. Its four partners ran the aggressive Ivest Fund, one of the stars of the short-lived Go-Go era described in Chapter 3. Ivest proved to be a meteor – it lit up the sky for a short moment and then burned out, its ashes floating gently down to earth.

1970: "Bonds Are Yesterday, Stocks Are Tomorrow"?

My new partners at Ivest *hated* bonds. When I proposed forming a bond fund in 1970, one of them quickly put the kibosh on the idea: *"Don't you realize that bonds are yesterday? Stocks are tomorrow."* This was shortly before the 50% market crash of 1972–1974. But I finally persuaded my colleagues to form an income fund, 60% bonds and 40% dividend-paying stocks. It proved to be a durable idea. Almost half a century later, in 2018, assets of Vanguard Wellesley Income Fund total $54 billion.

Then times changed – a little! We formed our first "pure" bond fund in July 1973 – now Vanguard Long-Term Investment Grade Fund – the first step in our gradual rise to overwhelming dominance in the bond fund sector of our industry.

At Vanguard's birth in 1974, our fund directors had barred Vanguard from providing investment advisory services to our funds, leaving that key task to Wellington Management Company. But as CEO, my job specifically included the responsibility of evaluating the investment performance of the funds managed by their adviser – yes, the very firm that had fired me only a few months earlier (see Chapter 3). That provision precipitated the creation of what would come to be our bond fund dynasty.

Municipal Bond Funds: The Door Swings Ajar

By September 1974, we were on our own. Fortunately, a door opened just a crack, and gave the new Vanguard an unexpected opportunity to pursue my interest in bond funds. In 1976, Congress passed legislation that allowed mutual funds to "pass through" municipal bond interest income to their shareholders free of income tax. Municipal bond funds quickly came into being as a new investment category, a permanent factor in our industry.

The first funds were "managed" municipal bond funds. As I explained in Chapter 5, they were run by portfolio managers with no limits on their ability to lengthen or shorten the maturity profiles of their portfolios, depending only on their view of market conditions. I simply couldn't imagine that these experts – or anyone else – could successfully time interest rate changes, which are the principle determinant of bond prices. (It was this same skepticism that led to my creation of the first stock index fund two years earlier.)

So – of course! – Vanguard took a different approach. We formed a series of three separate "defined-maturity" bond funds – long-term, intermediate-term, and short-term.[1] Each would hold to its particular mandate. With each series focused, *not* on shifting maturities but on strong credit quality, investors could decide for themselves what combination of risk and yield would best meet their financial goals.

The Door Opens Wide: Vanguard Becomes a Bond Fund Manager

Our innovative solution gave Vanguard a large competitive edge. By sorting the bond funds into three maturities, much of the "noise" in the performance of "managed" municipal bonds would be muted. When the comparative performance of such funds was sorted by maturities, the lowest-cost funds would be bound to win.

Given Vanguard's mutual structure and our rock-bottom costs, focusing on our bond funds with clearly defined maturities was the obvious strategy. Vanguard quietly became the fund industry's lowest-cost provider of bond funds.

To develop this strategy to its full potential, Vanguard needed to control the kinds of bond funds we would offer and to assume direct responsibility for their performance. It was high time for Vanguard to become the investment adviser to our municipal bond and money market funds, then run by Citibank N.A., and Wellington Management Company, respectively.

---

[1] In addition to the long-, intermediate-, and short-term municipal bond funds, Vanguard also offers a high-yield tax-exempt fund and a limited-term tax-exempt fund. Vanguard also manages seven state-specific defined-maturity tax-exempt funds.

So our next step was to eliminate that early provision that barred Vanguard from taking direct responsibility for the investment management of any of our funds. Fixed income funds – bond funds and money market funds – offered a great opportunity for Vanguard to get into active investment management. We waited until circumstances made that giant step possible.

Managing Vanguard's Fixed Income Funds

If the simple decision to create the first defined-maturity bond funds could be described as "brilliant," my choice of an external manager to run the new mutual funds was quite the opposite. We selected giant Citibank as the adviser to the funds. Alas, the bank's investment group was simply not up to the task. As 1980 began, Vanguard determined to terminate the relationship.

At the same time, our large ($420 million) money market funds were paying high fees to their then-manager, Wellington Management Company. This was the moment, I thought, to recommend to the Vanguard Board a giant step: having Vanguard replace Citi as manager of our municipal bond funds and replace Wellington as manager of our money market funds.[2] Simultaneously, Vanguard would build its own in-house management staff. This combination would give us "critical mass" for providing economies of scale.

The board meeting to discuss this sea change in Vanguard's charter was held in September 1980. It was contentious. On the one hand, given its erratic performance, replacing Citibank as adviser to the municipal bond funds was a nonissue. On the other hand, despite the savings generated for many of our shareholders, the dissolution of our relationship with Wellington brought forth old prejudices. Further, the retention of a new staff of bond professionals at Vanguard carried its own risks.

---

[2] We had arguably "broken the ice" in acting as an investment adviser to mutual funds when we created Vanguard S&P 500 Index Fund in 1975. Or not.

Vanguard Becomes a Fully Functioning Fund Complex

In the end, my recommendation to form an internal adviser to our bond funds, named Vanguard Fixed Income Group, carried the day, another important step in the expansion of Vanguard's responsibilities. As 1980 ended, we had become a fully functioning mutual fund complex, responsible for the administration and distribution services for all of our funds and investment management services for many of them. We also determined to apply the defined-maturity concept to our new taxable bond funds, and have our newly formed in-house staff manage them.

Enter the Bond Index Fund

The first leader of our new Fixed Income Group was Ian A. MacKinnon, whom I hired from Philadelphia's Girard Bank. I personally participated in Ian's regular monthly staff meetings. My oversight gave me confidence that this small group of experienced money management professionals could handle even more responsibilities. By then it was 1986, and I was certain that we could successfully run an index fund that would track the broad U.S. bond market.

The creation of Vanguard Total Bond Market Index Fund was yet another innovation that would come to dominate the world of fixed income investing. In mid-2018, the assets of its two (substantially identical) components – Total Bond Market Index and Total Bond Market Index II – total $355 billion, making it by far the world's largest bond fund. With a total of $1 trillion in its bond fund line-up, Vanguard is now the world's largest manager of fixed income mutual funds.

Vanguard: The Dominant Bond Manager

The addition of the bond index fund to Vanguard's internally managed asset base was followed by our creation of seven major additions to our menu of bond funds: three Admiral (lowest-cost) U.S. Treasury funds in 1991; the Intermediate-Term Investment-Grade (taxable) Fund in 1993; and Short-Term, Intermediate-Term, and Long-Term Bond Index Funds in 1994. This new wave of seven funds grew slowly but surely, with aggregate assets of $145 billion in early 2018.

Vanguard manages some $150 billion of bonds held in our balanced funds-of-funds, our LifeStrategy Funds and our Target Retirement Funds. We also manage more than $220 billion in money market fund assets. Together, Vanguard funds represent by far the largest aggregation of fixed-income mutual fund assets in the industry (see Exhibit 15.1).

Industry Leadership

Together, it is this combination of bond market index funds and their defined-maturity cousins (and, of course, our rock-bottom costs) that have brought Vanguard to its leadership in the bond fund arena (see Exhibit 15.2): from a mere 4% of bond mutual fund assets three decades ago, to 13% in 2005, to 23% today, a higher share than our three largest competitors combined.

Exhibit 15.1 Vanguard's Market Share of Bond Mutual Fund Assets, 1974-2018

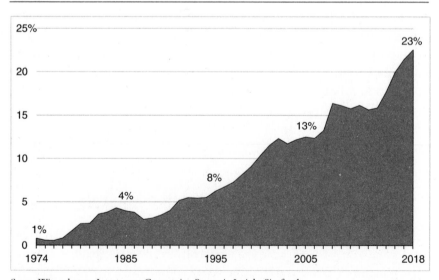

Source: Wiesenberger Investment Companies, Strategic Insight Simfund.

Exhibit 15.2   Managers of Bond Mutual Funds, Mid–2018

	Firm	Assets ($Bil)	Market Share
1	The Vanguard Group	1,041	23%
2	BlackRock	418	9
3	PIMCO	329	7
4	Fidelity	285	6
5	American Funds	146	3
6	Franklin Templeton	134	3
7	T. Rowe Price	115	2
8	Nuveen	110	2
9	JPMorgan Funds	104	2
10	Lord Abbett	99	2
	Other	1,833	40
	Total	4,612	100%

Over time, investors' perceptions of bond funds changed. The defined-maturity three-tier (or more!) approach became the industry standard. In mid-2018, all of Vanguard's original municipal bond funds are ranked among the industry's ten largest. Vanguard's taxable bond funds also follow the defined maturity strategy that we pioneered in 1977.

The Role of Bond Index Funds

What is the source of Vanguard's dominance in bond funds? The record is clear that it comes from a combination of the low costs that characterize all of Vanguard's funds, and our heavy reliance on bond indexing strategies. About 24% of all bond mutual assets are now indexed. Vanguard dominates this index sector, accounting for 58% of bond index fund assets, while BlackRock, the second largest bond fund manager, oversees 24% of bond index fund assets.

Lower Costs Equal Higher Yields

Our huge expense ratio advantage – engendered in part by the indexing strategy and in part by Vanguard's mutual structure – accounts for much of Vanguard's success (see Exhibit 15.3): the annual expense ratios of Vanguard's bond funds now average just 0.17%, some 40% below our closest competitor (0.27%), and 80% (!) below the industry norm of 0.87%.

Exhibit 15.3   Bond Mutual Fund Expense Ratios, 2017

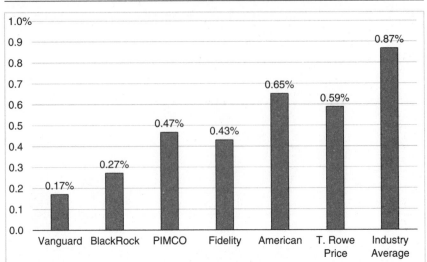

Source: Morningstar.

Other things held equal (as they pretty much are in a world of defined-maturity bond funds), lower fund expenses generate higher income yield to fund investors. The remarkably higher yields of Vanguard's bond funds, so critical for bond investors, are driven largely by our huge expense ratio advantage. Further, the absence of sales loads on our funds makes them far more attractive to individual investors in bond funds and corporate thrift plans, whose administrators have no interest in having company employees incur the unnecessary drag of sales loads.

"It's the Extra Yield, Stupid"

First, consider fund expense ratios (annual expenses as percentage of fund assets) for bond index funds versus actively managed bond funds.[3] Not

---

[3] Vanguard's actively managed bond funds carry expense ratios much lower than the industry average – even those that are managed by outside managers. For example, Vanguard GNMA Fund, with $25 billion in assets, carries an expense ratio of 0.14%. It is managed by Wellington Management Company for an advisory fee of a mere 0.01%. Don't cry for Wellington. In 2017, the firm was paid $2.5 million for its advisory services to GNMA Fund, and a total of $57.5 million for managing its $140 billion of Vanguard's bond fund assets.

Exhibit 15.4   Bond Fund Yields and Expense Ratios, 2018

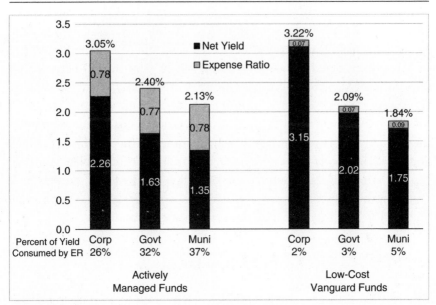

Source: Morningstar.

merely the yield differential itself, but the huge percentage of portfolio yield that is confiscated by the expenses borne by investors in actively managed bond funds.

Let's examine these differences in three bond categories. The income yield on the average active corporate bond fund – (see Exhibit 15.4) – comes with expenses of 0.78%, consuming 26% of the gross yield of 3.05%, leaving an actual net yield of 2.26%. Compare that outcome with Vanguard's corporate bond index fund: gross yield, 3.22%; expense ratio, 0.07%, consuming barely 2% of gross yield. Net yield, 3.15%: 35% (!) higher than the active corporate bond fund.

Similarly, actively managed government bond funds consume 32% of income versus 3% for the low-cost funds. For active municipals, 37% of income consumed versus 5% for the low-cost funds. Just imagine increasing an investor's net yield from 2.26 to 3.15% (corporates), or from 1.63 to 2.02% (U.S. governments), or from 1.35 to 1.75% (tax-exempt municipals) – *with no increase in risk.* Only a foolish investor would ignore the issue of fund costs.

The Drag of Sales Loads

Sales loads are another important factor. While nearly all bond *index* funds are available solely on a "no-load" basis, fully 2,300 share classes(!) of actively managed bond funds are available only by the payment of sales commissions to brokers and investment advisers. Today, those loads run in the range of 1 to 4% for bond funds, averaging about 2.5%. How much is 2.5%, you ask? Well, if you pay such a load, you relinquish more than your entire net investment income during the first year that you hold the fund's shares. There is no rational need for that sacrifice. Finally, were fiduciary duty to become the standard for mutual fund managers and distributors, we might see a sharp decrease – or even elimination – of many of the sales loads on bond funds.

Fiduciary Duty

Mutual fund managers and fund directors have a fiduciary duty to put the interests of investors first. But when fund expenses are consuming as much as 37% of a bond fund's yield and comparable index funds are consuming as little as 2%, we have no choice but to ask ourselves: "Have the fund directors who approved the advisory contracts that result in such confis-cation breached their fiduciary duty to shareholders? Have fund sponsors who distribute such funds violated their fiduciary duty? Have brokers who sell such funds to their clients failed to place their client's interests first?" It is high time for industry participants to examine the issue of the excessive fund costs that confiscate such mammoth portions of the invest-ment income earned on the vast majority of active bond funds.

The Future of Bonds . . . and Bond Funds

Most of today's bond investors have experienced only the sharp and unremitting drop in bond fund yields – and the corollary rise in bond prices – that has occurred over the past 35-plus years. The yield on the Bloomberg Barclays Aggregate Bond Index has plummeted from 14.6% at the close of 1981 (incredible) to 3.3% today, a decline of an incredible 83% (see Exhibit 15.5).

Exhibit 15.5 Bloomberg Barclays Aggregate Bond Index Yield, 1976–2018

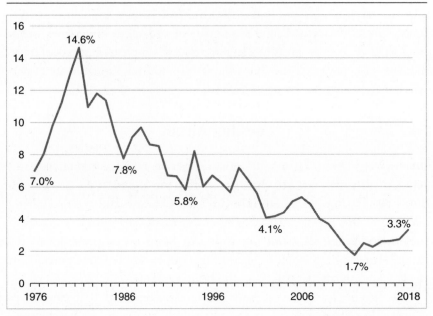

Source: Morningstar.

Today's low rates have led some experts to say that we're in a bond fund bubble, one that will soon burst and send yields soaring and prices tumbling. Since anything can happen in the financial markets, these predictions may or may not prove correct. But I believe that bursting bubbles are a concern largely for short-term speculators in bond prices, not long-term investors planning for their financial futures.

After all, if an investor purchases a 30-year U.S. Treasury bond paying an annual coupon of 3%, for the next three decades, that investor has made a bargain that will be honored – no bubble there! The investor will receive semiannual interest payments on schedule and will get the face value of the bond when it matures.

For the vast majority of investors, bonds should be bought and held for the long term, balancing relative price stability (short-term bonds) and high income (long-term bonds), rather than trading bonds in a vain attempt to capitalize on momentary fluctuations in market price.

Despite the current low interest rate environment, bond mutual funds have flourished. In 2017, cash flow into bond funds totaled some $335 billion, with about 50% of that total ($162 billion) invested in bond index funds. Given the remarkable advantages of Vanguard's long-time index fund strategy – lower costs, no sales loads, less confiscation of investment income – I believe that the index share of bond fund cash flow and assets will not only continue its historical rise, but even accelerate.

Looking Ahead

Of course interest rates will remain volatile and unpredictable, and bond quality will be key. But given the remarkable cost advantages based on its simple mutual, investor-first structure and the staggering economies of scale the firm has achieved for its shareholders, I see no reason that Vanguard cannot continue to build on its present base, to lead the field in the bond fund industry, and to be an active participant in the issues of the day affecting the bond market.

I'm no Pollyanna. As I look ahead, I understand that times will change. Believing that the future will closely resemble the past ("presentism") and ignoring the inevitable uncertainty of investing – and of life – is to forget the lessons of history. We'll talk more about that in Part III.

Chapter 16
Problems and Perspectives

C hapters 11 through 15 – the Vanguard fund histories – were focused, broadly speaking, on the oldest and largest of our funds, survivors that have had strong concepts and strong records of serving investors. But I do not want to leave the impression that decisions regarding fund strategies and adviser selections are either easy or assured of success.

Earlier in the book, I candidly confessed to the errors I made in creating Vanguard Specialized Portfolios (1984) and the Vanguard Horizon Funds (1995). These two examples attest to the reality that making investment decisions for marketing reasons is all too likely to ill-serve the investors who entrust their assets to the funds. Eventually, these decisions also ill-serve the managers that made them, for investors who are disappointed – even angry – are not likely to stick around forever.

But some of the failures in our funds have come only after many years – or even decades – of successful operations, less from flawed premises than from flawed implementation. I'm going to close this series of Vanguard fund histories with a capsule analysis of two such funds: Vanguard U.S. Growth Fund and Vanguard Asset Allocation Fund. Then I'll discuss Vanguard Growth Equity Fund, a fund with more opportunistic roots, a victim of (let's be honest) terrible timing.

Vanguard U.S. Growth Fund

Our U.S. Growth Fund began as Ivest Fund in 1959, created by my former Boston partners. It soared in the 1960s, then collapsed in the 1970s. In 1982, we separated Ivest into two portfolios, Vanguard U.S. Growth Fund and Vanguard International Growth Fund. Both funds would soon terminate their advisory contracts with Wellington Management Company and would retain new investment advisers.

We made wise choices for both. The adviser selected for U.S. Growth was Lincoln Capital Management, a Chicago-based manager with an experienced professional staff. Lincoln assumed responsibility on August 31, 1987, just six weeks before the stock market crashed on Black Monday, October 19, 1987. On that single day, the S&P 500 dropped 23%. But J. Parker Hall, Lincoln's leader, an industry legend, and the new portfolio manager, was unflappable. With his career-long focus on growth stocks, he had seen high volatility before.

From the time they took over the fund in mid-1987, Parker Hall and his team at Lincoln Capital Management built a fine record. U.S. Growth's return averaged 17.1% annually versus 15.6% for the S&P 500 through mid-2000, an impressive 14-year run. During Lincoln's tenure, the fund's assets increased from $150 million to $19 billion. But then it began to slip away.

Parker Hall retired in mid-2001, in the midst of the collapse of the information-age stocks of the New Economy, as all hell broke loose in the stock market. From its high in August 2000 to Lincoln's removal as the fund's adviser in June 2001, the S&P 500 dropped 14% while the U.S. Growth Fund fell by more than 44%.

The New Adviser Fails

I was no longer Vanguard's CEO when the problem began for U.S. Growth or when we switched advisers. But the record shows that in June 2001, Vanguard replaced Lincoln Capital with a new adviser, Alliance Capital Management. The fund's struggles continued under the new manager. As it happens, just as the firm was assuming its responsibilities, I met the new manager, Alliance's John Blundin.

At a reception in West Palm Beach, Florida, before I made an evening speech there, we had a curious exchange. John said, "I hear that you don't think that I can beat the S&P 500." I replied, tactfully,

"That would be a tough task for anyone." He answered, nicely enough, "Haven't you seen my past record?" (I knew only that he had been a star manager.)

After the change in advisers, things promptly got even worse for the shareholders of U.S. Growth. From the 2001 high through the low in 2002, the cumulative return on the U.S. Growth Fund was −70%, far worse than the −40% decline in the S&P 500.

In 2010, we terminated the advisory agreement with Alliance. Since then, U.S. Growth has followed a multimanager strategy, with William Blair Investment Management, Baillie Gifford Overseas, Jenison Associates, Jackson Square Partners, and Wellington Management Company each managing separate portions of the portfolio. Since 2010, annual returns for U.S. Growth Fund have averaged 18.7%, well ahead of both the S&P 500 (16.4%) and the average large-cap growth fund (16.7%).

Here are three lessons to take away from this example: (1) Good investment managers don't ply their trade successfully forever. (2) When a manager's strategy fails, hope for good luck when you select a successor. (3) Don't be fooled into believing that a manager's past performance is prologue to the future. (4) The multimanager strategy has generally worked well for the Vanguard funds that employ it, but is no panacea. *There are no panaceas.*

Exhibit 16.1 illustrates the relative cumulative performance of the U.S. Growth Fund versus the S&P 500. Essentially, we invest $1 into each portfolio in 1961 and calculate the cumulative return of both the U.S. Growth Fund and the S&P 500 Index. We then divide the S&P return into the fund's return. When the line is rising, the fund is outperforming the index, and vice versa. I call this sort of chart my 1/1 ("one over one") chart. I've found it extremely useful in evaluating the long-term success or failure of a mutual fund.

To have accumulated a cumulative return of 11,990% over 57 years in the fund versus a return of 20,269% for the S&P 500 is hardly likely to please its owners. (I've seen few charts with a relative return of 0.64 or below.) Perhaps even more striking is the exhibit's illustration of reversion to the mean (RTM). During the Go-Go era of the late 1960s and early 1970s, the then–Ivest Fund flew high, almost doubling the cumulative

Exhibit 16.1   U.S. Growth/S&P 500 Relative Cumulative Returns, 1961–2018

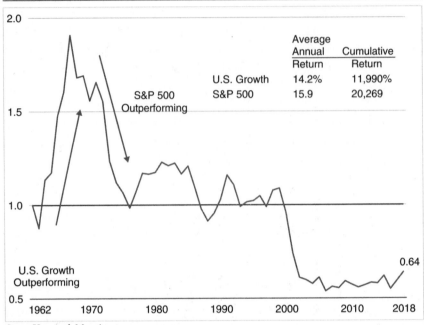

	Average Annual Return	Cumulative Return
U.S. Growth	14.2%	11,990%
S&P 500	15.9	20,269

Source: Vanguard, Morningstar.

performance of the index. But then RTM – and much worse – struck in the 1973–1974 bear market, and the fund badly underperformed.

Two more medium-term cycles of modest outperformance followed by underperformance preceded a disaster for the fund's investors. In the wake of the early-2000s bear market, the fund sank like a stone. Since then, Vanguard U.S. Growth Fund has stayed a bit ahead of the S&P 500, with no significant stretches of over- or underperformance.

Vanguard Asset Allocation Fund

My creation of Vanguard Asset Allocation Fund almost didn't happen. I was impressed with the extended record of legendary quantitative investor William L. Fouse and the firm he founded, Mellon Capital Management, and I was eager to retain Mellon as the investment adviser to a new asset allocation fund.

The fund's mandate would give its adviser complete discretion over tactical asset allocation – that is, the fund could change its mix of stocks and bonds depending on the adviser's convictions about future market returns. Several of Vanguard's directors were deeply skeptical of the idea that such a fund could prove successful over the long-term. Nevertheless, the board reluctantly approved the fund. Asset Allocation Fund began operations on November 3, 1988.

In essence, Asset Allocation Fund's default allocation was 60% equities (S&P 500 Index), with 40% in U.S. Treasury Bonds. Using a methodology based largely on the spread between the Treasury bond yield and the earnings yield on the S&P 500, Mellon would raise and lower the fund's equity ratio. Our comparative standard for evaluating the success of this fund was the return on a balanced portfolio with a fixed allocation ratio, 60% S&P 500 Index and 40% U.S. Aggregate Bond Index.

Such a relative yield methodology may seem too simple to produce consistent excess returns. But my, how well it worked! For almost two decades, from 1989 through 2007, Vanguard Asset Allocation Fund earned an annual return of 11.2%, a solid margin over the 10.0% return of its fixed-allocation 60/40 baseline. As 2007 ended, the fund's assets reached $11.6 billion.

It Worked … Until It Didn't

Then, abruptly, Mellon's approach stopped working. At the close of 2007, just as a 50% decline from the stock market's then-all-time high was about to begin, 100% of its portfolio was invested in equities. As I was no longer running Vanguard, I am in no position to explain how that could have happened.

In 2008, the fund's return was −36.3%, a far greater loss than the −22.2% decline in the balanced index standard. Asset Allocation then failed to recover much of that lost ground during 2009 and 2010. Over the full four years, from 2007 to 2011, the fund's cumulative return was *minus* 13.7% versus the *plus* 10.0% return on its balanced index target. By the time 2012 began, the fund's assets had tumbled to less than $2 billion, and Vanguard's management decided to merge the fund into our Vanguard Balanced Index Fund, with its fixed 60/40 stock/bond ratio.

Exhibit 16.2   Asset Allocation/Balanced Index Relative Cumulative
Returns, 1989–2011

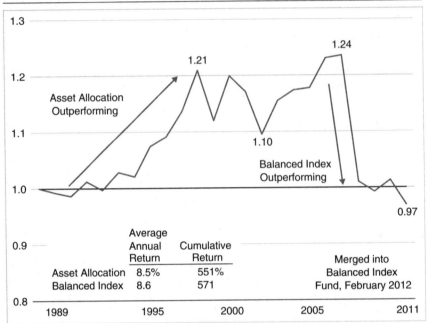

	Average Annual Return	Cumulative Return
Asset Allocation	8.5%	551%
Balanced Index	8.6	571

Merged into Balanced Index Fund, February 2012

Source: Vanguard, Morningstar.

As you can see from the one-over-one chart, the cumulative lifetime return of Asset Allocation Fund was almost exactly identical to the return of the 60/40 stock/bond Balanced Index Fund.[1] (That 0.97 figure at the bottom right is close to the 1.0 that would represent a perfect match.) But what a ride: way up through 1996, then two downs, then up again through 2006. Then the deluge. Mellon's strategy had stopped working, and the fund was finally merged into Vanguard Balanced Index Fund in early 2012.

Vanguard Growth Equity Fund

I accept my responsibility as the creator of the "new" Vanguard U.S. Growth Fund in 1983 and the Vanguard Asset Allocation Fund in 1988, but in 1996 they became the responsibility of my successors

---

[1] Balanced Index Fund's annual returns prior to its formation in 1993 are calculated on the basis of its 60/40 tracking standard.

at Vanguard. But I played no role in the adoption of Growth Equity Fund. Vanguard announced this event immediately following the stock market's peak in March 2000. My tenure as Vanguard CEO had ended four years earlier.

Vanguard Growth Equity began its life in 1992 as Turner Growth Equity Fund. It had been founded by its adviser, Turner Investment Partners. Before becoming part of Vanguard, the fund had built a remarkable record of annual returns, averaging 23.4%, far ahead of the 19.4% annual return of the S&P 500 Index.

Under Turner's management, the fund focused largely on technology stocks, riding the wave of the New Economy bubble in the stock market. But its asset base had remained small, just $200 million as 1999 came to a close. Vanguard proposed to bring the fund into its family, have it overseen by our firm's directors and our Portfolio Review Group, and continue to employ Turner as the fund's adviser.

The Past Was Not Prologue

The idea, apparently, was to build a much larger fund by capitalizing on Turner's past record. We were smart enough not to identify it as what it was – one more information-age fund that jumped on the fad of the day. When the tech bubble burst, Growth Equity tumbled.

During the first few months after adopting the fund, hundreds of millions of dollars poured in each month from performance-seeking investors (and speculators). Assets rose from $200 million at the close of 1999 to just under $1 billion in early 2001.

But the hopes of these opportunistic investors went unfulfilled, and the reputation of both Turner and Vanguard were tarnished. From 2000 to the market's low in early 2003, the fund's cumulative return was −61%, versus −38% for the S&P 500. Such a failure for our investors was simply intolerable.

By the close of 2002, the fund's assets had dwindled to $540 million. From there, they would again rise to $1.2 billion by the end of 2007 (largely as a result of the rising stock market), only to fall to $500 million when the S&P 500 experienced yet another 50% decline. By this time, the fund's performance was closely tracking the S&P 500,

Exhibit 16.3 Growth Equity Fund/S&P 500 Relative Cumulative Returns, 1992–2014

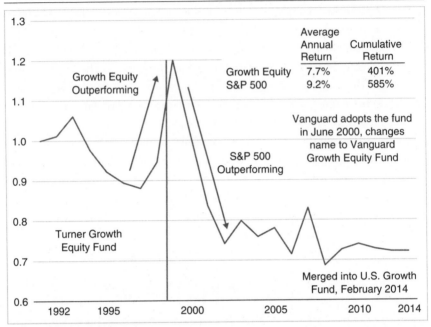

	Average Annual Return	Cumulative Return
Growth Equity	7.7%	401%
S&P 500	9.2%	585%

Source: Vanguard, Morningstar.

a far different approach than when it was originally acquired by Vanguard. The life of Vanguard Growth Equity came to an end on February 24, 2014, when it was merged into Vanguard U.S. Growth Fund.

As you can see from the one-over-one chart, Growth Equity Fund had a burst of strong outperformance during the New Economy bull market. But that performance went as quickly as it came, beginning just as Vanguard's adoption of the Turner Fund took place. The fund's performance never really got back on track.

Three Sad Stories, Three Challenged Funds

I need say only one more thing about my decisions on the selection of advisers for our U.S. Growth and Asset Allocation Funds, and the decision made by my successors by acquiring Growth Equity: *"This is a hard business."* Sometimes, as Tolstoy told us, "even the best generals make mistakes." But perhaps some mistakes can be avoided by adopting the following seven strategies: (1) a little more judgment; (2) a more thorough review of the holdings in a fund's investment portfolio; (3) an awareness that most funds outlive their managers; (4) the wisdom to understand that good marketing decisions are rarely good investment decisions; (5) that past performance means little in producing future returns; (6) "he who lives by the sword, dies by the sword." And yes, (7) that "relative predictably" is important, too. As always, understanding the past can keep us from making similar mistakes in the future.

I think it's fair to note that investors can successfully resolve each of the seven caveats just listed by the use of traditional index funds such as those tracking the S&P 500. During Vanguard's near half-century of existence, that is what I've been saying consistently. Simple it may be, but it has worked for the benefit of our investor/owners, and for our firm.

A Changing Asset Base

One more thing. As you read these histories, you may have noticed how the business of Vanguard and its predecessor Wellington Management has been dominated by a whole succession of distinct investment approaches. For example, 100% of our asset base in a single balanced fund from 1928 through 1958, only 4% of Vanguard's assets in actively managed balanced funds in 2018.

The percentage of Vanguard's assets in actively managed equity funds peaked in 1979 at 45%; only 9% in 2018. Active bond funds peaked in 1986 at 39%; 9% in 2018. In 1990, money market funds peaked at 39% of assets; 5% in 2018. Index funds are now Vanguard's largest class of investments, representing 74% of our total assets, up from zero in 1975.

Exhibit 16.4   Vanguard Asset Mix, 2018

Category	Peak Share of Vanguard Assets (Year)	Current Share of Vanguard Assets
Active Balanced	100% (1929–1957)	4%
Active Equity	45 (1979)	9
Active Bond	39 (1986)	9
Money Market	39 (1990)	5
Index Funds	74 (2018)	74

Source: Wiesenberger Investment Companies, Strategic Insight Simfund.

It took until 1990 for index funds to reach even 6% of Vanguard's asset base. Our early forays into different strategies and different "products" kept the firm alive until our early index strategy finally paid off. I see no reason that the 74% share of our assets in index funds will do anything other than increase during the era that lies ahead.

Of course Vanguard and our index funds will face stern challenges in the coming era. As stock valuations today are higher than historical norms, investors who are counting on historical rates of return to repeat are likely bound to be disappointed. Further, index fund assets are concentrated in just three firms – Vanguard, BlackRock, and State Street – and their burgeoning share of corporate ownership will doubtless be challenged. I describe some of these challenges in Part III, "The Future of Investment Management."

Part III
The Future of Investment Management

While in Parts I and II I focused on the history of Vanguard and our major funds, I take a different approach to Part III. In this section, I'll talk about the future of investment management. From a small number of boutique firms offering diversified portfolios of blue-chip securities, to the Go-Go era of high-flying stocks; to the rise of the money market fund, to the cult-of-personality era of star fund managers, to the index revolution initiated first by the traditional index fund (TIF) and then by the exchange-traded index fund (ETF), the history of the mutual fund industry is one of constant change. For better or for worse, that process of change is unlikely to cease during the years ahead.

In Part III, I'm going to make some predictions about three major challenges that the profession of investment management may face in the future. In Chapter 17, I'll discuss the need for the major firms in the mutual fund industry to "mutualize" so that they will finally place the interests of fund shareholders as their highest priority.

In Chapter 18, I'll focus on the battle to preserve broad-market S&P 500–like index funds from misguided academics whose work threatens their very existence, and the implications of the present dominance of index funds as corporate owners.

Finally, in Chapter 19, I anticipate the likelihood of new federal legislation largely affecting the mutual fund industry but also impacting existing institutional money managers of all types. I'll call this potential statute "The Financial Institutions Act of 2030," with that year being an arbitrary choice on my part. It would replace the antiquated Investment Company Act of 1940, which was designed largely to regulate the behavior of managers of "closed-end" funds, investment companies that barely exist today. The 1940 Act (inevitably) ignored many of the challenging issues facing the field of money managers today, including the implications of the present dominance of index funds as corporate owners. I'll close Chapter 19 by discussing several other important emerging issues, and, with a flourish, explain how all three chapters of Part III are united by a single theme: placing investors first.

Chapter 17
The Fund Industry Becomes Mutual

The Mutual Fund Industry: 1951 and 2018

The final sentence of my 1951 Princeton senior thesis is as good a place as any to begin this section:

> The [mutual fund] can realize its optimum economic role by the exercise of its dual function: to contribute to the growth of the economy, and to enable individual as well as institutional investors to have a share in this growth.

As we now know, the tiny $2.5 billion mutual fund industry that I studied in 1950–1951 has become a $20 trillion colossus. Mutual funds hold some 30% of the aggregate voting stock of U.S. corporations, vastly above our 1% ownership share in 1951. Thanks to the powerful secular rise in stock values that arguably began immediately following World War II, the fund industry has achieved quantum growth. Despite this growth, mutual funds as a group have failed to adequately fulfill their implicit promise to provide investors with an optimal share of the growth in the economy and the value of our public corporations. A share, yes, but not a fair share.

The Failure to Add Value

Almost a century has now passed since 1924, when the first U.S. mutual fund was incorporated. Yet only during the past several decades have investors come to fully embrace the truth that Vanguard holds self-evident: *Stock returns are ultimately created by corporations, and the financial system subtracts value from those returns.*

To reiterate, rather than wearing the royal clothes of market-beating professional management, the mutual fund emperor is wearing no clothes at all. In fact, it isn't only the mutual fund emperor who is naked, it is virtually the entire mutual fund empire. The returns earned for fund shareholders have been dragged down by excessive costs, making the industry unable to deliver on its implicit promise.

The concept that fund managers as a group could not add value to the wealth of their clients, once considered nearly heretical, is now broadly accepted. It has led to a disruptive revolution in the mutual fund industry, largely driven by the rise of index funds. The index revolution, in turn, has been led by Vanguard.

An Endorsement from Paul Volcker

I am hardly alone in fostering this heretical concept. It is also the opinion of one of our nation's greatest financial leaders of all time, Paul A. Volcker, chairman of the Federal Reserve Board from 1979 to 1987:

> *Over time, the stress on the value of index funds responded to the clear logic — a logic fully supported by the plain evidence — that most "active" money managers most of the time will not be able to "beat" the market. These days, after all, mutual funds largely are the market. On the average, they couldn't do better, even if they had no costs, operated with perfect efficiency, and incurred no taxes. With those hurdles to jump, very few funds can consistently outperform the averages.*

> *That's not an easy conclusion for money managers to accept. John Bogle has not won many popularity contests among his professional colleagues. Moreover, he himself would readily confess that the unique form of governance and style of management that he instilled in Vanguard is not easy to replicate.*

> *All of us dependent on mutual funds or other collective investment institutions to manage our savings, and that is most of us, owe thanks to John Bogle for insisting that our interests be placed front and center.[1]*

---

[1] Excerpted from Paul Volcker, foreword to *John Bogle on Investing: The First 50 Years* (Hoboken, NJ: Wiley, 2001).

An Absurd Structure

Paul Volcker's final sentence sets the stage for my consistent insistence that the interests of fund investors must "be placed front and center." To me, that means that mutual funds should be truly "mutual," owned and controlled by their own shareholders. With the single exception of Vanguard, that is nowhere the case today.

Vanguard is the only mutual fund complex in which the funds manage their own affairs. All other mutual funds contract with external corporations of one of these three types: (1) privately owned, (2) publicly owned, or (3) owned by domestic or foreign financial conglomerates.

In each of these three structures, separately owned management companies seek to maximize the return on their own capital, largely by generating increased fee revenues from the funds that they manage. But this goal directly conflicts with the goal of mutual fund shareholders – maximizing the return on their own capital, represented by their fund investments. Each dollar paid in management fees is a dollar out of the pocket of the mutual fund investor.

On the face of it, it seems absurd that, say, a $100 billion mutual fund complex – let alone one managing trillions – would need to hire an outside company to administer its affairs, to manage the investments of its fund shareholders, and to distribute the shares of the funds it manages to investors. Why shouldn't large fund companies manage themselves?

Structures That Contravene U.S. Public Policy

The answer is "it's always been that way." And so it has. But if this external management structure does not violate the letter of the fund industry's governing statute,[2] it surely violates its spirit. According to a 1981 decision of the Securities and Exchange Commission:

> One of the Act's basic policies is that funds should be managed and operated in the best interests of their shareholders, rather than in the

---

[2] The Investment Company Act of 1940.

interests of advisers, underwriters, and others. . . . The [Vanguard] funds are promoting this goal.[3]

Even earlier, in 1966, Manuel F. Cohen, chairman of the Securities and Exchange Commission from 1964 to 1969, described the reality, cited in Chapter 1. Because of its pungent accuracy, I repeat it here.

The principal reasons . . . funds are created and sold is to make money for the people who sell them and those who manage them.

Is it wrong to have mutual funds managed and operated under a structure designed to make money for their managers? Maybe . . . maybe not. But such a structure directly contravenes the policy standard set forth in the Investment Company Act of 1940.

"Independent Scrutiny"?

The Investment Company Act of 1940 also demands that investment companies must be subjected to adequate independent scrutiny. This provision, however, has been "more honored in the breach than the observance." Most independent directors (those ostensibly free of direct ties to a fund's management company) get paid much[4] and do little, tacitly accepting – without visible action – management behavior when it is less than ethical, fund performance when it is poor, existing fees when they are excessive, and marketing campaigns when they are misleading.

I am not alone in my skepticism about the performance of the independent directors of mutual funds. According to Warren Buffett, independent directors are supposed to behave "as Dobermans," but instead behave as "cocker spaniels with their tails wagging."[5]

Babies Grow Up

Yes, mutual funds are born as babies, nursed and then nurtured by their management company parents. Some, probably most, of these fund

---

[3] SEC Administrative Proceeding File No. 3-5281, February 25, 1981.

[4] The average annual compensation of independent directors serving on the boards of the five largest mutual fund companies is more than $400,000.

[5] Annual Meeting of Berkshire Hathaway Shareholders, May 2, 2009.

parents seek to serve their children/clients. But sometimes the parents are financial buccaneers who create funds that may be "hot," a fad for a moment in time but generating large fees. Sometimes, managers capitalize on their mutual fund franchise and sell their firms to new owners.[6] Warren Buffett has also spoken bluntly about the practice of fund managers who monetize their fiduciary duty and sell it to the highest bidder.

> *Why in the world don't the directors of [mutual] funds [whose manager has put their firm up for sale] simply select whomever they think is best among the bidding organizations and sign up with that party directly? The winner would consequently be spared a huge "payoff" to the former manager who, having flouted the principles of stewardship, deserves not a dime. The winner could surely manage the funds in question for a far lower ongoing fee than would otherwise have been the case. Any truly independent director should insist on this approach to obtaining a new manager.*

Like children, funds grow up. They may even mature. If the parents have done their job well, their children become independent, begin their own lives, and set their own standards. Not so in the mutual fund industry. Their funds have almost never been given the opportunity to become independent and run their own business.

In *Common Sense*, his 1776 call for overthrowing British rule of the American colonies, Thomas Paine used the same analogy:

> *We may as well assert . . . that the first twenty years of our lives is to become a precedent of the next twenty. . . . There is something very absurd, in supposing a continent to be perpetually governed by an island.*

---

[6] I've written frequently on both the anomaly of "serving two masters" (the shareholders of the manager versus the shareholders of the funds) and the dire consequences of public ownership of fund management companies. See *Common Sense on Mutual Funds: New Imperatives for the Intelligent Investor,* 10th anniversary edition (Hoboken, NJ: Wiley, 2009).

"The Vanguard Experiment"

Vanguard is a different case entirely. Its mutualization began when it was born – actually reborn – in 1974. Its formation was in part a simple recognition that a group of existing funds (notably Wellington Fund) had grown up and ought to be independent.[7] We called it "the Vanguard Experiment" in mutual fund governance. Our 180-degree departure from the traditional industry structure led directly to the creation of the index fund, now responsible for almost three-quarters of Vanguard's asset base and approaching one-half of the assets of all equity mutual funds.

The index fund principle has been copied widely, sometimes in the form of traditional index funds (TIFs), but far more often by exchange traded funds (ETFs). While our index strategy has been widely copied (if not always imitated!), our mutual structure, now with 44 years of demonstrated success, has yet to find its first follower.[8]

The Coming Age of Mutualization

I predict that the stagnant structure that characterizes all major mutual fund firms (except for Vanguard) will begin to change during the next decade or two. It is not merely the perversity of the present coun-terproductive structure that will force the change, but an increasing awareness of the critical importance of low costs in delivering successful investment outcomes for investors. Yes, the magic of compounding long-term returns, without the tyranny of compound-ing long-term costs.[9]

Despite Vanguard's unarguable success in the fund marketplace, there has yet been no movement whatsoever toward mutualization in

---

[7] See discussion in Chapter 2 on Exhibit 2.3.

[8] I often ask myself, "If I have no followers, how can I be considered a leader?"

[9] Too few investors are aware that, if the stock market's gross return is, say, 7% per year over 50 years (less than an investment lifetime for today's young investors), $1 will grow to $29.46. But, with annual costs estimated at 2% per year, $1 invested in a mutual fund that earns a net return of 5% will grow to just $11.47.

the fund industry. It's not that I haven't tried to spread the gospel, but that the opportunities have been rare.

Strike One: The IBM Funds

I waited – and waited – for my first opportunity to play a role in the first mutualization to follow our own. That opportunity came in 1994.

In an effort to help its employees save for retirement, IBM launched a group of mutual funds – predominately index funds – administered by a subsidiary called IBM Credit Investment Management Corp. With assets of $650 million in 1994, IBM decided to monetize the value of the mutual fund subsidiary and put it up for public sale. It retained a consulting firm to seek the highest bidder.

When I heard about the proposed sale, I quickly saw the obvious opportunity. Instead of making our proposal to parent IBM (which I assumed sought to make a large profit on the sale), we would make our proposal to the independent directors of the IBM funds themselves.

When the day came to present proposals to the fund directors, we were, if not welcomed, at least allowed to make our case. With Vanguard managing director Jeremy G. Duffield, we made our presentation: we would merge the IBM funds into the comparable Vanguard index funds, but would pay IBM *nothing*. However, through our rock-bottom costs, we would save the fund shareholders (IBM employees and retirees) $1.2 million in the first year and scores of millions of dollars in fees over time.[10]

We lost. The IBM subsidiary was sold to Rhode Island's Fleet Financial Group for $14 million.[11]

---

[10] Our proposal compared the expense ratio of our Vanguard 500 Index Fund expense ratio, then 0.19%, with IBM's 0.40%, a cost reduction of more than 50%. By 2018, the expense ratios on the Vanguard fund had plummeted to 0.04%, a 79% reduction.

[11] The arrangement with Fleet Financial or its successor may no longer exist, but the present investments of the IBM 401(k) retirement funds are largely index funds, carrying an average expense ratio of 0.12%. Bravo!

As Clear as a Conflict Can Be

I was angered by the decision. In my opinion, the funds' independent directors had placed the interests of parent IBM's shareholders ahead of the interests of the shareholders in the IBM funds to whom those directors had a clear fiduciary duty. I was so disgusted that I took a step that I had never taken before (nor since).

I met with *Wall Street Journal* reporter Sara Calian and recounted the story. Two days later, she gave the otherwise unnoticed event the coverage it deserved. Her article dominated the front financial page of the newspaper on April 26, 1994, under the headline "IBM Is Assailed Over Plans to Sell Funds."

In the course of writing her extensive article, Sara Calian telephoned the funds' three independent directors. One declined to comment. The second defended the decision. When she asked the third director, Professor Michael Tushman of Columbia University, about the transaction, she reported his response: "'I don't know anything,' and hung up the phone."

Strike Two: Putnam

A decade later, in 2007, a second opportunity for mutualization arose. Putnam Management Company, one of the early pioneers in the mutual fund industry, went public in a 1965 IPO, and in 1970 was acquired by insurance broker Marsh and McLennan.

The acquisition proved to be (a) a goldmine for Marsh and (b) a disaster for the shareholders of the Putnam Funds. One example: the misleading advertising and promotion of Putnam High Income Government Trust Fund. At a time when U.S. Treasury bonds were yielding 6%, the fund purported to offer a 12% yield. (Don't ask.) The High Income fund failed abjectly to measure up to that promise. Its dividend was slashed and its asset value tumbled, creating great harm to its largely retired shareholders who depended on the income from the fund for their living expenses.

Later, in the 2000–2003 bear market, most of Putnam's aggressive equity funds also plummeted. We cannot lay all of the responsibility for their collapse on Marsh's desire to maximize the return on their investment in Putnam. But the proposal to build earnings included the creation and aggressive marketing of highly risky funds with aggressive strategies. Their asset values fell even more precipitously than the market averages.

Ethical Failures

Performance failures, alas, were only part of Putnam's story. Ethical failures were another. The firm's managers were deeply involved in the "time-zone trading" scandals that enriched fund managers at the expense of fund shareholders. Essentially, big investors took advantage of an arbitrage opportunity by transacting at an international fund's net asset value calculated at 4 p.m. in New York, but based on closing market prices in Asia some 14 hours earlier. When New York attorney general Eliot Spitzer revealed that malpractice, the "opportunity" was erased.

All told, Putnam president Lawrence Lasser was paid a fortune in compensation (a reported total of several hundreds of millions of dollars) for enriching Putnam owner Marsh and McLennan, all the while impoverishing Putnam fund investors by diluting funds' assets via the "time-zone trading" scheme. (Lasser was fined by the SEC for misconduct. His fine was set at $75,000.)[12]

A Perfect Case

A test case for mutualization? No. *A perfect case.* Investment failure combined with ethical failure. Early in 2008, I met with the Chairman of the Board of the Putnam funds – deemed "independent" despite his prior service as a senior executive of Marsh and McLennan. I also talked to two putatively independent directors. My message: now is the opportunity to mutualize, to bring in a new independent management but retain existing staff, to slash advisory fees, and to create a new firm with a new mission. Their responses: "NO." "NO." And "NO."

---

[12] I present a more complete version of the Putnam story in my book, *The Clash of the Cultures: Investment vs. Speculation* (Hoboken, NJ: Wiley, 2012).

Later in 2007, Marsh sold Putnam to the Canadian financial conglomerate Great-West Lifeco for the astonishing amount of $3.9 billion. Once again, great for the owners of the manager, awful for the owners of the funds. During the ensuing decade, they have continued to earn returns that were undistinguished (or worse). It also was awful for the buyer, Great-West. Putnam's mutual fund assets have dropped from $250 billion in early 2000 to $72 billion in mid-2018 – a 70% decline in assets in a period when the cumulative return on the stock market has been 140%. Putnam will be a hard firm to save.

Two Strikes, Still at Bat

I take some satisfaction in being the instrument by which these examples of the mutualization that I proposed to the independent directors of the IBM funds and the Putnam funds come to see the light of day. Yes, both efforts failed. But the battle for placing the interests of fund shareholders first is far from over.

Of course, with the fund world as it is today, my optimism sounds callow, even stupid. The financial incentives in the fund industry are loaded in favor of fund managers. But change will come. Especially vulnerable are fund groups (1) that have a large asset base; (2) that have delivered poor performance; (3) where costs are high; (4) where management has behaved unethically; (5) where the terms of a proposed management company merger are closely scrutinized; (6) where the funds have a strong board of directors with a strong leader; and (7) when an increasingly tough fiduciary standard for fund officers and directors takes hold as U.S. public policy.

And yes, there is also *necessity*. In an ever-more-price-competitive industry, firms may need to mutualize in order to compete on price for the favor of investors, recognizing Adam Smith's dictum "Consumption is the sole end and purpose of all production." (Read: "The interest of the investor is the sole end and purpose of the mutual fund.") Mutualization is going to happen.

The SEC Speaks

In its 1965 report to Congress titled "Public Policy Implications of Investment Company Growth" (PPI), the issue of mutualization – described as "internalization" – was raised by the Securities and Exchange Commission. Here's what the SEC said.

The Commission is not prepared to recommend at this time the more drastic statutory requirement of compulsory internalization of the management function of all investment companies. Such a step would deal most directly with the adverse consequences flowing from the external management structure of the industry in the area of management compensation as well as with other aspects of the relationship between the funds and their external service organizations.

The prospect of profits from advisory contracts after a fund reaches adequate size has been the dominant motive for the promotion of investment companies. . . . The Commission believes that an alternative to the more drastic solution of compulsory internalization of managements should be given a fair trial. That alternative lies in applying to management compensation [a] standard of reasonableness.[13] *. . . This regulatory approach also can resolve the problems that exist in the area of investment company management compensation. If it does not, then more sweeping steps might deserve to be considered.*

Our public policy tolerance for today's inconsistency between the law (the Investment Company Act of 1940) and the industry's practices may engender a regulatory or even a legislative response to consider "more sweeping steps" and encourage mutualization.

Since the SEC wrote those words in 1965, assets of actively managed equity mutual funds have risen from $35 *billion* to $7.5 *trillion*. Yet the asset-weighted expense ratios of these equity funds has risen from 0.50% to 0.78%. The total expenses paid by investors in actively managed equity

---

[13] PPI was the basis for the 1970 amendments to the 1940 Act. But the SEC's attempt to set this standard for reasonableness was eroded by the fund industry and its lobbyists, and the strong language originally proposed was watered down.

funds has risen from $176 *million* in 1965 to $57 *billion*—an increase in expenses of over 32,000%, while assets have risen only 21,000%.

In sum, in an industry that realizes enormous economies of scale, nearly all those savings have been arrogated by fund managers for their own use and their own profits. None (actually less than none) have accrued to fund shareholders. It's high time to consider "more sweeping steps."

Chapter 18

The Challenge to the S&P 500 Index Fund[1]

I n addition to my battle to mutualize the large companies in the mutual fund industry, I'll also continue to battle for the survival of mutual funds as we know them: investment portfolios that are large, diversified, and often with holdings of numerous companies in a single industry. Their very existence has been challenged by a number of academic studies, and the S&P 500 Index Fund seems to be the bull's-eye of their target.

Honestly, I'm shocked by the need to defend the continued existence of what is often considered "the most important financial innovation that has been created for individual investors."[2]

As I've pointed out throughout this book, index funds have enjoyed remarkable success in the mutual fund industry. From a mere 2% of equity fund assets in 1987, index mutual funds will soon represent more than half of the assets of U.S. equity funds. Indeed, we can thank the index fund for changing the very way we think about investment management, and for bringing the importance of fund costs into the sunlight.

Despite this success (or perhaps because of it), in recent years index funds have come under attack on multiple fronts. Yes, it seems ridiculous that an innovation that has enabled investors to earn their fair share of the returns generated in our stock and bond markets is now under fire, not only from jealous rivals who are associated with active fund managers, but from academia as well.

---

[1] This challenge also applies to all large, diversified stock portfolios.

[2] I thank Burton Malkiel for this quote from the foreword to this book.

The Challenge from Wall Street

Of course Wall Street doesn't care much for index funds. Index funds undercut the notion that actively managed funds enhance the returns of investors; they don't generate advisory fees; and they typically engender little portfolio turnover. I regard the jealous criticism of indexing by some money managers as self-serving and callow, not worthy of a serious response.

No, "passive investing is [not] worse than Marxism," as suggested by a white paper from the asset management firm AllianceBernstein. And no, I don't accept the conclusion of a later op–ed in the *Wall Street Journal*, "Passive Investors, Don't Vote." Asset management firm Janus Henderson Investors argues that index funds should cede their voting rights to actively managed funds. That stock owners should cede their voting rights to stock renters seems beyond absurd.

The Challenge from Academia

I take far more seriously the attacks emerging from academia. These attacks are focused on what their authors describe as the problem of "common ownership." This small but growing body of literature claims that funds with large shareholdings in competing firms create anticompetitive incentives. For example, since an S&P 500 Index fund is a large shareholder in every publicly held airline company, the critics believe that the fund, expressly or tacitly, encourages airline managements not to compete with one another.[3]

While they have offered no compelling evidence – none – that this hypothetical problem exists, some academics have already suggested remedies. In "A Proposal to Limit the Anti-Competitive Power of Institutional Investors,"[4] Professor Eric Posner of the University of Chicago Law School; Glen Weyl, a principal researcher at Microsoft Research and visiting senior research scholar at Yale; and Professor

---

[3] Interestingly, only the airline industry is consistently cited to make this point. Almost all other industries are ignored.

[4] *Antitrust Law Journal*, 2017, 81(3).

Fiona Scott Morton of Yale recommend that large institutional investors, including actively managed funds and index funds alike, should be allowed to invest in only a single firm in any given industry.

One Company per Industry

Their position is that large holders of shares in all of the firms in a given industry at least tacitly encourage the companies to reduce wages and increase prices in order to maximize profits. If such behavior were proven, it would be deemed anticompetitive, and thus be in violation of the Clayton Antitrust Act of 1914.

If the proposal to limit large investors to one company per industry were to become law, it seems self-evident that it would undermine the broad diversification that is the traditional purpose of mutual funds run by active managers. But it would destroy index investing, including S&P 500 Index funds. It would also render substantially illegal the accepted principle of broad diversification for all large investment pools.

Defining an "industry" is no mean task. The authors fail to specify how many stocks an index fund would have to sell to comply. I've been writing to them for more than two years, seeking the answer to this simple question: Were their proposal to become law, how many stocks would an S&P 500 Index fund be allowed to own? Would the S&P 500 become the "S&P 143"? Or the "S&P 215?" Or the "S&P 350?" I've yet to receive a response.

How Many Industries?

The authors of the paper identify 49 distinct industries, but suggest that defining "industry" is no mean task. They say the number would be larger because they would define industries more narrowly. The S&P identifies 135 industries and sub-industries, which, strictly interpreted, would give us the "S&P 135" rather than the S&P 500.

The authors do not attempt to provide their own definition of what an industry is, outsourcing that responsibility to antitrust enforcement agencies (in the United States, the DOJ and FTC). The fact that U.S. government bureaucrats would make the decisions on defining an industry makes a bad situation even worse.

Why Seek to Destroy the Index Fund?

But that would be the least of the problems. Each of today's S&P 500 Index funds (and each total stock market index fund) could well select different companies in each industry and trade them as their prospects changed, simply one more form of active management, carrying higher costs. By doing so, they would cease to be index funds.

Each former S&P 500 Index fund would earn a different return. They would compete with one another for superior returns, and the notion that "cost makes the difference" would be lost in the competitive shuffle. The proposal, I think obviously, would destroy the index fund, despite the reality that it has been (correctly) described as democratizing the world of investing.[5]

The authors also blithely ignore the dire tax consequences to individual fund investors were index funds to divest themselves of hundreds of holdings (S&P 500 Index funds) or even thousands of holdings (total stock market index funds) accumulated over the years at much lower prices than those present today. I'm guessing that investors in such funds would realize capital gains in the range of $200 billion, and could be assessed potential taxes of some $25 billion. (Index fund investors in tax-deferred retirement accounts would not be subject to such taxes.)

Pascal's Wager: Consequences Must Outweigh Probabilities

I can't help being reminded of Pascal's famous wager on whether God exists. His conclusion: consequences must always outweigh probabilities. The probability that applying the one-company-per-industry policy to index funds would somehow reduce the monopoly power of corporations is vague and impossible to quantify. The consequences of that policy would destroy diversified investing by any large pool of capital. The S&P 500 Index fund, as we know it today, would vanish. The harm done to the investors who have entrusted their savings to index funds would be almost incalculable. Those extraordinary

---

[5] Even the index-driven $500 billion federal government's Thrift Savings Plan would lose its identity.

consequences must outweigh the remote possibilities that such a policy is necessary and in the public interest.

Yes, Index Funds Face Challenges

While I find much to criticize in the proposals to severely limit the corporate holdings of institutional investors, this is not to say that the remarkable growth of index funds and other pools of capital managed by financial institutions poses no public policy issues. Of course it does. If historical trends continue, a handful of giant institutional investors might one day hold voting control of virtually every large U.S. corporation.

Yes, U.S. index funds have grown to huge size, with their holdings of U.S. stocks doubling from 3.3% of their total market value in 2002, to 6.8% in 2009, and then doubling again to an estimated 14% in 2018. Other mutual funds now hold an estimated 20% of corporate shares, bringing the mutual fund total to almost 35%, the nation's most dominant single holder of common stocks.

Holdings of all U.S. financial institutions – including pension plans and thrift plans, as well as mutual funds – now hold 63% of all shares. We must carefully monitor this dominance of institutional ownership and its impact on the financial markets, corporate governance, and public policy. This will be a major issue of the coming era.

Concentration in Indexing

We must also consider the reality that the indexing sector itself has many of the characteristics of an oligopoly.[6] Just three companies – Vanguard, 50% of all index fund assets; BlackRock, 20%; and State Street Global, 10% – dominate the field with their collective 80% share of index fund assets. The oligopoly among these major index fund providers, if such it be, is a separate issue from that of corporate competition within given industries, but one that seems sure to arise when our

---

[6] While the classic oligopoly is represented by a few sellers who seek to raise the prices paid by their many buyers, the index fund "oligopoly" (if such it be) competes to lower prices, discouraging potential competitors whose goal is to charge the highest prices that the traffic will bear.

nation's policymakers inevitably turn their gaze to both the power and the concentration of institutional ownership of stocks.

That oligopoly, of course, is weird. It exists primarily because the indexing field attracts few new entrants – not because of high barriers to entry (although the scale enjoyed by the big indexers would be difficult to replicate by new entrants), but because their prices (expense ratios) have been driven to commodity-like levels. By early 2018, the expense ratio necessary to compete in the index fund marketplace had been driven down to as little as 0.04% of assets (four basis points).

"All the Darn Money Goes to the Fund Shareholders"

Low prices have led to low management profits. Indeed, Vanguard operates on an "at-cost" basis, earning no profit on its fund activities. Simply put, the reason most fund managers shun entry into the index fund arena is because "all the darn money goes to the fund shareholders."

One of the major reasons that we worry about oligopolies and monopolies to begin with is that they tend to cause prices for consumers to rise. Not so in indexing. Rather, as investors continue to understand the deleterious impact of investment costs, and as economies of scale increase for index fund providers, the expense ratios paid by index investors continue their inexorable march toward zero. Indeed, in August 2018, Fidelity announced two new index funds with an expense ratio of 0%.

We need more competitors in the index fund field, as the current concentration of such a large share of the ownership of our nation's corporations is both large and growing rapidly. But there is little or no financial incentive for active fund managers to join the fray – indeed the incentive (lower fees) is strongly negative.

Many observers expect that the share of corporate ownership by index funds will continue to present patterns of growth, and some observers believe that we need still more indexing and less active equity management. Some have even suggested that 80% would pose no issues. I disagree. If a handful of index managers hold 80% of all corporate voting shares, the largest would likely hold at least 30%. I do not believe that such concentration would serve the national interest.

Monopoly Power?

There is yet another major reason for my concern about the attack on the index fund. It's seen as part of a broad threat to our society that is increasing inequality among the nation's families and leading to a second Gilded Age. Two of the academics behind this attack are Glen Weyl and Eric Posner. On May 1, 2018, they wrote an op-ed in the *New York Times* titled "The Real Villain Behind Our New Gilded Age," laying the responsibility on "monopoly power." Of course they have a point when they assert:

> *In the past two decades, growth rates in the United States have fallen to half of what they were in the middle of the century. The share of income accruing to the top 1 percent has doubled since the 1970s, while the share of income going to all workers has fallen by nearly 10 percent. These are the marks of our new Gilded Age.*

I too am deeply concerned about these issues, and I suspect that many, if not most thoughtful citizens share my concerns. But these academics list institutional ownership of stocks in competing firms as *first* on their list of miscreants, ahead of corporate power over the labor markets and other new ways to achieve monopoly power. The authors assert that "as institutional investors obtain greater market share, consumers pay higher prices," but any proof of causation is conspicuous by its absence.

A New Gilded Age?

I can hardly deny that our society today has many of the attributes of the Gilded Age of the late nineteenth century. Much of today's wealth has been created in our financial sector. In the years ahead, all of those interested in the future of investment management must join the fight against largely unsupported theories that would have untold consequences for institutional investors and their clients, and destroy the single best option that our families have for investing to accumulate wealth: buying and holding shares in a broadly diversified, low-cost stock market index fund.

If the firms that manage money are to make the decisions that best serve our investors, our citizens, and our society, we need more than abstract statistical evidence, more than anecdotal evidence, more than sweeping generalizations. Pascal, after all, got it right. Consequences must outweigh probabilities.

Chapter 19

"The Financial Institutions Act of 2030"

T he future of investment management, to state the obvious, will be importantly determined by the makers of public policy. The mutual fund industry, now the dominant form of investment management, has been governed by the Investment Company Act of 1940 for almost 80 years now. Since 1940, the fund industry has changed in countless ways. Then, total industry assets were but $450 million, or 0.002% of today's $20 trillion industry. Then, the industry comprised 68 open-end funds; today there are 7,956.

The world of mutual funds has radically changed, not only in its growth, but also in its very character. How could the 1940 Act have contemplated the index fund? Yet index funds today (assets $7 trillion) represent 35% of mutual fund assets and nearly 50% of all equity fund assets. How could the 1940 Act have contemplated money market funds (now $2.7 trillion), or exchange-traded index funds ($3.4 trillion)? Yes, today's investment companies represent a vastly different industry in size, scope, and power than the industry that existed in 1940.

Indeed, the basic purpose of that 1940 Act was to regulate closed-end investment companies, which in 2018 have total assets of but $275 billion, only 1% of total investment company assets. Open-end (mutual) funds are totally dominant.

The Fund and the Fund Complex

Among the biggest flaws in the 1940 Act is that it focuses on regulating *individual investment companies* in a day when most managers offered but a single fund or two. Today, this is almost entirely a business of *multifund complexes*. The ten largest fund complexes, accounting for 63% of industry assets, manage an average of 184 funds. It is only common sense to have the fund management company as the new regulatory unit.

Perhaps the best example of the difference between fund and fund complex lies in the 1940 Act's provision that, in essence, limits a mutual fund from owning more than 10% of the voting stock of a single corporation.[1] I will not argue here that such a limit (or even a more general limitation) should apply to the aggregate investment of a given fund complex. But it would be naïve to assume, after such a sea change in the fund industry, that an ancient regulatory focus on individual mutual funds will prevail into eternity.

Public Ownership of Mangers

The 1940 Act also failed to contemplate the public ownership of fund management companies. Insurance Securities, Inc., one of the leaders in the industry of yore, became the first fund manager that attempted to sell itself to a new owner. The SEC vigorously opposed the sale,[2] but after a drawn-out legal battle, the commission lost its case in 1958. By 1960, public ownership of management companies began its surge, and soon a dozen fund managers followed suit. It took little time before giant financial conglomerates began to acquire fund management companies, public and private alike.

Today, public ownership in the mutual fund industry is the rule, not the exception. Among the 50 largest diversified fund managers, 41 are either publicly held (14) or owned by financial conglomerates (27). Eight remain privately held. Only one – Vanguard – is fund-shareholder-owned.

I'm no lover of regulation, but when the nature and structure of an industry is transformed, when a mom-and-pop industry becomes a colossus, and when too many fund managers earn public scrutiny

---

[1] Technically, this limit applies to only 75% of the investment company's assets. As a practical matter, however, that distinction has not been meaningful.
[2] Earlier in Part III, I reviewed other aspects of public ownership.

by their actions, the mutual fund industry must be subjected to more appropriate and meaningful regulation.

Institutional Investors and Corporate Governance

The Investment Company Act of 1940 almost totally ignored the broad subject of the role of open-end investment companies in corporate governance. The coming "Financial Institutions Act of 2030" (my guess as to the year) must not repeat the same omission. It seems self-evident that the holders of some 63% of the shares of U.S. corporations (mutual funds, pension funds, and other institutional investors) must play a decisive role in ensuring that our corporations are managed solely in the interests of their shareholders/owners.

Ownership has its rights, yes. But it also has its responsibilities. Present state law has proved inadequate to ensure the exercise of these responsibilities. We need a federal standard of fiduciary duty requiring that the institutions entrusted with the management of other people's money must put first the interests of the principals whom they serve, including a requirement that institutional investors be held accountable for the exercise of their proxy votes.

During the past decade, much progress has been made on developing more activist governance policies by mutual funds and other financial institutions, but there is still more to be done. The coming legislation must address the issue of institutional money managers as a whole, as well as their role in corporate governance.

The Narrow Ambit of the 1940 Act

Among the biggest flaws of all in the Investment Company Act of 1940 is that it is designed solely for investment companies. Of course that's easily explained: corporate pension funds did not then exist. (The first corporate pension fund wasn't formed until 1950, a full decade later.) Endowment funds were then of little significance. By far the largest institutional investors of the day were bank trust funds, whose regulation was presumed to be covered by our federal and state banking statutes.

In 1945, these various institutional money managers owned only 5% of the voting stock of publicly held U.S. corporations. Today, that total has soared to nearly 63%.[3] In substance, the ownership of corporate America has moved from individual stockholders representing their own interests to institutional stockholders who are, as a rule, agents for their principals—largely mutual fund shareholders and pension fund beneficiaries—whose investments they supervise and whose interests they are duty-bound to represent.

This radical change in the pattern of corporate ownership is more complex then it appears. For the managers of the largest mutual funds are also the managers of most of the large pension funds. In 2018, the top 300 institutional holders of U.S. equities held an estimated $17 trillion in U.S. stocks, 70% of the market capitalization of the Wilshire 5000. About half of those holdings were represented by mutual funds, the other half by pension funds and other investors. It is hard to imagine a sensible system in which different regulations would apply to each.

Implications of Index Fund Dominance

Index funds have often borne the brunt of criticism about the lassitude of the nation's money managers in the governance of the corporations whose shares they own and collectively dominate. They are an easy—and large—target. But while index funds are *passive* investors, they are increasingly *active* owners. Why? Because, as fiduciaries, they have few alternatives other than exercising their voting power.

When active money managers are unhappy with a corporation's management, operations, or strategy, they can simply sell the stock. Index funds, by their very nature, cannot do so. Their only alternative is to press the management for improvement, or change the management. Index funds as a group will soon have the voting power to do just that.

This concentration of voting power—in fact, it represents voting control—is a subject that deserves the prompt attention of the U.S. Securities Exchange Commission, the federal government, and our

---

[3] Accordingly, stock holdings by households has tumbled from 95% to 37%.

society. We need to develop principles and standards of conduct and operations for institutional money managers that, in the words of the preamble to the Investment Company Act of 1940, "serve the national public interest and the interest of investors."

My concerns are shared by many academic observers. In his draft paper of September 20, 2018, Professor John C. Coates of Harvard Law School focused on indexing and its reshaping of corporate governance, "controlled by a small number of individuals with unsurpassed power . . . practical power over the majority of U.S. public companies."[4] Professor Coates does not like what he sees, and offers tentative policy options – some necessary, all painful to contemplate. His conclusion: "The issue is not likely to go away." That conclusion is unarguable.

Two Other Investment Issues

There are too many more issues affecting institutional money management to catalogue here. But I will briefly mention two issues that concern me. First, we likely face an era in which stock and bond returns will be lower than historical norms. Managers of other people's money must do their best to ensure that individual investors, pension funds, and retirement plans alike are aware of that possibility.

I particularly worry about pension funds – especially, but not exclusively, state and local government pension funds – when their huge deficits come home to roost. I believe that pension managers have an obligation to make their opinions known about the assumed future returns on their investment portfolios. Today's prevailing assumption of a 7.5% future return seems far too aggressive.

Second, pension trustees must also be wary about the use and abuse of "pay-to-play" fees, often paid by state and local government pension funds as "finder's fees" to middlemen who offer contacts with supposedly superior managers of alternative investment strategies. Should not the "2030 Act" ban such fees, or at the minimum, require

---

[4] "The Future of Corporate Governance Part I. The Problem of Twelve." The use of 12 as the number of individuals with unsurpassed power is intended as an imprecise metaphor for a small number. My own number would be around six.

full disclosure of all fees paid to their investment advisers? Clear disclosure of the returns earned by each manager should also be required.

Fiduciary Duty: The Theme of Part III

The major recommendations involving "The Future of Investment Management" that I have described in these three chapters of Part III have one thing in common. All are designed to serve the individual investors of our nation who, directly or indirectly, have entrusted some $30 trillion of their savings to our financial institutions.

Looming over all of these changes – large and small alike – will be the gradual realization that institutional investors are, above all, fiduciaries, the stewards of the assets of our clients. The Department of Labor's enlightened fiduciary duty rule for sellers of retirement plans to investors has been eliminated by the new administration, and it is unclear how the SEC will deal with the issue. But, with or without government regulation, the fiduciary standard should shape everything that money managers do, and it should apply to any person or any firm that touches other people's money.

Yes, institutional money managers must truly act as fiduciaries, placing our clients' interests above all else. As the principal driver of our nation's financial, investment, and corporate governance systems, the industry must join with policy makers to seize this opportunity to begin to resolve the issues of the coming era, including management company ownership, preserving the present structure of index funds, concentration of voting power, and enlightened regulation and legislation. The goal must be policies that serve the interests of investors and the national interest as well.

PART IV

Personal Reflections

Much of the investing public seems at least vaguely aware of my career, my indexing insurgency, and my investment philosophy, all described in detail in the preceding chapters. In this final chapter of *Stay the Course*, I'd like to reveal a bit of who I am. How I've tried to serve society. Some of my joys, and some of my sorrows, even some of my fears (read carefully!). How much delight I've received from helping others – as, many decades ago, others helped me – along the road of life. I'd like to honor some of those who have influenced my life. To cite a few passages by others that I have found inspiring.

In this memoir of sorts, I present an alphabetical list of some of the things that are important to me – institutions that helped me to develop my mind and gave me the opportunity to give back to the community; some of the individuals who have helped shape who I am; some traits that shaped my character, and much more. This chapter is quite a departure from my typical writing style. I hope you enjoy it.

Yes, it's unusual, if not quirky, to organize this kind of material alphabetically. I resisted the temptation to use all 26 letters in the alphabet, which would have forced me into a box, and created the potential for producing awkward results. I hope each reader will find something lasting to benefit from and enjoy.

Chapter 20

What Really Matters
A Memoir

Advice. This ancient Persian proverb offers the best advice that I know for dealing with the inevitable ups and downs of life, the best times and the worse times alike: *This too shall pass away*.

American Indian College Fund. The more that I've studied our nation's history, the more that I've come to recognize that America's early Anglo-European colonists claimed that a land that belonged to others belonged to them. Ever since Columbus, American Indians have been shabbily treated by our invaders, by our own federal government, and by our society. I felt obligated to try to help right this wrong, and have made modest (if large for me) annual contributions to the American Indian College Fund, helping to support, I'm told, some 500 scholarships for young Native American men and women.

I served as a Trustee of the American Indian College Fund from 1996 to 2002, and each year I continue to receive photos of the smiling/serious faces of those young students, doing their best to find their place in our society.

"The Eagle and the Bear"

In 1996, while awaiting my heart transplant, I decided that, "just in case," I'd like to leave a remembrance at our family retreat on Placid Lake in the Adirondacks. Through the Lummi tribe of northwestern Washington State, I ordered a totem pole for my purpose. Carved by Native American artist Dale James, its height came to some 25 feet. For 22 years it has rested on a knoll overlooking the lake.

The totem pole, carved from a great cedar tree, came with its own legend, "The Eagle and the Bear."

Eagle called to the carvers of the people and said, "My time could be short. I am feeling the pull of two worlds, and when I see my wife and children I feel a great love and tenderness. I would have you carve me a great pole of remembering for them. A pole that tells of the family. A pole which speaks of the love of a man with the spirit of Eagle and a woman with the spirit of Bear, and their six children who will tell his story to their children's children."

Blair Academy.   This fine New Jersey boarding school was – and remains – among the principal cornerstones of my long life. Twin brother David and I began our studies at Blair in September 1945, and graduated in June 1947. (Brother William graduated in June 1945.)

Being away from our stressed home was the best thing for us. There was no way we could pay our tuition, but my beloved mother somehow persuaded Blair to take us in *gratis.* We held scholarships and worked jobs – waiters in the dining hall; in my senior year, waiter captain.

My experienced masters at Blair (four of whom had joined the faculty in 1912) seemed to see something worthwhile in me. They would not accept flawed work. Jesse Gage crushed me with a 40 on my first exposure to algebra, but I ended the year earning 100 on my final exam. Henry Adams and Marvin G. Mason corrected my English papers with a fury, and with red pens. The markups of my papers were not pretty sights, but my ability to write began under their tutelage.

Determined to overcome that slow start, I worked hard, graduated cum laude, and was named "best student." That may have been the first hint that I had the grit to stay the course.

Giving Back

Having been given so much, I wanted to give back. The Bogle Brothers Scholarship Fund has now helped enable more than 160 young men and women to attend Blair, and each year we add a dozen or so more. Bogle Hall (1989) and the Armstrong-Hipkins Center for the Arts (1999) were named to honor my parents, and then my grandparents.

I've also sought to serve my alma mater, mostly as an active member of the board of trustees from 1973 through 2002, and then as chairman emeritus to this day – 45 years of board membership, including 16 years as chairman. Leading a school board has its challenges. But I was lucky. My mentor was my remarkable predecessor, the late J. Brooks Hoffman MD, Blair Class of 1936. Brooks showed me the way.

Blair's Renaissance

The most important task for a chairman is when the time comes to select a new Head of School. For me, that time came in 1989. I sought a personable, energetic, young person who could lead Blair to the realization of its great potential. T. Chandler Hardwick (age 36) accepted our offer. With his wife Monie, Chan led Blair's renaissance, returning the Academy to its rank as one of the nation's top college preparatory schools.

A solid relationship between board chairman and Head of School is the key to good governance. It was essential to Blair's ascendance, and it was strengthened, I trust, by a self-imposed rule that I followed (most of the time!): "The Head of School is the boss. The chairman is there to help him whenever he asks." After giving Blair Academy 24 years of their lives, the Hardwicks moved on in 2013. The close friendship that Eve and I developed with them endures to this day.

What is the mission of Blair Academy? I can do no better than offer these words from a speech I gave to our alumni in 2007:

> *The task before our school is large, . . . to preserve, to protect and to defend this fount of liberal education, this island of opportunity, this community of teaching and learning. At Blair Academy, we give some of the most promising young men and women in our land the opportunity to learn more than they might otherwise have learned, to*

accomplish more than they might otherwise have accomplished, and to develop their character and their values more than they might otherwise have developed them. If these seem like unremarkable goals, I assure you that they are anything but. Such young citizens are the core of our civilization, our hope for years to come. . . .

Books.   I love writing books, and I have a "lover's quarrel" with the mutual fund industry. That combination has resulted in 12 books, 10 of which have helped to drive Vanguard's success as an industry rebel creating a new industry, one among those companies that consider "themselves insurgents, waging war . . . on behalf of an underserved customer," as described in Chapter 10.

Why do I write? Because I love to do it. Because writing takes those inchoate, rambling thoughts we all have rattling around in our brains and demands that they be focused and articulate, even impassioned. Because books outlive one's short existence on this planet.

My first book, *Bogle on Mutual Funds* (1993), and my sixth book, *The Little Book of Common Sense Investing* (2007), have been particularly popular with readers, and the nine others have also done well.[1] Sales of my books — so far! — total about 941,000 through mid-2018. Almost 1,000 readers have offered comments on Amazon, overwhelmingly positive (74% 5-star, 16% 4-star). I remember the pans better than I do the pats, but I won't soon forget two particular accolades for my *Little Book of Common Sense Investing* (Tenth Anniversary Edition, 2018). How could an author fail to revel in the headline and the review that follow:

1. *The oasis where every successful investor must eventually drink.*

2. *Wow, I just finished the book and never expected to be so entertained, I'm almost sad it's not longer just because I loved reading it so much. . . . Great advice for investing and written in a very easy to read style (it was like a close friend was giving me their honest advice). I also love that the book has been recently updated. But even if it's 10 years in the future and you're reading this review I think the book will still be very accurate and topical. John has done the investing world*

---

[1] You're reading my 12th and last (yes!) book, *Stay the Course: The Story of Vanguard and the Index Revolution* (Hoboken, NJ: Wiley, 2019).

another great service with this book and I highly suggest everyone read it (I already bought a second copy to give to a family member).

Buffett, Warren. The oracle of Omaha has been described as a better salesman than I am for the Vanguard 500 Index Fund. He's boosted it in seven Berkshire Hathaway Annual Reports. He's also put his money where his mouth is, including a winning bet that the S&P 500 would outpace a select group of hedge funds, and directing the trustee of his wife's estate to invest 90% of its assets in the Vanguard 500 Index Fund. Warren, that down-to-earth gentleman whom I first met 25 years ago, has also endorsed many of my books.

My personal highlight: at the Berkshire Hathaway 2017 annual meeting, held in a giant arena in Omaha before some 40,000 investors, Mr. Buffett gave me a generous "shout out."

Jack Bogle has probably done more for the American investor than any man in the country. . . . Jack could you stand up?

The applause was thunderous. I was embarrassed, overwhelmed, and delighted.

Communication. I've always recognized the need for us human beings to communicate with one another, directly, empathetically, honestly, personally, and, at best, elegantly. For an appraisal of my approach to communications, I rely here on my long-time aide and friend Jeremy Duffield. He is surely among the finest, best-schooled, and most integrity-laden individuals who have ever crossed my path.

Jeremy, an Australian who came to the United States in 1969, joined Vanguard in 1979, founded our Australian subsidiary in 1996, and ran it with entrepreneurial excellence until he left the firm in 2010. Here's how he described my communications style:

It helps to be compulsive about it − to be absolutely maniacal and disciplined about being a great communicator. . . . So the first lesson is you've got to work very, very hard at it . . . his books . . . his 575 speeches, [now 29] papers published in the Journal of Portfolio Management *and the* Financial Analysts Journal, *100 television appearances, 250 annual reports that he wrote to shareholders. . . .*

Perhaps the secret to Jack's impact is his ability to bring drama into the equation. A lot of that derives from his state of constant agitated moral indignation about the plight of the investor. There's no gray in Jack's thinking. It's moral absolutism.

"On Vanguard's Seas"

On a sobering note, Jeremy also wrote a poem to be read when I leave this mortal coil – a fine example of his own communications ability. I was deeply touched when I read, "On Vanguard's Seas":

> *On Vanguard's seas, the waves still flow*
> *With foaming crests, row by row*
> *That cover his resting place; and in the sky*
> *The gulls, still bravely singing, fly*
> *Scarce heard amid the guns below. . . .*
> *Take up my quarrel with our foe*
> *To you from failing hands I throw*
> *The torch; be yours to hold it high*
> *If ye break faith with those who die*
> *I shall not sleep, though winds still blow*
> *O'er Vanguard's seas.*

Determination.   Years ago I asked some friends and most members of my family what they thought was my single most important trait. Each came up with the same word: *determination.* I think they are likely on the right track, even as I recognize that while determination is necessary to achieve one's goals, it can sometimes result in a single-mindedness that is not particularly attractive. I'm also known for my contrarianism. ("There must be a better way.") I've also been cited for decisiveness, resilience, grit, and self-confidence (which, I pray, does not cross the line and become arrogance).

Dylan Thomas.   *Do not go gentle into that good night. Rage, rage against the dying of the light.*

Engine.   *The Little Engine That Could* offers the best brief advice for a successful career that I can imagine:

*I think I can. I think I can. I think I can. . . . I knew I could. I knew
I could. I knew I could.*

Family. My family has been an utter blessing, giving me a life that
is as complete as it could possibly be. The center of ours is Eve, my
wife of 62 years. She is loving, kind, strong, smart, and resilient. A few
years back, I was introduced to an audience that had been told that
we were then celebrating our 50th wedding anniversary. In the Q&A
period, the fifth question was "What's the secret?" Without a moment's
hesitation, I gave an answer that I could hardly improve on, even a
dozen years later, "Two secrets," I said. "First, marry a saint. Second,
never forget the two most important words in the English language:
'Yes, dear.'"

We've been infinitely blessed. Six children, 12 grandchildren, good
citizens all, healthy, happy, and dealing well with the challenges that are
part of the lives of every human being on our planet. And now six
great-grandchildren, all boys, two born in 2018.

Today, we see a lot written about the "work/life balance." As if
work were not part of life! But if the test is "the work/family balance,"
I have little doubt that I have been overbalanced on the work side of
the scale. Nonetheless, I did my best with family, and I believed that
they would all agree that I've earned more than a passing grade.

Forgiveness. I confess that I always kind of liked the simple message
"an eye for an eye and a tooth for a tooth." But I soon retreated to the
less severe "there can be no forgiveness without repentance." In 1974,
my former Boston partners abruptly cut short my career at Wellington
Management Company. It was hardball politics, for it was their investment failures that almost sank the company. So I returned to my earlier
philosophy: "The heck with asking for repentance, get revenge!" I soon
realized that heeding this maxim was eating away at me.

Then I learned of the mutual enmity between former U.S. presi-
dents John Adams and Thomas Jefferson. They were political enemies
until 1801, when Jefferson's presidency ended. Then their rift healed.
They became friends. Their long years of correspondence ended only
when both died on the same day, July 4, 1826, exactly 50 years after the
signing of the Declaration of Independence.

I was inspired by that story. So in 1991, 25 years after our merger agreement was signed on June 6, 1966, I decided to take the initiative to mend the rift and forgive my successors, even without their repentance. I met with Bob Doran and Nick Thorndike, leaders of the (dare I say) cabal that had axed me. My words were simple: "Twenty-five years is enough. Let's be friends." And so it would be. Indeed, when I spoke to a large audience at The Country Club (near Boston, for those not in the know), my forgiveness must have played a role in their graciously hosting a lovely small dinner there in Eve's and my honor. (I'm no hero. I confess that I can't quite get "an eye for an eye" out of my mind.)

God.   Is there a God? Yes.

Guardian angels.   As you read at the conclusion of Chapter 10, *No man is an island, entire of itself.* All my life I've depended on the support of others, never more than in my long struggle with heart disease. My first heart attack came on the tennis court in 1961, when I was but 32 years of age. The genetic disease, undiscovered for another decade, was arrhythmogenic right ventricular dysplasia (ARVD). Potentially fatal if not treated promptly, the heart fibrillations struck out of nowhere. Eve had to rush me to the hospital maybe 10 times (not easy for a mother of three, and later six, young children), where my heart would be electrically shocked into a normal rhythm.

This routine got rather tiresome. So I sought the top cardiologist in the nation. By consensus, it was Dr. Bernard Lown of Boston's Peter Bent Brigham (now Brigham and Women's) Hospital. Beginning in 1967, I became a patient of this superb physician (and remarkable human being who shared the Nobel Peace Prize – yes! – in 1985). He watched over me with intensity and deep caring, my prototypical guardian angel for two decades until 1987, when he could see that my frequent hospitalizations and visits to his Boston office were taking their toll on me.

Heart Transplant Wanted!

By then, my ARVD attacks, now treated in Philadelphia by experimental medicines, had become less frequent. But by 1996, half of my heart had stopped functioning. (Providentially, it was the right half; the left side does the pumping.) It was time to get a new heart.

At 65, I was but a marginal candidate, but Dr. Susan Brozena accepted me into the transplant program at Philadelphia's Hahnemann Hospital. (One door in the transplant unit said, "NO EXIT." That worried me.)

Potential recipients of new hearts are pretty much date-stamped, when they enter the hospital in a process (as I observed) "as democratic as a traffic jam." With continuous intravenous medicine, my flawed heart kept pumping for 128 days before a new heart (from a 26-year-old male, bless him) arrived on February 21, 1996. Two weeks later, after a bit of a struggle adapting to the transplant, I was home again. I knelt down and kissed the earth.

"Dr. B"

Since then, my cardiologist has been Dr. Susan Brozena ("Dr. B."), another prototypical guardian angel. Smart, experienced, professional, vivacious, charming, and up-to-the-moment with the pharmacology and complexity of transplant treatment (including anti-rejection drugs for the remainder of my life), she is primarily responsible for the extra 22 years of life that I've enjoyed to the fullest – likely a record for a 65-year-old transplant recipient.

Yes, Drs. Brozena and Lown have been incredible guardian angels. In my long life with two hearts, the first one flawed, the second less than perfect, I've also been watched over by a dozen or more other guardian angels. They know who they are, and to all of them I offer bountiful gratitude, from the bottom of my . . . well, heart.

There's apparently a psychological basis for survival over nearly six decades in dealing with heart disease and its aftermath. I'll let Dr. Lown describe it.

How were your major achievements possible with a heart struggling for the next uncertain pulse, for the next hesitating contraction? I marveled at your iron will and still do. The advances in medical science certainly added years to your life. Yet science alone does not account for the miracle of John Bogle.

You taught me a deeper truth: that surviving against great odds demands intangibles not readily measured by the metrics of science – above all the might of the human spirit that defines our self-awareness. It includes a commitment to serving others, a fearless sense of transience, and a joy in making a difference. Such a self-image enabled you to cultivate a web of devoted family and intimate friends, to bond with the future even when it was merely a shimmer of possibility. Thereby you gained a hold on a meaningful life.

Hedgehog and the fox. The quotation that follows was found, circa 670 BCE, in a fragment of writing of the Greek philosopher Archilochus:

The fox knows many things,
But the hedgehog knows one great thing.

For me, this idea provides an insight into our nation's money managers. We have an army of sly foxes who survive and prosper by knowing many things about complex markets and sophisticated marketing. The hedgehogs in the field know only one great thing: that investment success is based on simplicity – plain service and honest stewardship. (Alas, the hedgehogs in the field are few.) Do I need to tell you in which category I cast Vanguard's lot?

Impartial spectator. The words that follow, written by Adam Smith in *The Theory of Moral Sentiments* (1759), need no embellishment:

What is it which prompts the generous to sacrifice their own interests to the greater interests of others? It is the impartial spectator who calls to us, with a voice capable of astonishing the most presumptuous of our passions, that we are but one of the multitude, in no respect better than any other in it; and that when we prefer ourselves so shamefully and so blindly to others, we become the proper objects of resentment, abhorrence, and execration.

It is from him only that we learn the real littleness of ourselves. It is this impartial spectator . . . who shows us the propriety of generosity and the deformity of injustice; the propriety of reining the greatest interests of our own, for the yet greater interests of others . . . in order to obtain the greatest benefit to ourselves.

It is not the love of our neighbor, it is not the love of mankind, which
upon many occasions prompts us to the practice of those divine virtues. It
is a stronger love, a more powerful affection, the love of what is honourable
and noble, the grandeur, and dignity, and superiority of our own characters.

Now, please read those passages once more. Maybe twice.

Investment **Company Institute.** From 1969 to 1974, I served on
the board of the ICI. That era was a central part of my career. There
I found two great mentors, ICI President Robert Augenblick and
Chairman D. George Sullivan, then-executive vice president of Fidelity.
They were consummate leaders, and they showed me the way.

Today's ICI leadership mystifies me. It is quick to spring to the
defense of the investment management companies that control our
nation's mutual funds, often at the expense of mutual fund shareholders. Shouldn't its name be changed to the "Investment Managers
Institute" (IMI) to reflect its true function?

The fund industry calls out for reform. Are advisory fees too high?
Has aggressive marketing gotten out of hand? Are fund directors truly
independent? Why do index fund returns outpace the returns of the
vast majority of actively managed funds? Are brokerage commissions
being used to serve the interests of shareholders or the interests of
managers?

This list only begins a long menu of subjects that I believe should
have found their way onto the agenda of the ICI's annual General
Membership Meeting (GMM). But none did. In the hope of finding at least a hint of introspection on those and other issues, I used
to attend those meetings. Alas, each year I'd come back to Vanguard
empty-handed.

ICI Chairman, 1969–1970

In the interest of full disclosure, I served for five years on ICI's
Executive Committee. As ICI chairman from 1969 to 1970, I worked
to develop the compromise passage of the Investment Company
Amendments Act of 1970. (Not sure how proud I am of that!) I
brought four subsequent ICI chairmen into the fund industry. I created the index mutual fund, which now represents nearly one-half

of the equity mutual fund assets of its members. And I founded the ICI's largest member — and largest dues-payer. Even those credentials, however, were insufficient to merit an invitation to speak at the ICI's 2017 GMM, as suggested by a 2017 article about me in *The Times* of London. Go figure!

"**Jo.**" **Josephine Hipkins Bogle.** My mother, Jo (1896–1952), was a saint. Yes, beautiful, utterly charming, vivacious, a joy to everyone who was lucky enough to know her.

To this day, I don't know how, given an uneasy marriage and constant financial strain, she held herself together. Her firstborns were twin daughters who did not survive their birth. Yet I never saw my mother wince or weep or complain about the challenges that she faced.

She devoted her life to her three boys, doing her best to have us grow up with solid friends (a home run) and to make sure that we got the best education imaginable (a grand slam).

For all three sons, "Hello, Blair Academy!" For her youngest son, "Hello, Princeton University!" Providentially, she lived to see me graduate, and snapped a photo of me (I still have it) on her little Hawkeye camera as I strode across the stage and received my diploma, *Magna Cum Laude in Economia.* Eight months later she was gone. But not gone from my eternal love and memory. Never.

Lake Placid. Ever since 1958, Eve and I have enjoyed our family retreat in New York on Placid Lake, where our children and grandchildren and great-grandchildren now come and go all through the summer. We love our ancient place, its expansive old boathouse, especially our electric boat (*Blue Heaven*), and our lake. I've memorialized the lake with this prayer.

> *For the beauty of our Earth*
> *For the glory of our skies*
> *For our mountains ever there*
> *For the Placid Lake we prize.*
> *Lord of all, to thee we raise*
> *This our hymn of grateful praise.*
> *Amen.*

Life. In his 1938 play, *Our Town*, Thornton Wilder tells us the story of a few ordinary people in Grover's Corners, New Hampshire. The central character is a young woman named Emily Webb. She gets married, but dies after giving birth to her second child. Years later, the spirits of the cemetery allow her to leave her grave for a day to revisit her family in Grover's Corners. She is pained by what she observes—how little the living appreciate the joy of everyday life—and returns early to her grave. To paraphrase the character Emily's dialog:

> *Goodbye mama. Goodbye papa. Goodbye world. . . . I didn't realize it goes so fast. All that was going on in life and we never noticed. Oh earth, you're too wonderful for anybody to realize you. Do any human beings ever realize life while they live it . . . every, every minute? . . . That's all human beings are. Just blind people.*

Mentors, protégés, and friends. This subject could take a whole chapter, but I've condensed it, and mention names only where necessary.

My first great mentor was James P. Harrington, Princeton (BSE Class of 1947; PhD Class of 1950), and manager of the Princeton Athletic Association student ticket office. Jim, who held an engineering degree, set standards that I would do my best to honor for the rest of my life: responsibility, reliability, timeliness, diligence, and punctilious accuracy. We (with his wife Anne) worked together for two years as I served as assistant manager and then manager. We remained close friends until time and distance took their toll.

In 1951, I graduated from Princeton and joined Wellington Management Company. Founder Walter L. Morgan, Princeton Class of 1920, was my mentor. But he was not alone. Executive vice president Joseph E. Welch, sales vice president A.J. Wilkins, and general counsel Andrew B. Young, Esq., all seemed eager to share with me the knowledge that they had accumulated during their long careers. Could they have seen something in me that was worth mentoring? They must have. At his death at age 100, I had known Walter Morgan for 50 years. I later learned that he considered me "the son he never had."

Proteges

During nearly all my career, I've relied on a series of "assistants to the president," usually fairly young men with undergraduate degrees, and often graduate degrees as well. I've worked with a dozen of these protégés over the years, and their career outcomes have been remarkably diverse. Some have earned considerable business success; others less so. Some remain friends today; some, doubtless busy, have made no connections with me for two or more decades. Indeed, I have come to conclude that, as a broad generalization, it is unwise to assume that today's protégés will remain tomorrow's friends. (I'm not suggesting that gratitude for one's mentor, while it might be nice, should necessarily be eternal.) As a group, my assistants have lit up my life.

Other Friends

Today's list of my best friends is quite extensive enough . . . and surely diverse enough: One of the nation's most respected leaders of a giant firm focused on alternative investment strategies. Two distinguished professors of finance. My classmates of Princeton, Class of 1951 (we're vanishing fast!), and another Princetonian, Class of 1949, who served as Chairman of the Federal Reserve Board. The couple that led Blair Academy for 24 years.

Plus a special friend I grew up with whom I've now known for 75 years. A former CEO of a major mutual fund complex. A U.S. senator from the Midwest. A money manager in a family office who was kind enough to charter a Cessna Citation to fly Eve and me and a few of our children to Omaha for the Berkshire Hathaway Annual Meeting in 2017. The managers of two of the nation's largest university endowment funds. Three editors, one directing a major regional newspaper, one a brilliant observer of interest rates, and another the former managing editor of *Time* magazine.

*   *   *

Finally, two closing, "shout-outs," one for Erica and Loretta, my pals in the Vanguard Galley who serve our crew so ably, day after day, and one for Bob and Billy and their colleagues who drove me on my commutes and trips, arriving timely and safely.

Friendship, it turns out, is where you find it. Paraphrasing a song from the musical *South Pacific*,

Once you have found friends, never let them go.

National Constitution Center.   In 1998, a fine opportunity for me to serve our nation arose. It was then that my tenure as chairman of the National Constitution Center began. When my predecessor, Philadelphia mayor Ed Rendell, was named to lead the Democratic National Committee, he felt he should leave the board. With then-president Joe Torsella, he asked me to serve as the new chairman. I declined: "You have a lot of candidates on the board who would be far more effective than I to lead the board. Anyway, I can't spare the time to do it!"

"A Real Chairman?"

But they pushed, and, with time of the essence, I agreed . . . "but only until you can find a real chairman." Seven years later, in 2005, I stepped down as chairman, succeeded by one former president of the United States (William Jefferson Clinton) and then by another (George H. W. Bush). My seven years flew by like a whirlwind: leading the board, fund raising, planning, testifying before Congress, helping this great undertaking move from idea to reality. Please be clear. Joe did the lion's share of the heavy lifting. (See my comment about a chairman's role in "Blair Academy," earlier in this chapter.)

Our National Constitution Center museum now stands proudly at the north end of Philadelphia's Independence Mall, with Independence Hall anchoring the south end. At our ground-breaking ceremony in 2000, I spoke right before President Clinton's inspired address on "what it means to be a citizen of the United States of America." Our grand opening took place on July 4, 2003.

I was thrilled to contribute to a great American mission: to bring the Constitution into the lives of our citizens. Working with president Torsella, a Rhodes Scholar, was a delightful experience. In 2016, he was elected Treasurer of the Commonwealth of Pennsylvania. Joe was a wonderful (senior) partner during an era in which I could follow my passion of devotion to our nation, her values, and her institutions.

Presidents.   In 1969, at the New York World's Fair, I had just completed my trip on a moving walkway past Michelangelo's *Pieta*. There, I recognized a familiar face, seemingly standing alone and without bodyguards. It was Harry S Truman, and I shook the hand of a U.S. president for the first time.

My second handshake took place in the White House on May 27, 1970. After a sharp drop in the stock market, I was invited to a dinner called by the White House with 35 other CEOs and officers of Wall Street firms. The gathering was designed to calm the nerves of investors. (You can't make this stuff up.)

"Mr. President . . . "

When President Richard M. Nixon called for questions, no one else stood up, so I did. "Mr. President, in view of your campaign pledge to bring us all together, what are you doing about the growing gaps between our generations and our races?" He was clearly thrown off-balance by a question like that from a typically friendly Wall Street audience, and responded uneasily. As we exited the State Dining Room, we met face-to-face and shook hands. He didn't seem amused.

I later met Lyndon Johnson at a dinner of about 30 people in New York City. He signed a photograph of himself for me and one for my youngest son, Andrew. I framed it and presented it to him.

Two More Presidents

Serving as chairman of the Constitution Center also gave me the opportunity to work with my first two successors: William Jefferson Clinton and George H. W. Bush. I came to know President Clinton fairly well; he wrote a lovely foreword to the second edition of my book *Enough: True Measures of Money, Business, and Life*, published in 2010.

I observed many characteristics that these men seemed to have in common: presence, intelligence, speaking skills. But each had his own idiosyncrasies. President Truman was terse. When we met, President Nixon seemed nervous. (I can't imagine why.) President Johnson, self-confident, almost to the point of arrogance. President Clinton, with an extraordinary charisma that showed through at a one-on-one meeting as clearly as in a State of the Union speech. (He graciously signed copies of *Enough* – as the author of the foreword – for each of my 12 grandchildren.) President George H. W. Bush, who seemed more to the manor born in Connecticut than the hard-bitten Texan he sought to become.

Press on, regardless.   This biblical motto goes all the way back to St. Paul's admonition, "press on." It was introduced as a family motto by my uncle Clifton Armstrong Hipkins, long-time commodore of the Greenwich (Connecticut) Yacht Club. He named his boat *Press On, Regardless*, an inspiring challenge. But don't forget this: The motto means not only "press on" when times are tough, but also "press on" when times are easy. That's what "regardless" means.

Princeton.   *Stranger, you have reached the noblest home on earth.*

More than two millennia after Sophocles wrote these words (they come from *Oedipus at Colonus*), they were etched on a plaque on Goheen Walk on the Princeton campus. The inscription resonates with me today as the best summary of the role played by Princeton University in my life. As an undergraduate, as I noted earlier, I was awarded generous scholarships, worked diligently on my studies, and, as a freshman, worked as a waiter in the university's magnificent dining halls.

Picked Out of Obscurity

In my sophomore year, I was picked out of obscurity (as I like to say) as a waiter in our dining halls and named by the manager of the Athletic Association student ticket office, Jim Harrington (see "Mentors, protégés, and friends," earlier in this chapter), to serve as his assistant manager; I became his manager a year later. The work involved enormous responsibility and long and hard hours, especially during the Tigers' 1950 football season, when we earned the Ivy League championship. I watched every kickoff, but never saw a game. (There was work to be done.) Basketball season was less demanding; baseball season was, in terms of tickets sold, a laugher.

From D+ to A+

I loved the work and sought for ever more responsibility. But the duties were time-consuming, and during a terrible first semester in 1948, my grades tumbled to the danger point. But they got better. Semester by semester, my 3s (Cs) and a 4+ (D+), rose to 2s and finally to 1s (Bs and As), capped by a 1+ on my senior thesis, another example of my early determination to stay the course.

During my college years, it was pretty much "all work and no play." But I made some great friends, and regularly attend our annual class reunions. I proudly march in the colorful P-rade each year, and also still participate in periodic Princeton seminars, often on the subject of "Ethics and Finance."

Scholarships and Fellowships

I've also spent much time with the fine young men and women who have held Bogle Brothers Scholarships, so far 160 students and counting. I also remain involved as a sponsor of the Pace Center for Civic Engagement. In 2016, thanks to a generous gift to Princeton from my son, John C. Bogle Jr., and his wife Lynn, the John C. Bogle Fellowships in Civic Service program was established. In 2017, 28 freshman members of the Class of 2022 were awarded fellowships that funded their summer internships in civic projects. What a joy it is to help these young people along the road of life!

This son of Princeton has been honored beyond measure by his beloved alma mater: the Woodrow Wilson Award for Distinguished Achievement in the Nation's Service (1999), an Honorary Doctor of Laws Degree (2005), and "One of the 25 Most Influential Princetonians of All Time" (2008).

From the university's alma mater, 1951 version.

In praise of old Nassau, my boys,
Hurrah, Hurrah, Hurrah.
Her sons will give, while they shall live
Three cheers for old Nassau!

Quakers. While I was baptized as an Episcopalian and attend a Presbyterian church (a tad irregularly) with my family, I have come to believe that, deep down, I'm truly a Quaker. I do my best to honor those stern Quaker values personally. In retrospect, I see that my life and my design for Vanguard reflect many of the basic Quaker values that William Penn fostered – simplicity, economy, thrift, efficiency, service to others, and the conviction, in the words of Quaker founder George Fox, that "the truth is the way." (I confess that I'm not so strong on some of the other Quaker values; in particular, consensus, patience, silence, and humility.)

Staff. Where would I be without my veteran assistants Emily Snyder (33 years at Vanguard) and Michael Nolan (17), and our associate Kathy Younker (16)? Nowhere! Could this book about Vanguard and the index revolution – written by the founder of both – have been published without their enthusiastic participation and infinite patience? Maybe. But it would have been less of a book – far more arduous – have taken far longer, and been far less fun.

Teaching and learning. When I'm asked what is the secret of a life well-lived, I often answer, "First rule: get out of bed in the morning. If you don't do that, not much will happen. Then, every day, teach something and learn something. Along the way, give an enthusiastic compliment to a deserving soul whom you may have never before met. Then you've earned a great night's sleep. You'll get it. When you awaken the next day, repeat these rules."

Tennyson. The closing words of Alfred Lord Tennyson's poem "Ulysses" (1842) begin as the oarsmen of his launch sweep Ulysses out to his flagship for one last voyage:

> . . . *Come, my friends*
> *'Tis not too late to seek a newer world.*
> *Push off, and sitting well in order smite*
> *The sounding furrows; for my purpose holds*
> *To sail beyond the sunset,*
> *until I die. . . .*

Though much is taken, much abides; and though
We are not now that strength which in old days
Moved earth and heaven, that which we are, we are –
One equal temper of heroic hearts,
Made weak by time and fate, but strong in will
To strive, to seek, to find, and not to yield.

T. **Rowe Price.** This is a firm that I've always admired – right up there with Dodge and Cox and Dimensional Fund Advisers – for professional conduct, low-key marketing (or none), and good people. When my one-time assistant, then-executive vice president of Vanguard, James S. (Jim) Riepe, left Vanguard for T. Rowe Price in 1980, I was crestfallen at the loss of my heir-apparent. But I was confident he had found the perfect home. (I was right!)

But T. Rowe Price has put me into an awkward position. Back in 1994, in order to collect current information about Vanguard's peers, I made a token investment in the stock of T. Rowe Price, Incorporated, the publicly held investment adviser to the Price mutual funds. I bought 100 shares at $42 per share, a total cost of $4,200.

A Great Investment

I've received the firm's glossy but interesting annual reports ever since, but paid little attention to the stock price. But, my goodness, I made a great investment. Those 100 shares have split five times, and I now hold 3,200 shares. At Price's market price of $121 per share in mid-2018, my casual investment of $4,200 in 1994 is now worth $384,000. My annual dividend of $8,960 is more than double that of my initial investment. Is it really a good idea for me to have so much invested in one of our major competitors? That's the "awkward" part.

As founder of a mutual company in which the lion's share of profits are returned to fund shareholders rather than to management company owners, I marvel at the enormous profitability of T. Rowe Price and our peers in the mutual fund business, generated in part by management and marketing, but largely by the soaring prices of stocks in the great bull market and the staggering economies of scale available in managing mutual funds. But the lion's share of those economies of scale have been arrogated by the managers to themselves, and barely shared with the mutual fund clients whom the officers and directors of mutual funds are duty-bound to serve.

Work. I've been working since I was nine years old, beginning as a newspaper deliverer, store clerk, postal worker, and waiter. I worked my way through school and college waiting on tables (and also worked during summer vacations and holiday breaks). After college, I worked to build my career in the mutual fund business.

In all my working career, however, I've had only a single job that I could call real "work": when I was a pin-setter in the bowling alley of the Sea Girt (New Jersey) fire department. Other than that, all of my work has been fun, productive, and deeply fulfilling, even with a spiritual element.

The joy of work was beautifully expressed by Thomas Carlyle:

> *Blessed is he who has found his work; let him ask no other blessedness. . . . There is a perennial nobleness and even sacredness in work.*

Lin-Manuel Miranda described Alexander Hamilton's standards for getting ahead in one's work in his hit Broadway musical *Hamilton*. To paraphrase:

> *The founding father with no father,*
> *Got farther, by working harder,*
> *by being smarter, and by being a self-starter.*

Mr. Miranda described Hamilton this way to NPR, "All in the strength of his writing, he embodies the word's ability to make a difference."[2]

Hamilton would, I think, endorse the spirit of Carlyle's words, reflected, even enhanced, by the words of this familiar hymn:

> *Work, for the night is coming,*
> *Under the sunset skies;*
> *While their bright tints are glowing,*
> *Work, for the daylight flies.*
> *Work till the last beam fadeth,*
> *Fadeth to shine no more;*
> *Work, while the night is darkening,*
> *When man's work is o'er.*

---

[2] www.npr.org/2017/12/26/572622911/lin-manuel-miranda-on-disney-mixtapes-and-why-he-wont-try-to-top-hamilton.

You . . . and me . . . and the universe.   My final reflection starts with an existential issue that applies to you, dear reader, and to me, and to every other human being who exists on the face of our planet Earth.

We may think of ourselves as small, merely a single one of Earth's seven billion (plus or minus) human beings. Yes, we enjoy the beauty of living. But we live for only a brief moment in time and space, and then we move on. But we're far *less* important than that.

Our Earth is but a single planet in the solar system, which in turn is part of the Milky Way galaxy, our huge galaxy 100,000 or so light-years in diameter. Our galaxy, in turn, is but one of at least 200 billion galaxies in our universe, each galaxy with more than 100 billion stars. If you want to measure the relative importance of a single human being, just do the math!

And yet . . . and yet to dwell on our own insignificance in the grand scheme of things doesn't seem particularly useful. There's work to be done here on Earth, and we'd best get on with it. We might begin by acting, before it's too late, to save our own planet. Beyond that, our task is to live productive lives, to raise our families, to contribute to our communities, and to serve to our nation and our global society.

Each of us human beings must be the best that we can be, helping others – especially those less privileged – along the road of life. We must leave everything that we touch better than it was when we found it. Yes, we are here for only a short while, but isn't it our obligation to make the most of every moment of it?

We must remind ourselves each day that "even one person can make a difference." (Remember to apply that axiom to one's self!) That's the way that I've strived to live my own imperfect life, maybe even why I've survived for so long. Looking back from the vantage point of my 90th year on Earth, I can easily imagine that my mission of serving investors and the values I've established for Vanguard, the firm that I founded in 1974, will endure.

Stay the Course

I've usually used the phrase "stay the course" as one of the great rules of investment success. Ignore the day-to-day fluctuations in the stock market and focus on the long-term growth of the U.S. economy. But as I complete this memoir, "stay the course" is also a splendid rule for fighting our way through the inevitable ups and downs of the short spans of our existence on this Earth, and for enjoying a productive and honorable life well lived.

Index

Page numbers followed by *e* refer to exhibits.

BOOKS BY
JOHN C. BOGLE

1994   *Bogle on Mutual Funds: New Perspectives for the Intelligent Investor*
        —Foreword by Paul A. Samuelson

1999   *Common Sense on Mutual Funds: New Imperatives for the Intelligent Investor*
        — Foreword by Peter L. Bernstein

2001   *John Bogle on Investing: The First 50 Years*
        —Foreword by Paul A. Volcker, Introduction by Chancellor William T. Allen

2002   *Character Counts: The Creation and Building of The Vanguard Group*

2005   *The Battle for the Soul of Capitalism*
        —Foreword by Peter G. Peterson

2007   *The Little Book of Common Sense Investing: The Only Way to Guarantee Your Fair Share of Stock Market Returns*

2008   *Enough. True Measures of Money, Business, and Life*
        —Foreword by William Jefferson Clinton, Prologue by Tom Peters

2010   *Common Sense on Mutual Funds,* 10th anniversary edition, fully revised and updated
        —Foreword by David F. Swensen

2011   *Don't Count on It! Reflections on Investment Illusions, Capitalism, "Mutual" Funds, Indexing, Entrepreneurship, Idealism, and Heroes*
        —Foreword by Alan S. Blinder

2012   *The Clash of the Cultures: Investment vs. Speculation*
        —Foreword by Arthur Levitt

2017   *The Little Book of Common Sense Investing,* 10th anniversary edition, fully revised and updated

2018   *Stay the Course: A History of Vanguard and the Index Revolution*
        —Foreword by Burton G. Malkiel